Strange Love

Critical Perspectives Series

Series Editor: Donaldo Macedo, University of Massachusetts, Boston
A book series dedicated to Paulo Freire

Strange Love

Or How We Learn to Stop Worrying and Love the Market

Robin Truth Goodman
and Kenneth J. Saltman

ROWMAN & LITTLEFIELD PUBLISHERS, INC.
Lanham • Boulder • New York • Oxford

ROWMAN & LITTLEFIELD PUBLISHERS, INC.

Published in the United States of America
by Rowman & Littlefield Publishers, Inc.
4720 Boston Way, Lanham, Maryland 20706
www.rowmanlittlefield.com

12 Hid's Copse Road, Cumnor Hill, Oxford OX2 9JJ, England

British Library Cataloguing in Publication Information Available

Library of Congress Cataloging-in-Publication Data
Goodman, Robin Truth, 1966-
  Strange love : or how we learn to stop worrying and love the market / Robin Truth
Goodman and Kenneth J. Saltman.
     p. cm. — (Critical perspectives series)
  Includes bibliographical references and index.
  ISBN 0-7425-1634-2 (alk. paper) — ISBN 0-7425-1635-0 (pbk. : alk. paper)
     1. Capitalism—Moral and ethical aspects—United States. 2. Power (Social sciences)—United States. I. Saltman, Kenneth J., 1969- II. Title. III. Series.

HB501 .G623 2002
330.12'2—dc21

2001048265

Printed in the United States of America

♾™ The paper used in this publication meets the minimum requirements of American National Standard for Information Sciences—Permanence of Paper for Printed Library Materials, ANSI/NISO Z.39.48–1992.

Contents

Introduction

This is a book about oppressive power today. Stanley Kubrick's Cold War classic dark comedy *Dr. Strangelove: Or How I Learned to Stop Worrying and Love the Bomb* may then seem to be an inappropriate reference for the title to take. After all, the Cold War has thawed, ideas such as mutually assured destruction are no longer common parlance, and there no longer seems to be a red menace threatening democracy and free markets. We won the war and we won it without Slim Pickins having to ride the H-bomb bronco style into what Ronald Reagan referred to as the Evil Empire.

Yet, the collapse of the ideological nemesis of the United States has not conferred to most citizens the fruits of victory—freedom and wealth. As political power has concentrated in the nether realms of the corporate elite, as political parties are increasingly indistinguishable ideologically,[1] and as access to power for most citizens appears as unapproachable as ever, the promise of democracy appears to have eluded our victory.[2]

But at least we got free markets.

Well, not really.

If access to political power seems as remote as ever, then access to capital is even farther, not only for U.S. citizens but for the bulk of the world's population. While corporate news media heralded economic boom at the millennium's turn, disparities in wealth have reached greater proportions than during the Great Depression[3] with the world's richest three hundred individuals possessing more wealth than the world's poorest forty-eight countries combined, and the richest fifteen have a greater fortune than the total product of sub-Saharan Africa.[4]

1

According to the most recent report of the United Nations Development Pro-
gramme, while the global consumption of goods and services was twice as big
in 1997 as in 1975 and had multiplied by a factor of six since 1950, 1 billion
people cannot satisfy even their elementary needs. Among 4.5 billion of the
residents of the "developing" countries, three in every five are deprived of access to basic infrastructures: a third have no access to drinkable water, a quarter have no accommodation worthy of its name, one-fifth have no use of sanitary and medical services. One in five children spend less than five years in
any form of schooling; a similar proportion is permanently undernourished.[5]

Austerity measures imposed by world trade organizations such as the
World Bank and the International Monetary Fund ensure that poor nations stay poor by imposing "fiscal discipline," while no such discipline
applies to entire industries such as defense, entertainment, and corporate
agriculture that are heavily subsidized by the public sector in the United
States. While the official U.S. unemployment rate hovers around 5 percent, the real wage has steadily decreased since the seventies, to the point
that not a single county in the nation contains one-bedroom apartments
affordable for a single minimum-wage earner.[6] Free trade agreements
such as NAFTA have enriched corporate elites in Mexico and the United
States while intensifying poverty along the border.[7] Free trade has meant
capital flight, job loss, and the dismantling of labor unions in the United
States and the growth of slave labor conditions in nations receiving industrial production such as Indonesia and China. But perhaps the ultimate failure of liberal capitalism is indicated by its success in distributing
Coca-Cola to every last niche of the globe while it has failed to supply in-
expensive medicines for preventable diseases or nutritious food or living
wages to these same sprawling shanty towns in Ethiopia, Brazil, and the
United States. Forty-seven million children in the richest twenty-nine nations in the world are living below the poverty line. Child poverty in the
wealthiest nations has worsened along with real wages as national incomes have risen over the last half century.[8] The effects of globalization on
world populations are a far cry from freedom. As Stephen Sholom writes:

> In developing countries nearly 1.3 billion people do not have access to clean
> water, . . . 840 million people are malnourished. . . . Even in the industrial
> countries, globalization has taken a grim toll. One person in eight suffers
> from either long-term unemployment, illiteracy, a life-expectancy of less than
> 60 years, or an income below the national poverty line.[9]

In the face of what the victory of the Cold War looks like globally, the sounds
of triumph at the global ascendancy of liberal capitalism echo with the same
mad call of joy emanating from Slim Pickins as he descends on the bomb to
the obliteration of himself and the world. Yeeeee Hawwww!

One must identify sources other than the "Soviet Threat" to explain widespread feelings of powerlessness, insecurity, and political defeatism at a time when protesters are denied permits to march for the allegedly "extremist," "radical" causes of health care, racial equality, and housing. Since the end of the Soviet Union, the "Rogue State," the "drug war," and the "terrorist threat" have bolstered the rise of the security state and obscured public focus on domestic priorities while excluding the public from participation in foreign policy decisions. If the ultimate spectre of destruction hanging over the world of the Cold War was the mushroom cloud, nuclear winter, and long half-lives of radiation, today it is global capitalism and what Ellen Meiskins Wood calls the "new imperialism," which is "not just a matter of controlling particular territories. It is a matter of controlling a whole world economy and global markets, everywhere and all the time."[10] The project of globalization according to *New York Times* foreign correspondent Thomas L. Friedman "is our overarching national interest" and it "requires a stable power structure, and no country is more essential for this than the United States"[11] for "it has a large standing army, equipped with more aircraft carriers, advanced fighter jets, transport aircraft and nuclear weapons than ever, so that it can project more power farther than any country in the world. . . . America excels in all the new measures of power in the era of globalization."[12] As Friedman explains rallying for the "humanitarian" bombing of Kosovo, "The hidden hand of the market will never work without the hidden fist—McDonald's cannot flourish without McDonnell Douglas, the designer of the F-15. And the hidden fist that keeps the world safe for Silicon Valley's technologies is called the United States Army, Air Force, Navy, and Marine Corps."[13]

The impoverishing power of globalization is matched by the military destructive power of the new imperialism that enforces neoliberal policy to make the world safe for U.S. markets. Kosovo is a case in point.

> If we assume that NATO was acting on imperialist motives, we are unlikely to be surprised at the failure of its action to help the victims, whose conditions became palpably worse after the bombing began. We are unlikely to be surprised at the destruction of the country's infrastructure which will, as in Iraq, do far more harm, and for much longer, to innocent civilians than to their oppressors. We are unlikely to be surprised at the destruction perpetrated by the NATO military machine, the immediate killing and maiming of civilians by bombs, and the long-term killing and maiming of this and future generations, by ecological catastrophe through the bombing of refineries and chemical plants (which is nothing short of biological warfare), and the use by the U.S. of depleted uranium, which is not a million miles away from nuclear war.[14]

During the Cold War it was hard to put a happy face on nuclear holocaust. Kubrick probably came as close as anybody but this was not a lighthearted laughter. No one really emerged from the theater after seeing *Strangelove* free of nuclear worry and now in love with the bomb. However, despite the savage and brutal effects of global capital—effects not seen since the time of the robber barons and the Great Depression—the new imperialism, global capital, and the ideologies known as neoliberal that bolster it are appearing today in such varied places as mass media, school curricula, and multicultural literature as not merely a happy face. Global capital and the "new imperialism" that expands it are appearing as love.

This violent imperialism increasingly takes the duplicitous guise of humanitarianism—what Noam Chomsky has dubbed "The New Military Humanism":

> "The New Internationalism" was hailed by intellectual opinion and legal scholars who proclaimed a new era in world affairs in which the "enlightened states" will at last be able to use force where they "believe it to be just," discarding "the restrictive old rules" and obeying "modern notions of justice that they fashion." . . . The Soviet Union, and to some extent China, set limits on the actions of the Western powers in their traditional domains, not only by virtue of the military deterrent, but also because of their occasional willingness, however opportunistic, to lend support to targets of Western subversion and aggression. . . . With the Soviet deterrent in decline, the Cold War victors are more free to exercise their will under the cloak of good intentions but in pursuit of interests that have a very familiar ring outside the realm of enlightenment. The self-described bearers of enlightenment happen to be the rich and powerful, the inheritors of colonial and neocolonial systems of global domination.[15]

Globalization does move forward through policy initiatives and the military force to back them. However, it is not predominantly guns that keeps Americans consenting to the evisceration of social services while the Pentagon's budget "a decade after the fall of the Berlin Wall and with no credible 'enemy' in sight—sat at $268 billion during the Clinton years. . . . That's four times more than Russia spends and about eight times more than China."[16] Then there is the special $112 billion Clinton authorized in 1999 for the Pentagon over the next six years and the political consensus of the necessity for a missile defense system (even as feasibility tests have failed) and the $400 billion appropriation for three new tactical aircraft programs and the continued expenditure of $2.5 billion per plane on the B-2 bomber—a plane designed to penetrate the air defenses of the Soviet Union, a nation that no longer exists. Dr. Strangelove himself would be sending back the weapons.

With the terror attacks of September 11, 2001, that destroyed the World Trade Center and damaged the Pentagon, the Bush administration was given full license by Congress to further increase military spending to fight America's "new war on terrorism." The ironies of the expanded military build-up include:

1. It was global military build-up that created massive animosity towards the United States around the world.
2. The United States funded, trained, and supported this new adversary to fight the Soviets and other enemies, as it had done with the Sandanistas in Nicaragua, Saddam Husseim in Iraq, and Noriega in Panama. By representing the issue as a family matter, the parodical magazine *The Onion* highlights the extent to which U.S. militarism is at odds with democracy.

Bush Sr. Apologizes to Son for Funding Bin Laden in '80s

Midland, TX—Former president George Bush issued an apology to his son Monday for advocating the CIA's mid-'80s funding of Osama bin Laden, who at the time was resisting the Soviet invasion of Afghanistan. "I'm sorry, son." Bush told President George W. Bush. "We thought it was a good idea at the time because he was part of a group fighting communism in Central Asia. Sounds weird. You sort of had to be there." Bush is still deliberating over whether to tell his son about the whole supporting-Saddam Hussein-against-Iran thing. (*The Onion* 37, no. 34, September 26, 2001)

3. Just as missile defense was an inappropriate response to existing threats, the conventional force build-up is an inappropriate and excessive response to an enemy that Bush himself has described as a "faceless coward" or a nation that cannot afford to feed its own people.

These unending armaments are not aimed at U.S. citizens, forcing them to go along with the mad misuse of public funds to expand a globalization system that is failing them and the world. While some—labor unionists, environmentalists, progressives—have taken to the streets to challenge globalization, what keeps most people consenting to and even risking their lives for globalization is largely the successes of corporate cultural production. Mass mediated ideologies of neoliberalism function pedagogically in a variety of ways: (1) market triumphalism, or the disseminating as common sense the notion that there are no alternatives to the current order of capitalism and that consumerism is the only possibility of self-definition, self-fulfillment, patriotism, and the only path to success; (2) creating a sense that the nation-state's power is diminishing before the relentless growth of trade and financial networks while simultaneously fantasizing a paranoid defensiveness around borders between races and nations; (3) making the private sphere sacred by defining freedom as an innocent, sentimental space where government cannot enter; (4) projecting anti-federalism as redemptive, or a vilification of the state at all levels (with the exception of military, security, or policing action), and representing the state as inherently authoritarian because it imposes restrictions on capital; (5) representing ignorance as a virtue, and knowledge as purely instrumental, so that learning falls into the service of a service economy; (6) building an ambivalence around technology as both the only protection from evil and the sure course towards universal destruction. In curricula, literature, and film, such ideological claims have been made common sense in order to school citizens in the virtues of corporate power over democratic power, the beauty of global aggression, the innocence of markets, and the new imperialism as a form of love.

FORECAST

Strange Love: Or How We Learn to Stop Worrying and Love the Market is about the corporatization of education as well as about how education is the means through which globalization is achieved, in part, through the corporatization of identities, values, notions of citizenship, and the broader social and political field. We unravel what we are calling "strategies of neoliberal benevolence" promoted in both corporate curricula and corporate mass media. *Strange Love* shows how multiple cultural forms are presently drawing on discursive traditions of sentimentalizing the family, humanitarianism, and compassionate action in order to sanctify the private and eradicate the very notion of the public and the political, to replace the language of community and solidarity with the language of radical individualism, affect, and the personal. *Strange Love* situates the values projected through corporate, multicultural, and mass-mediated curricula within current policies easing the internationalization of capital. Corporate and neoliberal powers are creating the conditions of their expansion by masking oppression in narratives about childhood innocence, philanthropy, humanitarianism, and family compassion. As Arvind Rajagopal asserts, "the task of educating individuals into modern citizenship occurs at least as much through markets as it does through politics."[17] *Strange Love* studies corporate power's destructive expansion through its use of traditional discourses of schooling and values of benevolence.

Strange Love is also concerned with how teaching critical consciousness can make the conditions for social change. It argues that educators can and, indeed, must show how cultural representations are supporting a power structure in the interests of multinational capital and at the expense of democracy. Teachers can draw on the insights of critical pedagogy in order both to expose and to challenge the feel-good sentiment in which the mainstream media is cloaking corporate expansion and neo-imperialism. This book aspires to help teachers critique such cultural representations and expose the cruelties of neoliberal practices, pointing to the ways that the power structure is reinforced, but also envisioning ways of constructing more equitable and just futures and alternatives.

At stake here is not only a form of academic investigative journalism that exposes particular corporations and cultural producers such as Michael Milken's Knowledge Universe, BPAmoco, Scholastic, Time-Warner, Waste Management, Monsanto, and ExxonMobil for their unethical practices and cynically self-interested war on the public sector, though with the rise of the corporate media monopoly, academic work is a more likely place to find investigative journalism than news media. Such corporate influence over culture also limits creativity and the sense of the possible. While *Strange Love* does indeed offer examples of how multinational corporations are infiltrating public education through pro-corporate propaganda, it would be inadequate to understand corporate curriculum as merely propaganda or as merely what goes on in schools. In the words of Henry Giroux, "'Pedagogy' . . . is about linking the construction of knowledge to issues of ethics, politics, and power and to challenging the institutions and ideologies that are setting in place regimes of racism, sexism, hatred, and poverty."[18] Highlighting the pedagogical dimension of all corporate cultural production points to the hegemonic struggle over meanings that cultural production engages. As Judith Butler writes,

> Distinct from a view that casts the operation of power in the political field exclusively in terms of discrete blocs which vie with one another for control of policy questions, hegemony emphasizes the ways in which power operates to form our everyday understanding of social relations, and to orchestrate the ways in which we consent to (and reproduce) those tacit and covert relations of power. Power is not stable or static, but is remade at various junctures within everyday life; it constitutes our tenuous sense of common sense, and is ensconced as the prevailing epistemes of a culture. Moreover, social transformation occurs not merely by rallying mass numbers in favour of a cause, but precisely through the ways in which daily social relations are rearticulated, and new conceptual horizons opened up by anomalous or subversive practices.[19]

In the context of this book, pedagogy refers not only to teaching and learning but to how the struggle over meaning constructs identities, frames issues and understandings, produces values and desires, and promotes particular visions for the future. Critical pedagogy as a counter-hegemonic practice involves holding those in power responsible for their cultural productions. *Strange Love* does not only concern questions of pedagogy as teaching and learning nor is it simply about the possibility to challenge corporate public school curriculum. As well, *Strange Love* argues that the pedagogical needs to be understood as a constitutive element of all cultural politics. As Henry Giroux has significantly elaborated,

Educational work is both inseparable from and a participant in cultural politics because it is in the realm of culture that identities are forged, citizenship rights are enacted, and possibilities are developed for translating acts of interpretation into forms of intervention.[20]

Strange Love demonstrates how corporate values currently provide the conceptual basis through which schooling is understood. The logic of the corporation (through languages of management, efficiency, and choice as well as through the emphasis on methods and standardization) affects educational policies from privatization, vouchers, and magnet and charter schools to standardized testing, inner city school closings, defunding, technologization, and increased surveillance. The corporatized school prepares for the corporatist future.

FAMILY VALUES

In the post–Cold War world, a family values rationale justifies the repackaging of military action as humanitarian action. One can easily read this in the coverage of Kosovo. A *Time* magazine Special Report on Kosovo shows on its cover a Madonna-like woman holding a baby at her breast. The headline reads, "Are Ground Troops the Answer?"—tying the intentions of military action into a loving and redemptive image of mother and child. The top photograph of the *New York Times* front page (15 June 1999) exhibits a KLA solider holding a gun in one hand and a little girl in the other. Affectionately hugging the soldier with one arm, the little girl holds up two fingers of her other hand in a sign of victory.

The war coverage used family imagery to justify a global and even a military defense of privacy. The constant return, in the press coverage, to images of the reuniting family serve to create the family as pure privacy, love, and safety, a pure moral goodness sanctified and untouched by technologies of aggression, evil states, or the movement of history. This defense of privacy would form, in turn, an ideology of private interest and private enterprise that were really being projected as the goal of the war. Not incidentally, a spate of films such as *Three Kings* appeared in 1999, suggesting that the real problem with the massive human rights abuses of the Gulf War were the way the war interrupted business, hindered the distribution of consumer goods, and hurt families. Corporate lobbying for the expansion of NATO, the corporate support of the 1999 NATO summit, and the consolidation of corporate military contractors all testify to the interests multinational companies have in the furtherance of the war effort in particular, but also future militarization more generally. In this setting, the family is simply a tool to make aggressions seem both benign and redemptive as NATO force clears new territories for economic infrastructures benefiting private companies in their expansion into new enclaves.

The pursuit of profit on the part of corporations depends on the reproduction of families and their consumption patterns. The life cycle—birth, marriage, childrearing—is defined through successive stages of products, from toys and weddings to houses, entertainment, appropriate clothing, cars, and furniture. We are criticizing here not affective relations between people, but rather a symbolic structure that limits people's capacities for imagining any possibilities for the future except for a world saturated in consumption, where minds are ensconced in corporate slogans while credit and identity become one, where the desire to consume becomes the primary motivation for an array of cruelties easing the corporate colonization of everything. Part of what capitalism depends on is a continually expanding economy, so social values need to be configured for continually expanding consuming practices. This involves producing ever-diversifying and changing needs.

There have been a number of theories to explain why the nuclear family has become such a dominant form of social organization in modernity—from Engels who identifies it as the first form of class division ushering in the primary form of social struggle under capitalism;[21] to Freud who identifies the family as the foundation of civilization; to Lévi-Strauss who sees marriage as the primary form of trading and alliance;[22] to Foucault who sees the bourgeois family as the primary place where power operates in its regulation of bodies;[23] to Danzelot who shows the family emerging in response to the failings of philanthropy, the rise of juvenile justice, and the subsequent need of mothers to take charge of the newly privatized practices of preventive health care and education;[24] to the contemporary Christian right who defines it as a return to morality following the unraveling of the moral fabric of the counterculture sixties. However, the current and incessantly repeated return to the family in many popular representations and political discourses needs to be addressed, as Nancy Fraser has pointed out, because the idea of the family has been used as the primary organization for the distribution of social goods—in the welfare system and elsewhere—and the primary justification for many present inequalities. Set up as a way to facilitate production under industrialization, the traditional family, Fraser argues, is no longer a valid arrangement for funneling public funds or legislating equal access, as the demands of the contemporary economy are often forcing the traditional family to unravel, requiring forced mobility, lack of attachments, instability, increasing working hours, double incomes, and the like.[25] Not only does the holdover of family imagery in most mainstream political rhetoric demonize gays and lesbians as the anti-family, but it also serves to scapegoat non-whites as the evil seed of social disintegration, accusing them of not taking family values seriously enough.

Family values discourse depoliticizes the social by designating the family, rather than the citizen or the society as a whole, as the foundational social unit. When Margaret Thatcher said that there is no England, there are only English families, she was actively redefining social responsibility from the public (in the form of government support) to the private in the form of the family. The privatization of social responsibility through the elevation of the family to the fundamental social unit renders a state in the service of the private sphere. When the impeachment of a president hinges on the idea of illicit sexuality, a real political dialogue of the administration's failings gets precluded. The symbolism of the family ends up decimating any notion of the public good. Responsibility for social services like health care, education, basic needs, shelter, and the like is shifted to the family. The danger of this shift is that it creates a historical amnesia around the fact that in the past there were social services, instead harking back to a nostalgic moment in which an idyllic *Leave It to Beaver* family could provide (but never really did). The neoliberal state contributes public revenue to the furtherance of private profit-seeking activities rather than to programs dedicated to public welfare and public interest. It also contributes to a central tenet of market ideology—namely, that the good of private enterprise is the good of society.

Within such representations, the family is not a political entity. For example, we see the family take over where political concerns are most pressing. When right-wing radical Timothy McVeigh bombed a federal building in Oklahoma City, the event was framed in terms of the actions of a loner attacking innocent children in a day-care center. Emotional press coverage of the children killed in the building's day-care center, along with sentimental photographs of firemen carrying infants out of the flames, did not merely eclipse but also replaced the political issues and conversation surrounding domestic right-wing terrorism, for example, issues concerning how the relationship between a government and its citizens ought to be defined. This can be seen, too, in the federal attack on David Koresh's Branch Davidian compound in Waco, Texas. Waco was staged in the mainstream press as the government's botched attempt to route out a family that was bursting the seams of morality through rape, incest, drugs, the stockpiling of weapons, and child sacrifice. The spectacle of horror seething from the attack on the sacred social unit of the family replaced meaningful public discussion of the implications for a society composed of multiple political factions competing for different agendas. Focusing on the family hindered a consideration of the relationship of the incident to broader public concerns about the role of the state in both policing and supporting the private ones. In both examples, the liberal imperative for consensus and the effacement of right-wing dissent instead took the form of family-centered pathos or a narrative about dysfunctionality and psychological deviance.

In *The Democratic Paradox*, Mouffe warns that the refusal of "third way" liberals and former Marxists to admit the constitutive agonism at the core of the social increasingly results in the rise of right-wing populism as the only viable form of political dissent:

> The very legitimacy of liberal democracy is based on the idea of popular sovereignty and, as the mobilization of such idea by right-wing politicians indicates, it would be a serious mistake to believe that the time has come to relinquish it. . . . Democratic logics always entail drawing a frontier between 'us' and 'them', those who belong to the 'demos' and those who are outside of it. . . . Until recently, the existence of contending forces was openly recognized and it is only nowadays, when the very idea of a possible alternative to the existing order has been discredited, that the stabilization realized under the hegemony of neoliberalism—with its very specific interpretation of what rights are important and non-negotiable—is practically unchallenged.[26]

The rise of the Reform Party, the successes of David Duke and his National Organization for European American Rights, the militia movement, increasing incidents of right-wing domestic terrorism, and George W. Bush's talk of compassion as he defends racist institutions and practices and admits members of the Confederacy into his cabinet, all testify to the dangers of denying the conflictive nature of social life. In this context, the turn to the besieged family in endless representations needs to be understood as a part of the inability of neoliberalism to admit dissent. The failure of such 'center-left' politicians as Bill Clinton to take political positions ideologically distinct from the right resulted in the inability of U.S. political discourse to amount to more than squabbles over family values. Worries about Oval Office sex, divorces, and other private family matters toppled many politicians who should have been toppled for failing to represent the interests of their constituents in matters such as labor rights, civil rights, and environmental destruction. Representations of the family function politically and pedagogically to produce consensus around issues of private morality, simultaneously eradicating dissent over crucial public issues.

Representations of the family convey a fetishistic sense that the family is in dire danger, assaulted by sin and cruelty from every imaginable figure of villainy, from outer-space aliens in a movie like *Independence Day* to the tyranny of the state in *Life Is Beautiful* to, say, organized crime or the perfidies of disease or sleazy teachers or natural disasters or drugs or pornography or killer nineteen-year-olds with guns.[27] Whereas in the seventies TV programs like *The Partridge Family* or *The Brady Bunch* or *Sanford & Son* took divorce or widowhood as a matter of course, not necessarily posing problems that would threaten the social bonding of the family, in the nineties the family seems on the verge of massive devastation, fragile and weakened by any new social force from technology to gay and lesbian marriages to day-care centers. This phenomenon has arisen in conjunction with a backlash on feminism, a squeezing of the workforce, and a downgrading of salaries.

Women are being blamed for working. Feminism can thus be condemned as at best elitist, at worst useless, as it was in *Time* magazine's 1999 issue on "Is Feminism Dead?" Feminism can sometimes even seem no longer relevant as, it can be claimed, women have already reached high management levels, or detrimental because their professionalization leads to the abandonment of children and thus to the growth in pathologies, street crimes, drug abuse, and the like. Blaming women for working limits the popular understanding of feminism's political agenda, making it seem that feminism is concerned only with access to professional careers, so that some feminist traditions' integral involvement with questioning distributions of wealth and with challenging white supremacy can be overlooked, dismissed, and even erased. The assumption in such advocacy is that children are better off and healthier with stay-at-home moms. In most regards, this assumption is embedded in a racist hierarchy of values. As many black feminists have argued, "Like their men, Black women have worked until they could work no more. Like their men, they have assumed the responsibilities of family providers. . . . Unlike the white housewives, who learned to lean on their husbands for economic security, Black wives and mothers, usually workers as well, have rarely been offered the time and energy to become experts at domesticity."[28] The fear of working women and working moms is thus implicated in a fear of cultural values being blackened and de-classed as dysfunctionality, and other crimes enter into homes of those in power. The movie *Traffic* shows this: when the mother lets down her vigilance, the nice white daughter of the drug czar becomes embroiled in black cultures of deviance through becoming addicted to drugs, destroying the picture-perfectness of the white family. What is more, this tendency to blame working women for social problems evolves into a contingent tendency to blame non-working women for social problems, as in the welfare debates. For example, whereas working class and poor women are being accused of poor parenting for *not* working, professional class mothers are being accused of poor parenting *for* working. What seems like a contradiction here is not really a contradiction. A discourse about women's labor is replacing a recognition of class warfare. As Valerie Amos and Pratibha Parmar have written, "Internationally, while Black and Third World women are fighting daily battles for survival, for food, land, and water, western white women's cries of anguish for concern about preserving the planet for future generations sound hollow. Whose standards of life are they trying to preserve?"[29]

Similar to the 1999 films *Life Is Beautiful* and *Enemy of the State*, the Kosovo conflict is a story about a repressive state (the Serbs, with the criminal, power-corrupted Milosevic at their head) that threatens private space and sovereignty by endangering the family. The conflict in Kosovo actually stages a very similar conflict as the one featured in *Life Is Beautiful*. Nazi imagery was used time and again to describe the atrocities of the Serbs, even while their systematic removal of the ethnic Albanians from the province of Kosovo was incessantly compared to the Holocaust. The collapse of Nazi imagery into representations of the Serbs was neatly set off from contingent images of NATO soldiers as benevolent fathers and Albanian mothers as figures of redemption. Such Nazi imagery reflects a patriarchy in disarray where the father abuses his excessive authority. Military technology becomes the means through which the family is saved.

The protection and salvation of the family are launched in this deification of private industry through images of war machinery. These images of military power are meant to glorify corporate efficiency and to testify to the superiority of capitalism. CNN reports of the war in Kosovo were interspersed with Lockheed-Martin commercials. This massive military contractor reminded viewers that it does not only produce the weapons of war but also improves the domestic front. Their warplanes happily fly through computer-generated U.S. neighborhoods. (In reality, part of what Lockheed-Martin does domestically is destroy families by participating in the privatization of federal family services).[30] In many instances, the family images in the Kosovo coverage seem almost organically connected to such images of military technology. The cover photograph of *Time's* Special Report, for instance, shows the Albanian mother breast-feeding her child, but the child's face is invisible, folded inside a bundle of blankets. Two weeks later, the article "Who Will Save the Children?" in *People* starts with a photograph of children running across Kosovar fields towards flying army helicopters. The helicopters here stand spatially in the same place as the mother in the former photograph, giving the same sense of salvation and safety as the mother does in the Special Report. The mother's nourishment seems to blend into the army's presence. The mother figure with her deadened eyes represents a technological fulfillment, the deployment of salvational instruments to defend the innocence of children.

News coverage of Littleton assigned blame for this horrific event to the Internet, video games, movies, schools, violence on TV, and, significantly, to poor parenting. The message conveyed suggests that pedagogical sites like the media and schools are demonic, vampiristically sucking away at children's brains as Lucy did on her gravestone in Bram Stoker's *Dracula*. Such pedagogical influences are here part of a unified assertion about the failure of the adequate policing of youth. Instead of being a potential field for creating resistant identifications, mass media characterizes pedagogy as failed families and mothers. As *Time* asks in a post-Littleton article considering if "character education" would fix the problem of youth violence,

"Where are the parents?"[31] If the kids were building bombs in the garage and stockpiling semi-automatic weapons in their bedrooms, why didn't the parents know about it? *Time* magazine begins its report with a picture of Dylan Klebold being cared for by his mother many years before the incident, with the caption reading that Dylan "grew up in what friends called a happy home."[32]It is the subsequent absence of such proper mothering—a loosening of everyday surveillance—that leads to, then, the catastrophe, suggesting that if this family love had continued, there would have been no violence.[33] The coverage makes clear that Klebold's mother was a professional psychologist specializing in job placement for the disabled. The same *Time* magazine article goes on to talk about Dylan Klebold's "disturbed fictions," which he wrote in his creative-writing class, about "Satan opening a day-care center in hell."[34] The press coverage of Dylan's disturbed fantasies bolster a sense of dereliction pervading in the mother's absence, the complete undermining of social control in the image of the working mother.

The perceived crisis in the family is not just a representational field existing in some ethereal state. It is actually guiding social policies as well as globalization initiatives in very real ways. As Tipper Gore, in the wake of Littleton, urges parents to keep a sharper eye on their kids' moods or depressive urges,[35] and parents in general are encouraged to turn in their kids for "suspicious" behavior, there is an emphasis in the coverage—paralleling the Kosovo coverage—on sentimental reunions between parents and children, as though such reunions ensure the return to social order. *People*, for example, gives the testimony of Zak Cartaya who, in the midst of the Columbine shooting, while hiding under the desks in the choir room, managed to make a telephone call to his mother and tell her that he loved her. "I had to be sure I told my mom I loved her in case I died,"[36] he confessed. Like the link to God during the Christian last rites, the call to the mother at the moment of death serves to re-establish the family as order, goodness, and the site of survival at a time when it has been disrupted by the chaotic explosion of violence and immorality.

It can be said that the growth of state military action abroad is producing the ideological support for the shrinkage of state social action at home. The family functions as the core principle behind the rise of technological power, the very structure through which a military might can assert itself in a territorial takeover. Here is the contradiction: on the one hand, the state military action defends the sacred family unit abroad, while on the other hand, on the domestic front, the family is seen as the limits of the state, responsible in itself for everything from child care to the enforcement of moral behaviors in every corner. While Kosovo was discussed in the media as a maiden-in-distress, in need of the military father to protect her from villainy, rape, and pillage, on the home front the danger to the family is staged as the "bitch's own fault," as the working mother takes the blame for the child's deviant behavior, or the welfare mother needs to stand on her own and stop sucking from the system.

THE PUBLIC AND THE PRIVATE

On both an ideological and material level, attacks on feminism and blaming social problems on women's work or poor family values can be seen as resulting from widespread corporatization and the privatization of the social sphere. They shift public responsibility onto the private sphere by claiming that the private family, rather than the collective public, should maintain the social order. This shift of responsibility towards the private sphere is happening concomitantly with a strident ideological anti-federalism. Anti-federalism proclaims that the public sphere, in the form of an overly burdensome state, is at the root of social rot and degradation and that limits need to be placed on its influence. The family, in this sense, becomes representationally the safe haven against the recklessness of public involvement, including, for example, feminism and other social movements. On the ideological plane, this configuration between the public and the private means that any attempt to define and defend a public role seems to fall into a defense of the state, as the state seems, in the popular mind, to be the primary source of an entrenchment in a public will which curtails individual freedoms. The idea of the public seems only possible as an operation of the state, even though in actuality the state is only one possible place to negotiate and build public power.

Strange Love is therefore concerned with how narratives about private life and freedom are being used to protect corporate powers and actions which are inimical to private life. It therefore points to how the increasingly global movement of capital redefines the relation between public and private.[37] As multinational corporations grow more powerful, state power shrinks not only in terms of the welfare state but also in the defunding of public spaces like schools and parks, as well as in the privatization of state disciplinary functions like military contracting[38] and police,[39] not to mention educational testing and accreditation.[40] Part of this redefinition, as well, has occurred as a result of social movements such as feminism and gay/lesbian liberation which have publicized private life and politicized subjectivity. Legislatively, civil rights to privacy in search and seizure have been reduced while the powers of private businesses now fall under the protections like the First Amendment, previously serving civil liberties and privacy.

The pressing question here is how the new distribution of powers between public and private life affects material distribution and the distribution of cultural-valuation (how the cultures of different groups come to be valued differently). As philosopher Nancy Fraser has shown, the division between public and private life has been instrumental in determining material distribution: "It is clear, too, that the old forms of welfare state, built on assumptions of male-headed families and relatively stable jobs, are no longer suited to providing this protection [against economic uncertainty]."[41] A reconfiguration of private life which results from the new global economy is certainly manifesting itself in different arrangements for family living and is influenced by different cultural traditions interacting in zones of production. Immigration and migrant labor have been a major factor in defining new relations between public support and private freedoms, as children are denied school enrollment on the basis of language ability, or their "failure" as students—the standard argument against bilingual public education—is attributed to inadequate parental attention and dysfunctional family life. Material distribution, Fraser points out, must be understood in relation to culture. "Struggles for [cultural] recognition," she formulates, "occur in a world of exacerbated material inequality—in income and property ownership; in access to paid work, education, health care, and leisure time; but also, more starkly, in caloric intake and exposure to environmental toxicity, and hence in life expectancy and rates of morbidity and mortality."[42]

The state remains a dominant mechanism for defending public life, as it has traditionally been seen through institutions like welfare and public schooling, which are currently, and tragically, being dismantled. Though clearly the nation-state has historically been an arm of capital, it has also created and/or funded institutions serving the public good, it continues to be a key site of struggle, and it is certainly worthwhile to think through the following:

1. In what ways can the state still support the public interest?
2. How can economic distributions be equitably relegated without state interventions—are there other types of institutions that can perform this function? "Any conception of the public sphere," Nancy Fraser contends, "that requires a sharp separation between (associational) civil society and the state will be unable to imagine the forms of self-management, interpublic coordination, and political accountability that are essential to a democratic and egalitarian society"[43]
3. In what ways and under what terms, indeed, *can* a public free of the state *be* imagined, created, and developed, both nationally in terms of a civil society, and internationally in terms of global labor and global social movements? One sees now that international bodies of justice, finance, and distribution are being formed, and it is crucial therefore to envision how such institutions can induce a more just world.

Modernist and postmodernist political theories have offered a spectrum of possibilities for thinking of ways of resisting what is becoming a major ideological assault on the public, providing arguments for supporting the public sphere as a defense for democracy. A Habermasian notion of the public sphere, for example, relies on the state to secure and legitimate democratic communication among citizens. "The constitutional state as a bourgeois state," explains Habermas, "established the public sphere in the political realm as an organ of the state so as to ensure institutionally the connection between law and public opinion."[44] One of the problems with Habermas's model of liberal democracy, however, is that it relies too much on the idea of rational communication among subjects, particularly subjects thinking freely and versed in the values of enlightenment through their increased access to books of literature, art, and philosophy. Not only does such a viewpoint not take into account unequal distributions of access to learning, but it also begs the question of whose knowledge counts. As Habermas himself points out about the eighteenth century establishment of the public sphere, "Women and dependents were factually and legally excluded from the political public sphere."[45] As well, this Habermasian logic also assumes that the free reading of cultural texts determines the interpretation, so that all subjects reach consensus as to rules, procedures, and assumptions. Habermas's focus on free communication and interpretive communities of the eighteenth century means that he does not consider current corporate controls of meaning in the culture industry and how the range of possible interpretation are at least partially already a product of the distribution of money and power and thus already embedded in ideology.

Alternatively, a theory of radical democracy has offered a way of thinking about difference, rather than consensus, as constitutive of the public sphere. Unlike Habermas, Chantal Mouffe has shown how democracy depends on conflict and antagonism, or on Wittgensteinian language games, rather than on consensus, so that deliberation is radically indeterminate. For her, liberal democracy relegates difference to the private sphere, whereas the public is composed of consensus reached through rules and procedures. Mouffe believes that differences need necessarily to be brought into spaces of public deliberation, particularly establishing a democratic ethos where the general good can be considered in relation to individual rights as posed under liberalism. "We should acknowledge and valorize," she insists, "the diversity of ways in which the 'democratic game' can be played, instead of trying to reduce this diversity to a uniform model of citizenship. This would mean fostering a plurality of forms of being a democratic citizen and creating the institutions that would make it possible to follow the democratic rules in a plurality of ways."[46] The problem here is that differences—including differences based on material access, like differences in class—become a matter of subjective identifications and individuation, obfuscating an explanation of how identifications are anything other than cultural or aesthetic questions of taste, or again today how identifications are produced largely through corporate mass media. Indeed, Mouffe envisions class as just another category of difference, another nodal point on the chain of equivalencies. As Mouffe emphasizes justice through politics, the idea of the economic as a pivotal basis for political fairness disappears. Again, the political economy of meaning production, including the production of taste, is left out in favor of a model of negotiating language-meanings between equal parties with equal access to the negotiating table.

The shortcomings in these models of a democratic public sphere result from their focus on the language of communication in a region free of political interventions and impositions, in other words, a space of communication existing between public citizens separate from the state, exterior to the political yet affecting it. This clearly conforms to the way democracy has been defined in the interests of corporate deregulation. In a world where the rights to reap profits free from controls become the discursive equivalent of "free speech," it is absolutely essential that a model for democratic public communication and deliberation include the possibility of state or other types of institutional guidance as a lever for justice, where justice would necessarily include material redistributions. The need for an institutional body to assure economic fairness continues until international organizations for the expansion of economic justice are formed and methods of enforcement are enacted to counter the opposing force—towards the growing powers of accumulation on the parts of rich, corporate elites worldwide— promised by the IMF, the World Bank, NATO, and other such global coalitions. Thus we believe that selective elements of the democratic liberal tradition need to be maintained, particularly in terms of institutional and legal supports for freedom, though we would substitute ideas about collectivity, social justice, and the public good for the individuation which the liberal discourse on private rights so uncompromisingly assumes. As Zygmunt Bauman astutely points out, individual liberty *"can only be a product of collective work. . . .* We move today though towards *privatization of the means to assure . . . individual liberty."*[47]

Vital, in this regard, is Antonio Gramsci's notion of civil society, where there is an interaction between private apparatuses for the production of meaning ("hegemony") and the direct domination of the state:

> In this form of regime ["The State as *veilleur de nuit* " or "The State as policeman] . . . , hegemony over its historical development belongs to private forces, to civil society—which is "State" too, indeed is the State itself. . . . We are still on the terrain of the identification of the State and government—an

identification which is precisely a representation of the economic-corporate form, in other words of the confusion between civil society and political society. For it should be remarked that the general notion of the State includes elements which need to be referred back to the notion of civil society (in the sense that one might say that State = political society + civil society, in other words hegemony protected by the armour of coercion). In a doctrine of the State that conceives the latter as tendentially capable of withering away and of being subsumed into regulated society, the argument is a fundamental one. It is possible to imagine the coercive element of the State withering away by degrees, as ever-more conspicuous elements of regulated society (or ethical State or civil society) make their appearance. . . . What is involved is the reorganisation of the structure and the real relations between men on the one hand and the world of the economy or of production on the other.[48]

This notion of civil society allows us to imagine a civil society forming as part of the State and yet distinct from its coercive functions in order to institute more just material distributions.

Because of the consolidation of corporate mass media, meanings, language, and significations are themselves the basis for both economic relations and culture. So while on the one hand it is still possible to distinguish public ownership and control of institutions, it becomes very difficult to locate public culture. What stands in for public culture are the privately owned yet widely disseminated productions such as TV talk shows, talk radio, and the corporate Internet community. The question is how to expand genuinely public cultures and places—that is, how to shift control of public space to more people. It must be recognized, following Gramsci, that struggles over pedagogy are fundamentally implicated in struggles over the relation between public vs. private power. As such, pedagogical questions point to the potential role of teaching, learning, and cultural production in expanding the public sphere and hence democratic participation. Concomitantly, what needs to be theorized and developed is a notion of the public that is neither reduced to the state nor reduced to private enterprise, but yet takes into account the influence of both. We do not have the scope of foresight to predict the future of the state or the market, but we feel confident in predicting that the death of a notion of the public is akin to the end of the possibility of democracy.

To exemplify the themes that the book will take up, we now use an analysis of how the media's reporting on the tragedy at Columbine High School interrelates with their simultaneous coverage of the war on Kosovo. We use this juxtaposition to explore how sentimental family discourses and popular representations of schools are currently tied to calls for increased enforcement policies protecting market expansion and global war.

COMING HOME TO KOSOVO

Fifty years ago, movies were homogenous, meant to appeal to the whole
family. Now pop culture has been Balkanized. . . . Recent teen films,
whether romance or horror, are really about class warfare. In each movie,
the cafeteria is like a tiny former Yugoslavia, with each clique its own fac-
tion: the Serbian jocks, Bosnian bikers, Kosovar rebels, etc. And the horror
movies are a microcosm of ethnic cleansing.
              —*Time* magazine, reporting on the shootings at Columbine

As mass mediated news accounts of the war in Kosovo were expressed
through stories of families abroad, the school shooting in Littleton, Col-
orado, refocused the nation's attention on violence at home. As the
story unfolded, "The Littleton Massacre" and "The Kosovo Massacre"
began to merge, elements of one bleeding into the other. On 20 April
1999—Hitler's 110th birthday—two white boys calling themselves the
Trenchcoat Mafia shot and killed twelve of their fellow students and
one teacher before turning their guns on themselves. This event was a
tragedy that caused terrible, even devastating sadness for many people.
The enormous, spectacular coverage of the event—of the magnitude of
the 1992 L.A. uprising—however, participates in broader public dialogues, particularly in the way it works to assign blame variously to er-
rant parents, crazy kids, lack of adequate policing, and violent video
games while exonerating the institutions of power—particularly in the
ways they configure economic, political, and social agency. How many
black kids died in the United States that day because of violence and
guns, and why is that information so comparatively hard to access, particularly during a media spectacle that is highlighting the dangers that
kids confront in public schools? In reality, violence in schools has diminished in the past ten years even while people perceive there to be
more violence in schools.[49] Even more relevant, how many Serbian and
ethnic Albanian kids were killed in NATO bombings that day?

The 20 December 1999 issue of *Time* magazine featured exclusive coverage of "The Columbine Tapes: The Killers Tell Why They Did It, the Five
Home Videos They Made Before Their Death, What the Families are Doing to Prevent Another Tragedy." The cover shows Eric Harris and Dylan
Klebold assessing their damage from a frame of the school cafeteria
surveillance video. Open *Time* magazine and immediately following the
contents page is a two-page advertisement for Internet search engine
AltaVista (see pp. 22–24). The advertisement displays the Lockheed Martin F-16 fighter plane in an exploded blueprint diagram with every part
labeled and with the external body of the plane invisible so that the interior is revealed, as in Wonder Woman's aviational aesthetic. The AltaVista

search box overlaying the schematic reveals a search for "Who will guide my sleigh tonight?" Another box headed "AltaVista Shopping" contains a first category "find product" and is filled in "F-16"; the second category "compare with" is filled in with "Reindeer." Turn the page and the advertisement continues with Santa's sled being pulled by an F-16, a weapon that U.S.-led NATO used to bomb Serbia "back to the stone ages."

Thanks to the F-16s top speed of 1,320 mph, Santa will be delivering your presents faster this holiday season. Furthermore, the F-16's armament of one 20mm M61A1 three-barrel cannon with 515 rounds and 20,450 pounds of ordnance guarantees the safe arrival of those presents.

At the top of the page an elf sips a soda and accompanying text reads,

Who needs elves when you have AltaVista Shopping.com? At AltaVista Shopping.com you can research products you know nothing about: stereos, computers, TV's, digital cameras and Pokémon toys, for example. There are 126 different Pokémon characters and over 2,000 licensed Pokémon toys on the market. Only one of them is going to win you most-favored parent status for the coming year. We can help you find out which.

At the bottom of the page, eight cute out-of-work, clearly non-unionized reindeer are accompanied by a search box that reads, "Where can I sell eight tiny reindeer?" Between the three pages of AltaVista ads, *Time* Managing Editor Walter Isaacson editorializes on "Why We Went Back to Columbine." The title, which references a slew of recent stories on returning to Vietnam after a quarter of a century, is headed by a photograph of triumphant white boy high school football players with the caption: "Healing the Wounds: Columbine celebrates its recent state championship."

On one level there is nothing particularly new here in *Time*'s spread. The white male violence of football, toy weapons, violent video games, and global imperialist ventures such as Vietnam and Kosovo arise as the tools for recovering the health of youth and family threatened by the insane and random joyride of the gun-toting Columbine murderers. The AltaVista ad restores the innocence of technology and violent aggression— Internet technology that Klebold and Harris used in their little war. The ad recuperates the Web technology to innocence by associating it with the destructive NATO attack done in the name of love or at least humanitarian intervention but also by associating it with consumerism.

The "innocent" culture of violence transforms imperialist slaughter into Christmas morning family love and fuzzy cuteness. It portrays as healing and recovery violent team sports that emulate war—Columbine High School football team's "state conquest." It mutates military hardware into

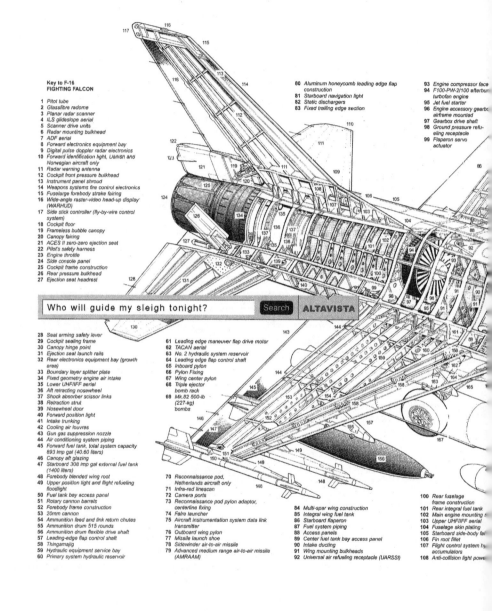

Key to F-16 FIGHTING FALCON

1 Pitot tube
2 Glassfibre radome
3 Planar radar scanner
4 ILS glideslope aerial
5 Scanner drive units
6 Radar mounting bulkhead
7 ADF aerial
8 Forward electronics equipment bay
9 Digital pulse doppler radar electronics
10 Forward identification light, Danish and Norwegian aircraft only
11 Radar warning antenna
12 Cockpit front pressure bulkhead
13 Instrument panel shroud
14 Weapons systems fire control electronics
15 Fuselarge forebody strake fairing
16 Wide-angle raster-video head-up display (WARHUD)
17 Side stick controller (fly-by-wire control system)
18 Cockpit floor
19 Frameless bubble canopy
20 Canopy fairing
21 ACES II zero-zero ejection seat
22 Pilot's safety harness
23 Engine throttle
24 Side console panel
25 Cockpit frame construction
26 Rear pressure bulkhead
27 Ejection seat headrest

28 Seal arming safety lever
29 Cockpit sealing frame
30 Canopy hinge point
31 Ejection seat launch rails
32 Rear electronics equipment bay (growth area)
33 Boundary layer splitter plate
34 Fixed geometry engine air intake
35 Lower UHF/IFF aerial
36 Aft retracting nosewheel
37 Shock absorber scissor links
38 Retraction strut
39 Nosewheel door
40 Forward position light
41 Intake trunking
42 Cooling air louvres
43 Gun gas suppression nozzle
44 Air conditioning system piping
45 Forward fuel tank, total system capacity 893 imp gal (40.60 liters)
46 Canopy aft glazing
47 Starboard 308 imp gal external fuel tank (1400 liters)
48 Forebody blended wing root
49 Upper position light and flight refueling floodlight
50 Fuel tank bay access panel
51 Rotary cannon barrels
52 Forebody frame construction
53 20mm cannon
54 Ammunition feed and link return chutes
55 Ammunition drum 515 rounds
56 Ammunition drum flexible drive shaft
57 Leading-edge flap control shaft
58 Thingamajig
59 Hydraulic equipment service bay
60 Primary system hydraulic reservoir

61 Leading edge maneuver flap drive motor
62 TACAN aerial
63 No. 2 hydraulic system reservoir
64 Leading edge flap control shaft
65 Inboard pylon
66 Pylon Fixing
67 Wing center pylon
68 Triple ejector bomb rack
69 Mk.82 500-lb (227-kg) bombs
70 Reconnaissance pod, Netherlands aircraft only
71 Infra-red linescan
72 Camera ports
73 Reconnaissance pod pylon adaptor, centerline fixing
74 Faire launcher
75 Aircraft instrumentation system data link transmitter
76 Outboard wing pylon
77 Missile launch shoe
78 Sidewinder air-to-air missile
79 Advanced medium range air-to-air missile (AMRAAM)

80 Aluminum honeycomb leading edge flap construction
81 Starboard navigation light
82 Static dischargers
83 Fixed trailing edge section

84 Multi-spar wing construction
85 Integral wing fuel tank
86 Starboard flaperon
87 Fuel system piping
88 Access panels
89 Center fuel tank bay access panel
90 Intake ducting
91 Wing mounting bulkheads
92 Universal air refueling receptacle (UARSSI)

93 Engine compressor face
94 F100-PW-2/100 afterburn turbofan engine
95 Jet fuel starter
96 Engine accessory gearbo airframe mounted
97 Gearbox drive shaft
98 Ground pressure refueling receptacle
99 Flaperon servo actuator

100 Rear fuselage frame construction
101 Rear integral fuel tank
102 Main engine mounting s
103 Upper UHF/IFF aerial
104 Fuselage skin plating
105 Starboard side-body fai
106 Fin root fillet
107 Flight control system hy accumulators
108 Anti-collision light powe

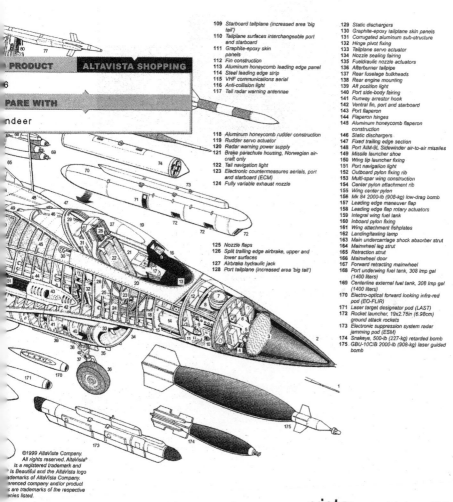

109 Starboard tailplane (increased area 'big tail')
110 Tailplane surfaces interchangeable port and starboard
111 Graphite-epoxy skin panels
112 Fin construction
113 Aluminum honeycomb leading edge panel
114 Steel leading edge strip
115 VHF communications aerial
116 Anti-collision light
117 Tail radar warning antennae

118 Aluminum honeycomb rudder construction
119 Rudder servo actuator
120 Radar warning power supply
121 Brake parachute housing, Norwegian aircraft only
122 Tail navigation light
123 Electronic countermeasures aerials, port and starboard (ECM)
124 Fully variable exhaust nozzle

125 Nozzle flaps
126 Split trailing edge airbrake, upper and lower surfaces
127 Airbrake hydraulic jack
128 Port tailplane (increased area 'big tail')

129 Static dischargers
130 Graphite-epoxy tailplane skin panels
131 Corrugated aluminum sub-structure
132 Hinge pivot fixing
133 Tailplane servo actuator
134 Nozzle sealing fairing
135 Fueldraulic nozzle actuators
136 Afterburner tailpipe
137 Rear fuselage bulkheads
138 Rear engine mounting
139 Aft position light
140 Port side-body fairing
141 Runway arrestor hook
142 Ventral fin, port and starboard
143 Port flaperon
144 Flaperon hinges
145 Aluminum honeycomb flaperon construction
146 Static dischargers
147 Fixed trailing edge section
148 Port AIM-9L Sidewinder air-to-air missiles
149 Missile launcher shoe
150 Wing tip launcher fixing
151 Port navigation light
152 Outboard pylon fixing rib
153 Multi-spar wing construction
154 Center pylon attachment rib
155 Wing center pylon
156 Mk 84 2000-lb (908-kg) low-drag bomb
157 Leading edge maneuver flap
158 Leading edge flap rotary actuators
159 Integral wing fuel tank
160 Inboard pylon fixing
161 Wing attachment fishplates
162 Landing/taxiing lamp
163 Main undercarriage shock absorber strut
164 Mainwheel leg strut
165 Retraction strut
166 Mainwheel door
167 Forward retracting mainwheel
168 Port underwing fuel tank, 308 Imp gal (1400 liters)
169 Centerline external fuel tank, 308 Imp gal (1400 liters)
170 Electro-optical forward looking infra-red pod (EO-FLIR)
171 Laser target designator pod (LAST)
172 Rocket launcher, 19x2.75in (6.98cm) ground attack rockets
173 Electronic suppression system radar jamming pod (ESM)
174 Snakeye, 500-lb (227-kg) retarded bomb
175 GBU-10C/B 2000-lb (908-kg) laser guided bomb

alta^{vista:} smart is beautiful

www.altavista.com

a fashion show for viewers to identify with destructive power (AltaVista's motto adorning the F-16 blueprint is "Smart Is Beautiful"). Central to this recovery of the "innocent" culture of violence is the transformation of justice into the act of consumption. The final text of the ad reads:

Can I really purchase military aircraft online? Let's put it this way: if military aircraft were available for purchase by the general public, we'd not only find it for you, we'd find you a deal that would make the Defense Department jealous. That said, AltaVista Shopping.com lets you scour the entire Web for just about anything you can buy, even if we don't sell it.

What is so shocking and even terrifying in this spread is an open admission that U.S. military aggression in such places as the Balkans and Iraq is fundamentally about the expansion of markets.

Yet the big lie at work here is the suggestion that the dropping of bombs is the same as the dropping of consumer goods (the expansion of markets) and all in the name of the preservation of childhood innocence as the stronghold of a civilization severely menaced when these values go awry. The ad suggests that destruction is really about the enrichment of the place being bombed because it is about the expansion of American wealth, markets, and consumer goods. While multinational corporations did line up to take advantage of infrastructural rebuilding, some estimates placed former Yugoslavia's recovery time from the bombing at fifty years. Perhaps more pertinent, those places that have agreed to Americanization without bombs have also suffered terribly from "structural adjustment." If Isaacson's interceding headline "Why We Went Back to Columbine" resonates with a spate of articles about why we went back to Vietnam, that is because the bombing of Kosovo as a part of the new imperialism really is a return to Vietnam and Isaacson's headline is simultaneously about how *Time* magazine's return to Columbine is also a return to Vietnam.

In fact, the imperialist venture of bombing Kosovo is replicated in the call for increased discipline, mostly in inner cities, that followed the Columbine massacre. As Harris and Klebold let a slew of bullets loose on the suburban kids who were calmly eating their lunches or studying chemistry before the attack, the tragedy of a cruel Milosevic performing ethnocide came home. The need for the intervention to defend the defenseless Albanians blurred into the need to defend our kids at home through increasing police enforcement of inner cities. Reflected in the coverage of the Columbine massacre, Kosovo thus appeared as the exporting of the inner city. Columbine coverage entered a discourse on youth innocence that is essentially an imperialist discourse assigning criminality to the colonized. It thus treats youth differently depending on race and class. As Harris and Klebold created public Web site paeans to Hitler, declared hatred for blacks, Asians, and Latinos, still no one believed white kids from the sub-urbs were capable of such violence. As Henry Giroux points out,

> If these kids had been black or brown, they would have been denounced not as psychologically troubled but as bearers of a social pathology. Moreover, if brown or black kids had exhibited Eric Harris and Dylan Klebold's previous history of delinquent behavior, including breaking into a van and sending death threats to fellow students over the Internet, they would not have merely been given short-term counseling. On the contrary, they would have been roundly condemned and quickly sent to prison.[50]

In the words of Patricia Williams, Klebold and Harris

> seem to have been so shrouded in presumptions of innocence—after pro-fessing their love for Hitler, declaring their hatred for blacks, Asians and Lati-nos on a public Web site no less, downloading instructions for making bombs, accumulating the ingredients, assembling them under the protec-tively indifferent gaze (or perhaps with the assistance) of parents and neigh-bors, stockpiling guns and ammunition, procuring hand grenades and flak jackets, threatening the lives of classmates, killing thirteen and themselves, wounding numerous others and destroying their school building—still the community can't seem to believe it really happened "here." Still their teach-ers and classmates continue to protest that they were good kids, good stu-dents, solid citizens.[51]

What *Time* and AltaVista add to this scenario is that this presumption of innocence saturating the Columbine coverage promotes the innocence of the imperialist mission in Kosovo.

Similar to the public conversation at the beginning of the Gulf War, end-less articles debating the Kosovo air war focused on the danger of a ground war that would get the United States embroiled in "another Viet-nam." As Noam Chomsky points out, there has been a long project in the mass media of getting the public to overcome the "Vietnam Syndrome." That is, the conservative restoration of the last three decades has involved making global aggression and the murder of combatants and non-combat-ants in foreign nations once again palatable to the public. Yet, Kosovo is different from Vietnam and the hot wars of the Cold War in that the ven-tures of militarized globalization since the end of the cold war are still not viewed by the public as worth U.S. lives. Writes Ellen Meiskins Wood,

> In his Manifesto [for the Fast World], [Thomas L.] Friedman explains that Americans, who "were ready to pay any price and bear any burden in the Cold War," are unwilling to die for that "abstract globalization system." That's why "house-to-house fighting is out; cruise missiles are in." He could just as easily have said "that's why ground troops are out and high-tech

bombing is in. We don't want to die ourselves for globalization, but we don't mind killing others."[52]

For Wood, part of what successfully undercut popular and particularly left opposition to Kosovo, unlike Vietnam, was the pretense of humanitarian intervention that mystified the imperialism.

> We now have what some have called "human rights imperialism," based on a conception of human rights in which the particular interests of the U.S. and its arbitrary actions have effectively displaced the common interests of humanity and the international instruments designed to represent them. The notion of "human rights imperialism" nicely captures the mystification that seems to have swayed a lot of people on the left in the case of Kosovo.[53]

Open claims in news outlets as to the humanitarianism of the bombing were matched by a spate of popular war films such as *Saving Private Ryan* and culminating in *The Patriot* and *Pearl Harbor* that brought the "good war" theme back after a long stretch of "bad war" Vietnam films.

If pre-Kosovo *Saving Private Ryan* reinvented the public and political motives for World War II as the redemption of the private and apolitical maintenance of the family, then post-Kosovo *The Patriot* took this theme even further, suggesting that the American Revolution—the good war par excellence—was about nothing but family. "What difference does it make if I'm ruled by a tyrant three thousand miles away or by three thousand tyrants one mile away," orates Mel Gibson's character at the South Carolina meeting about whether to enter the war on the side of the colonies, just before joining up to defend his southern plantation family. In other words, fighting for the politics of democracy poses dangers to the preservation of the family and, in fact, Gibson's two eldest sons get killed in the fray.

The film further portrays the disruption of the family by showing the British enslavement of the black plantation farmhands who claim to be working as free labor, the system many characters in the film insist the revolutionaries are defending. In the film, the black plantation laborers explicitly claim to be working as free labor rather than as slaves (until the tyrannical British arrest them and turn them into slaves), even though the images of black labor are surely borrowed from a cultural repertory of traditional, familiar images from slavery. The film suggests that the war was about freeing the slaves in defense of ideas about self-determination and free will (represented in the defense of the family against state authoritarianism), the goal of the "good war." It is only when the British threaten this self-determination—by entering the home and killing one of the kids, and by enslaving black labor—that a defense campaign can be taken up. Just as the AltaVista ad replaces fanciful toy reindeer with real fighter planes, in *The Patriot* Mel Gibson's character melts down his dead son's toy lead soldiers into bullets. The campaign against Kosovo involved getting over the "Vietnam Syndrome" to return to the "good war" by reinventing imperialist aggression as a loving gift, associating it with the childhood innocence of Rudolph the Rednosed Reindeer and Santa Claus himself. Merry Christmas, Kosovo. Merry Christmas, Serbia.

Dr. Strangelove feels envy.

WAR GAMES

The Columbine shooting coverage was also a return to the battlefield. As mentioned, Isaacson's title "Why We Went Back to Columbine" references the return to Vietnam after twenty-five years in order to open markets. It is contextualized with a photo of Columbine's football team conquest captioned, "Healing the Wounds: Columbine celebrates its recent state championship." Isaacson begins,

> I want to explain why we returned to Columbine this week, running a chilling cover photo and stories about killers we would rather forget. . . . We sent a team back to Littleton, Colo., to investigate what actually motivated the killers and find out what they were really like. What could we learn about how to spot—and deal with—the demons that can lurk inside the souls of seemingly average kids? . . . Assistant managing editor Dan Goodgame, who led our team, is the father of three schoolkids and the husband of a teacher, and he was sympathetic to the concerns of the survivors and others in the community.[54]

It is, perhaps, a coincidence that the leader of *Time*'s team that went in search of "answers" about Columbine is named "Goodgame." It is not, however, a coincidence that Isaacson uses the metaphor of the "good game" to discuss the Columbine recovery, health, and healing. The AltaVista ads link global trade and military competition between nations to parental competition for children's love. "Only one [Pokémon toy] is going to win you most-favored parent status for the coming year."

It is not only the editorial and the AltaVista spread that refer to gaming. Page after page of *Time* is filled with "news" and advertisements that tout the salubrious power of gaming as well as its dangers: Headline page eight—"Is Your Dog an Athlete?" "Border collies . . . get psychotic if they don't have work."[55] Page nine: "Enter to win the APC Home Power Protection Package." Two page spread on twelve and thirteen advertising ClearStation.com: "I'm simply going to move to the sidelines until the trend becomes more clear." Turn the page and Mohegan Sun Casino asks, "Who needs caffeine? Experience the rush of 190 gaming tables, over 3,000 slot machines. . . . All in a setting that'll blow you away." Turn the page and see James Bond, the regal and suave gamer extraordinaire who blows away his opponents, pitching an Omega watch. Turn the page and find a colorful two page spread with a man on the Olympic rings transforming into mercury and information for a Web application called Akamai, "Why embrace mediocrity and risk indifference when intensity and impact are at your fingertips." Turn two pages and a girl shoots hoops in an idyllic black and white photo of the heartland as State Farm Insurance tells us that "She learned about life in a world of broken glass and blacktop where nothing is given. Especially to those trying to play a man's game. . . . State Farm is a proud supporter of women's sports and women's dreams. Little girls have big dreams too." Turn the page and the daily game of the stock market advertises Compaq computers. Turn again and the new MobilExxon oil conglomerate tells us that their anticompetitive merger is in fact, "A future where the best combination of ideas, technology and talent will win." A page turn later and an arthritis drug called Vioxx has a two page spread of a father and son on a soccer field, "Vioxx can help make it easier for you to do the things you want to do. Like sitting down on the grass to watch your kid's game." But you may not be sitting too long as, "Commonly reported side effects included upper respiratory infection, diarrhea, nausea, and high blood pressure." Other news content of *Time* is, of course, also framed in terms of competition from the education article on the dangers of cheating to the "Winners and Sinners of 1999" column to the Columbine tapes feature itself.

The difficulty that parents, teachers, and the police had in identifying the violent outbursts of Harris and Klebold owes, in part, to the normalcy of such competitive violence that saturates not only *Time* magazine's reporting and advertisements but pervades mass media more generally, particularly as it sells the public on globalization. Such a fine line between "healthy" and "pathological" competitive violence became particularly blurry as Bill Clinton himself said after the tragedy, while continuing the bombing campaign on Kosovo, refusing diplomatic solutions, "We must teach our children . . . to resolve their conflicts with words, not weapons."

The Columbine story involves regularly repeated acts of playing: "Eric Harris adjusts his video camera a few feet away, then settles into his chair with a bottle of Jack Daniels and a sawed-off shotgun in his lap. He calls it Arlene, after a favorite character in the gory Doom video games and books that he likes so much. He takes a small swig. The whiskey stings, but he tries to hide it, like a small child playing grown-up."[56] "It's going to be like f—ing Doom. Tick, tick, tick, tick-Haa! That f—ing shotgun is straight out of Doom."[57] "It's easy to see the signs: how a video-game joystick turned Harris into a better marksman like a golfer who watches Tiger Woods videos."[58] Whereas Clinton equates "playing grown-up" with playing with words, Harris and Klebold equate "playing grown-up" with the violence of adults like Clinton and the valorization of violent competition more generally.

News coverage downplayed the fact that Harris and Klebold were re-solving a conflict in a way consistent with the competitive violence sur-rounding them. Instead *Time* opts to emphasize the shooters' thirst for fame. A photo in the *Time* coverage of angry and imposing-looking football play-ers is titled, "The classmates Harris and Klebold felt immense rage toward all, not just jocks." Yet later commentary reveals the extent to which the shooters did seek revenge against the violent culture that targeted them.

> Evan Todd, the 255-lb. defensive lineman who was wounded in the library, describes the climate this way: "Columbine is a clean, good place except for those rejects," Todd says of Klebold and Harris and their friends. "Most kids didn't want them there. They were into witchcraft. They were into voodoo dolls. Sure, we teased them. But what do you expect with kids who come to school with weird hairdos and horns on their hats? It's not just jocks; the whole school's disgusted with them. They're a bunch of ho-mos, grabbing each other's private parts. If you want to get rid of some-one, usually you tease 'em. So the whole school would call them homos, and when they did something sick, we'd tell them, 'You're sick and that's wrong.'"[59]

Time's commentary, in the tradition of nineteenth century sciences of race, positions Harris and Klebold as uppity, mutinous colonized subjects prac-ticing magical curses against the righteous, governing elite. Because Har-ris and Klebold practice voodoo and because they are "homos," the jocks, like nineteenth century colonials, serve as defenders of the morality on which civilization is founded and which was threatened by the evil su-perstitious practices and the unlawful, ungodly sexual proclivities. The superstitious violence of Harris and Klebold is used to justify the disgust and then the violence of the morally upholding jocks.

Remarkably, *Time* uses the above quote as evidence that the shooters were not responding to systematic cruelty by other students. Instead, the article emphasizes a desire for celebrity. However, in the following article, "The Victims: Never Again," the father of victim Daniel Rohrbough says, "Jocks could get away with anything. If they wanted to punch a kid in the mouth and walk away, they could. Had I known this, my son wouldn't have been there. They did nothing to protect the students from each other."[60] Rohrbough's statement clearly attests to how the thin façade of innocence barely covered a vicious culture of violence. The tapes them-selves reveal the killers' motive to settle a score at being unable to com-pete: "Harris recalls how he moved around so much with his military family and always had to start over, 'at the bottom of the ladder.'"[61]

The *Time* coverage charges that the police, parents, and the community failed to see how Harris and Klebold's violent fantasies were motivated not so much by the desire for revenge as ultimately the desire for celebrity.

Because this may have been about celebrity as much as cruelty. "They wanted to be famous," concludes FBI agent Mark Holstlaw. "And they are. They're infamous. It used to be said that living well is the best revenge; for these two, it was to kill and die in spectacular fashion."[62] The emphasis on the killers' desire for fame in the coverage downplays the extent to which the shootings were politically motivated as Giroux and Williams show, but the emphasis on fame as an alibi also effaces the extent to which the shootings took the competitive culture of violence to its logical extension, even as the boys turned themselves into commodities, notorious for an instant. Harris and Klebold were even willing to sacrifice their own lives to win at the game they had been losing for years.

There is an overwhelming sense in the coverage that police and parents lost the competition with the kids by failing to see the signs, failing in the shootout at the school, and due to the suicides even losing the satisfaction of a legal trial to see authority restored symbolically. Just as endless Vietnam films of the 1970s and 1980s brought to national consciousness a notion of the Viet Cong as an enemy that could not be seen, everywhere and nowhere, simultaneously culpable aggressors and innocent victims, media coverage surrounding Columbine and Kosovo framed youth simultaneously as innocent victims in need of saving and as violent aggressors hell-bent on destruction. The Vietnam films produced a nostalgia for a good war in which the enemy was visible, thereby replacing a meaningful public discussion of the motives for U.S. imperial aggression with a suggestion that the real problem behind a war that cost roughly 60,000 U.S. and over 2 million Vietnamese lives, was that the United States was denied an opportunity to fight the good fight. Such representation both denies the politics undergirding U.S. global aggression and transforms the aggressor into the victim. Similarly, Columbine coverage produced nostalgia for the "good school" with its innocent culture of violence exemplified by white boy warriors on the football field. The coverage denies the relationship between the pervasive culture of violence that structures the lived realities of school for many students and the broader social structures that such violence serves.

It is precisely this connection that *Time*'s editor denies in the "Why We Returned to Columbine" editorial. Says *Time* editor-in-chief Norman Pearlstine, defending *Time*'s sensationalist coverage, "It's not our tendency to sensationalize crime or do covers on the crime of the week. Sometimes, however, a shocking picture—of a wartime execution, a brutality, a kid with a gun—along with an analysis of the tale behind it serves to focus our eyes on things we would prefer to ignore but instead should try to understand."[63] Yet, not unlike the Vietnam War practice of measuring success through body counts, understanding and even justice ultimately become the compilation of the most possible minute details of the event by *Time*'s team, thereby replacing with spectacle a meaningful discussion of the role that the innocent culture of violence plays in maintaining a social order in the service of the corporation.

CHAPTER BREAKDOWN

Strange Love seeks to answer the question of how varied cultural forms—in this case, curricula, multicultural literature, and popular films—educate the public ideologically. While such ideological analysis of cultural politics is hardly unique in the fields of cultural studies and critical education, *Strange Love* marks the entry into critical education of a global critique of cultural politics that reveals the extent to which domestic stories such as the Columbine school shootings justify global aggression, and conversely the way that representations of the global mediate the coverage of domestic incidents and social policy. That is, *Strange Love* interrogates the relationship between the political economy of globalization and the new human rights imperialism and the cultural politics that educate the public into complicity with it through such narratives as family, war, politics, privatization, and innocence. While much has been written about the policy of the new human rights imperialism, very little has been written about the cultural pedagogical project accompanying and supporting it. *Strange Love* looks to the ways education itself is being infiltrated by corporate curricula that make the most destructive elements of the new imperialism appear as their diametrical opposite.

The book has three parts. Each part comprises two chapters. Part I details how corporate initiatives in education are presenting themselves as philanthropy, entertainment, and even progressive pedagogy when in reality they are part of an attack on the public sector and democracy; part II shows the ways some recent multicultural and postcolonial literature purports to further democratic inclusion and "humanize the other," yet we show how it supports neoliberal doctrine and neoliberal foreign and domestic policies which undermine democracy in multiple ways and tend towards destroying others abroad for corporate profit; part III shows how two recent popular films appear to champion family and childhood innocence when, in fact, they function to deny the social and sanctify the private sphere and consumerism.

Chapter 1: Junk King Education. Michael Milken is sold to the public in mass media as a benevolent savior of education when in fact he is spearheading a destructive move for a hostile corporate takeover of education and the redefinition of education as a private rather than a public good.

Chapter 2: Rivers of Fire: Amoco's iMPACT. Amoco distributes a science curriculum which promotes their notion of "progressive pedagogy" as entertainment, fun, and love. Following on the critique of the corporate raid on education as recounted in the previous chapter, this chapter focuses specifically on how the corporate curriculum functions as both ideology for corporate culture and as diversion from what this oil giant is doing globally. The curriculum does not mention Amoco's use of science for its profit-seeking domestic and overseas destruction of the environment, displacement of indigenous peoples, human rights violations, or the undermining of democracy.

Chapter 3: A Time for Flying Horses: Oil Education and the Future of Literature. Keri Hulme's novel *The Bone People*, winner of Mobil Oil's Pegasus Prize as well as the Booker Prize, has been hailed by scholars in postcolonialism and multiculturalism as a celebration of family, spiritual healing, and Maori recognition. Following on the prior chapter's critique of the oil industry's intervention in public school curriculum, this chapter shows how the novel, widely read as postcolonial higher education curriculum, celebrates international finance and presents nature as ripe for corporate exploitation while attacking public institutions and labor.

Chapter 4: The Mayor's Madness: So Far from God. Ana Castillo's acclaimed Chicana novel *So Far from God* receives praise for setting up ideals of a caring feminist community. Yet, its anti-federalism and critique of public institutions in conjunction with its celebration of the private, bolsters cruel ideologies that are enacted in such policies as New York City Mayor Rudolph Giuliani's attacks on the homeless. Following from the prior chapter's discussion of corporate influence in seemingly progressive higher education curriculum, this chapter is concerned with how individualist values promoted through particular versions of multicultural higher education curriculum are feeding ideologies that justify the gutting of the public sphere.

Chapter 5: Enemy of the State. Equality and freedom appear as major concerns of this popular 1999 film. However, this chapter, the first of two chapters on media pedagogy, discusses how these seemingly democratic values are transformed by the filmmakers into equality as the effacement of difference, and freedom as the freedom to consume the vast array of commodities advertised by the film. Ideal for neoliberal vilification of the public sphere, as in *So Far from God*, the public appears as the enemy of ethnic difference and affective human communities in this film.

Chapter 6: A Hilarious Romp Through the Holocaust. Academy Award winning *Life Is Beautiful* stresses the virtue of parental sacrifice for the protection of children and youthful innocence. However, as this chapter discusses, the film shows how the political is demonized through making political knowledge seem dangerous to children, defining freedom as the free pursuit of business and public action as an obstacle to private happiness and affective human relations. This chapter discusses how the neoliberal ideology promoted in *Life Is Beautiful* poses the private family and business in a cosmic battle against the evils of the public sphere. Expanding the prior chapter's discussions of the ideologies of anti-federalism, this analysis shows how film promotes values that endanger youth by propagating ideologies favorable to the privatization and elimination of the welfare state designed to protect them.

Strange Love is fundamentally concerned with possibilities of resistance and the politics of hope, in short with changing the social vision of the world that corporate capitalism imposes. In doing so, *Strange Love* takes Cultural Studies beyond its current entrenchment in representational analysis, image wars, and the aesthetics of recognition, arguing that culture is vitally connected to the building of political agendas and policy. As Edward Said writes,

> For in an age of the mass media and . . . the manufacture of consent, it is Panglossian to imagine that the careful reading of a few works of art considered humanistically, professionally, or aesthetically significant is anything but a private activity with only slender public consequences. Texts are protean things; they are tied to circumstances and to politics large and small, and these require attention and criticism. No one can take stock of everything, of course, just as no one theory can explain or account for the connections among texts and societies. But reading and writing texts are never neutral activities: there are interests, power, passions, pleasures entailed no matter how aesthetic or entertaining the work.[64]

Strange Love is concerned with how teaching critical consciousness can make the conditions for social change. It offers educators tools to show how cultural representations are political, supporting a power structure in the interests of multinational capital and at the expense of democracy. Teachers can draw on the insights of critical pedagogy in order both to expose and to challenge the feel-good sentiment in which the mainstream media is cloaking corporate expansion and neo-imperialism. Critical pedagogy, writes Giroux, "as a form of political activism refers to a deliberate attempt by cultural workers to influence how knowledge and subjectivities are produced within particular social relations."[65]

NOTES

1. While the Democratic and Republican parties seem to differ on social policy issues such as abortion, both affirm the justice of corporate capital, frequently conflating democracy with liberal capitalism.

2. As Zygmunt Bauman points out, "Even those who think they know what is to be done throw the towel into the ring when it comes to deciding who—what

kind of an effective institution—is going to do it." *The Individualized Society* (Malden, Mass.: Polity, 2001), 53.

3. Chris Hartman, ed., "Facts and Figures," www.inequality.org/factsfr.html, 18 September 2000 (Shifting Fortunes). "Since the mid-1970s, the most fortunate one percent of households have doubled their share of the national wealth. They now hold more wealth than the bottom 95 percent of the population." James D. Wolfensohn, "The Other Crisis," www.worldbank.org/html/extdr/am98/jdw-sp/am98-en.htm, 6 October 1998. In a report to the World Bank's Board of Governors, James D. Wolfensohn attests, "Across the world 1.3 billion people live on less than $1 a day; 3 billion live on under $2 a day; 1.3 billion have no access to clean water; 3 billion have no access to sanitation; 2 billion have no access to power." Bauman, *The Individualized Society*, 115. In the United States alone, "by far the richest country in the world and the homeland of the world's wealthiest people, 16.5 percent of the population live in poverty; one fifth of adult men and women can neither read nor write, while 13 percent have a life expectancy shorter than sixty years."

4. Bauman, *The Individualized Society*, 115.

5. Bauman, *The Individualized Society*, 114.

6. "Index," *Harper's*, July 2000.

7. Jerry W. Sanders, "Two Mexicos and Fox's Quandary," *The Nation*, 26 February 2001, 18–19. "According to data from the 2000 consensus, fully 75 percent of the population of Mexico lives in poverty today (with fully one-third in extreme poverty), as compared with 49 percent in 1981, before the imposition of the neoliberal regimen and, later, NAFTA. Meanwhile, the longstanding gap between the northern and southern regions, as manifested in poverty, infant mortality, and malnutrition rates, has grown wider as the latter has borne the brunt of neoliberal adjustment policies. Chiapas, for example, produces more than half of Mexico's hydroelectric power, an increasing portion of which flows north to the maquiladora zone on the Mexico–U.S. border. Yet, even including its major cities of Tuxtla Gutiérrez and San Cristóbal de las Casas, only half of Chiapanecan households have electricity or running water. Additional water sources have been diverted to irrigate large landholdings devoted to export-oriented agriculture and commercial forestry, while peasant farmers have suffered reductions in water and other necessities as well as an end to land reform, even as they have endured a flood of U.S. agribusiness exports that followed the NAFTA opening. According to the Mexican government's own official estimates, 1.5 million peasants will be forced to leave agriculture in the next one to two decades, many driven northward to face low-wage maquiladoras on one side of the border and high-tech militarization on the other."

8. John Williams, "Look, Child Poverty in the Wealthy Countries Isn't Necessary," *The International Herald Tribune*, 24 July 2000. See also Chris Hartman, ed., "Facts and Figures": "Nine states have reduced child poverty rates by more than 30 percent since 1993. These states include Tennessee, Michigan, Arkansas, South Carolina, Mississippi, Kentucky, Illinois and New Jersey. Michigan is a prime example of a national trend, in that even the recent dramatic improvement did not counter the losses of the previous 15 years, in which its poverty rate increased 121 percent. In California, the number of children living in poverty has grown from 900,000 in 1979, to 2.15 million in 1998 (Columbia University)."

9. Stephan Shalom, "The State of the World," *Z-Net,* www.lbbs.org/CrisesCurEvts/Globalism/14shalom.htm, 14 September 1999.

10. Ellen Meiskins Wood, "Kosovo and the New Imperialism," in *Masters of the Universe?* edited by Tariq Ali (New York: Verso, 2000), 199.

11. Thomas L. Friedman, *The Lexus and the Olive Tree* (New York: Farrar Straus Giroux, 1999), 373.

12. Friedman, *The Lexus and the Olive Tree,* 304.

13. Friedman, *The Lexus and the Olive Tree,* 373.

14. Wood, "Kosovo and the New Imperialism," 199.

15. Noam Chomsky, *The New Military Humanism: Lessons from Kosovo* (Monroe, Maine: Common Courage Press, 2000), 4–12.

16. Ken Silverstein, *Private Warriors* (New York: Verso, 2000), ix.

17. Arvind Rajagopal, "Thinking Through Emerging Markets: Brand Logics and the Cultural Forms of Political Society in India," *Social Text 60,* 17, no. 3 (Fall 1999), 134.

18. Henry A. Giroux, *Stealing Innocence: Youth, Corporate Power and the Politics of Culture* (New York: St. Martin's Press, 2000), 25.

19. Judith Butler, "Restaging the Universal," in *Contingency, Hegemony, Universality: Contemporary Dialogues on the Left,* edited by Judith Butler, Ernesto Laclau, and Slavoj Zizek (New York: Verso, 2000), 13–14.

20. Giroux, *Stealing Innocence,* 25–26. "Making the political more pedagogical requires that educators address how agency unfolds within power-infused relations, that is, how the very processes of learning constitute the political mechanisms through which identities are produced, desires are mobilized, and experiences take on specific forms and meanings. This broad definition of pedagogy is not limited to what goes on in institutionalized forms of schooling; it encompasses every relationship youth [and adults] imagine to be theirs in the world. So to understand and overcome today's assault on youth [and the public sector more broadly], educators need to rethink the interrelated dynamics of politics, culture, power, and responsibility and redefine their own political role."

21. Frederick Engels, *The Origin of the Family, Private Property and the State,* edited by Eleanor Burke Leacock, translated by Alec West (New York: International Publishers, 1972). "In an old unpublished manuscript written by Marx and myself in 1846, I find the words: 'The first division of labor is that between man and woman for the propagation of children.' And today I can add: The first class opposition that appears in history coincides with the development of the antagonism between man and woman in monogamous marriage, and the first class oppression coincides with that of the female sex by the male.

22. Claude Lévi-Strauss, *The Elementary Structures of Kinship,* trans. Rodney Needham and James H. Bell (Boston: Beacon, 1971).

23. Michel Foucault, *The History of Sexuality: An Introduction,* vol. 1, translated by Robert Hurley (New York: Vintage Books), 1978. "[During the monotonous nights of the Victorian bourgeoisie,] sexuality was carefully confined; it moved into the home. The conjugal family took custody of it and absorbed it into the serious function of reproduction. On the subject of sex . . . the couple imposed itself as model, enforced the norm, safeguarded the truth, and reserved the right to speak while retaining the principle of secrecy. A single locus of sexuality was ac-

knowledged in social space as well as at the heart of every household, but it was a utilitarian and fertile one: the parents' bedroom."

24. Jacques Danzelot, *The Policing of Families*, translated by Robert Hurley (Baltimore: Johns Hopkins University Press, 1997).

25. Nancy Fraser, *Justice Interruptus: Critical Reflections on the "Postsocialist" Condition* (New York: Routledge, 1997), 42.

26. Chantal Mouffe, *The Democratic Paradox* (London: Verso, 2000).

27. Sigmund Freud, "Fetishism," in *Sexuality and the Psychology of Love*, edited by Philip Rieff (New York: Collier Books, 1963), 216. *Fetishistic* here is meant in a Freudian sense, where there is recognition that the thing has disappeared but that it still appears as a fantasy of representation, "a sort of permanent memorial to itself"—"the perception has persisted and . . . a very energetic action has been exerted to keep up the denial of [the loss of the object perceived]."

28. Angela Y. Davis, *Women, Race & Class* (New York: Vintage Books, 1981), 231–32.

29. Valerie Amos and Pratibha Parmar, "Challenging Imperial Feminism," in *Feminism & 'Race'*, edited by Kum-Kum Bhavnani (Oxford: Oxford University Press, 2001), 30.

30. William P. Ryan, "The New Landscape for Non-Profits" *Harvard Business Review*, 24 November 1999.

31. Andrew Ferguson, "Character Goes Back to School," *Time*, 24 May 1999, 68.

32. Eric Pooley, "Portrait of a Deadly Bond," *Time*, 10 May 1999, 26.

33. Terry McCarthy, "Warning: Andy Williams Here. Unhappy Kid," *Time*, 19 March 2001, 24. This logic of maternal abandonment has continued to pervade post-Columbine school shootings, for example, when Andy Williams shot Bryan Zuckor and Randy Gordon and wounded thirteen others at Santee High School in California in the spring of 2001. "Things weren't great at home either," reports *Time*. "Williams' parents had divorced when he was 5, and he rarely saw his mother after that. Several friends said he would automatically call their mothers Mom."

34. Pooley, "Portrait of a Deadly Bond," 30.

35. Tipper Gore, "Drop the Stigma," *Time*, 10 May 1999, 32.

36. Bill Hewitt et al. "Sorrow and Outrage," *People*, 3 May 1999, 97.

37. By *public*, we mean publicly funded institutions (schools, roads, etc.), popular participation in decision-making through civil society (public intellectuals, civic groups, elections, protests, public gatherings, public assemblies, citizen groups, collective action, the Internet, militias, etc.). By *private*, we mean civil liberties and protected spaces for political action where corporate power is limited.

38. See Silverstein's *Private Warriors* for an extended illustration of the global privatization of armed forces. This includes private mercenary forces but also the corporate backed expansion of NATO and the consolidation of military contractors to only Lockheed Martin and Boeing, to name a few examples.

39. For a discussion of the interrelation among privatization, capitalist ideology, and the police and prison system see Christian Parenti, *Lockdown America: Police and Prisons in the Age of Crisis* (London: Verso, 1999); and Joel Dyer, *The Perpetual Prisoner Machine: How America Profits from Crime* (Boulder, Colo.: Westview Press, 2000).

40. For a discussion of the relationship between educational reform initiatives, corporatization, and militarization see Kenneth J. Saltman's *Collateral Damage: Corporatizing Public Schools – A Threat to Democracy* (Lanham, Md.: Rowman & Littlefield, 2000). For a discussion of the privatization of higher education, see Stanley Aronowitz, *The Knowledge Factory: Dismantling the Corporate University and Creating True Higher Learning* (Boston: Beacon, 2000).

41. Fraser, *Justice Interruptus*, 42.

42. Fraser, *Justice Interruptus*, 11.

43. Fraser, *Justice Interruptus*, 92.

44. Jürgen Habermas, *The Structural Transformation of the Public Sphere: An Inquiry into a Category of Bourgeois Society*, translated by Thomas Burger with Frederick Lawrence (Cambridge, Mass.: MIT Press, 1989), 81.

45. Habermas, *The Structural Transformation of the Public Sphere*, 56.

46. Mouffe, *The Democratic Paradox*, 73.

47. Zygmunt Bauman, *In Search of Politics* (Stanford, Calif.: Stanford University Press, 1999), 7.

48. Antonio Gramsci, *Selections from the Prison Notebooks*, edited by and translated by Quintin Hoare and Geoffrey Nowell Smith (New York: International Publishers, 1971), 261–63.

49. See "Facts About Violence Among Youth and Violence in Schools," a study published by the Centers for Disease Control and Prevention's National Center for Injury Prevention and Control and the 1999 Annual School Safety Report published by the U.S. Department of Education. Both show decreases in school violence in the nineties. Both reports suggest that schools are some of the safest places that kids can be. See also, Mike Males, *Scapegoat Generation* (Monroe, Maine: Common Courage Press, 1996).

50. Giroux, *Stealing Innocence*, 8.

51. Patricia J. Williams, "The Auguries of Innocence," *The Nation*, 24 May 1999, 9.

52. Wood, "Kosovo and the New Imperialism," 196–97.

53. Wood, "Kosovo and the New Imperialism," 195.

54. Walter Isaacson, "Why We Went Back to Columbine," *Time*, 20 December 1999, 6.

55. Kenneth Miller, "Is Your Dog an Athlete?" *Time*, 20 December 1999, 8.

56. Nancy Gibbs and Timothy Roche, "The Columbine Tapes," *Time*, 20 December 1999, 40–41.

57. Gibbs and Roche, "The Columbine Tapes," 42.

58. Gibbs and Roche, "The Columbine Tapes," 44.

59. Gibbs and Roche, "The Columbine Tapes," 50–51.

60. Andrew Goldstein, "The Victims: Never Again," *Time*, 20 December 1999, 53.

61. Gibbs and Roche, "The Columbine Tapes," 44.

62. Gibbs and Roche, "The Columbine Tapes," 42.

63. As cited in Walter Isaacson, "Why We Went Back to Columbine," *Time*, 20 December 1999, 6.

64. Edward Said, *Culture and Imperialism* (New York: Vintage 1994), 318.

65. Giroux, *Stealing Innocence*, 30.

1

Junk King Education

The kindness in my father's eyes took nothing away from his serious message. "Never forget," he said sternly, "Businesses are built on trust, and trust starts with the balance sheet."

—Michael Milken[1]

In the 1980s, Michael Milken was sent to prison for his illegal financial dealings—fraud and insider trading. However, his legal activities in the junk bond market[2] were destructive to companies, to retirees, and to the general public. He was a major factor in the savings and loan collapse, which cost the public billions. He invented the junk bond market, and after failing to reap sufficient rewards from personally investing in junk bonds, he profited enormously by selling risky junk investments to publicly backed savings and loans. He promoted and pioneered the use of junk in hostile corporate takeovers, which destroyed businesses, labor unions, and job security while enriching only a tiny corporate elite, and prominently contributed to the rise of the corporate media monopoly. He promoted greed as a public virtue and still claims that his destructive profit-seeking behavior is the essence of democracy.

Since his early release from prison, Milken has been building the first education conglomerate that is aimed at transforming public education into an investment opportunity for the wealthy by privatizing public schools, making kids into a captive audience for marketers, and redefining education as a corporate resource rather than a public good vital to the promotion of a democratic society. In Milken's own words, his entry into education is a direct continuation of his financial activities. He calls his destructive financial practices the democratization of capital. He describes his vulture-like relationship to public education as the democratization of knowledge. In both cases, democracy does not refer to public control over public resources but rather intensified corporate control over public resources and public decision-making power. Part of what is so disturbing about Milken's predatory move into education is that the popular press has hailed it as redemption for a man with a tainted history. In reality, Milken's predatory financial activities, which bilked the public of billions while making him a billionaire, are continuing in education.

In his defenses of privatization, Milken is suggesting that he is benefiting children, giving them opportunities within a corporate future where the competition will make it increasingly difficult for them to participate in the economy.

> Education must address individual needs. Rapid corporate evolution and frequent restructuring—including downsizing, rightsizing and outsourcing—mean an employee can no longer rely upon a "job for life." We believe that those who have the ability to learn and apply new skills are most likely to achieve career success and personal fulfillment.
>
> —Knowledge Universe Vision Statement

Corporate culture appears to be solving the problems of schooling by remaking the school in the image of the corporation. What Milken is not saying is that he himself is actively sponsoring and building that cutthroat future with no job security, low pay, and exploitative work conditions. Instead, Milken sells a corporate aesthetic as educational improvement, suggesting that problems with schools are technical problems instead of social problems like the distribution of public resources.

What Milken has in store for education is more than the transformation of school kids into a captive audience for corporate commercials. Knowledge Universe and the other "lifelong learning" companies seek to reinvent the school on the model of the corporation. With the advent of the industrial age, curriculum specialists concerned themselves with standardizing knowledge, disciplining students, organizing the time and space of school in accord with the industrial principles of scientific management.[3] Today the wild drive for "computer literacy" for teachers and students, the emphasis on instructional technology, and the general faith in technology as an inherently educative and liberating force belies another yet more disturbing faith—a (radically misguided) faith in the corporation to provide employment, fair work conditions, security, and a general state of bounty for the student, for the nation, and for the world. Historically, corporations have proven their lack of concern with the welfare of the world's citizenry from the slave trade, to colonization, to the exploitation of industrial labor and child labor, to the gutting of the public sphere through corporate welfare, to the cultural elevation of greed and selfishness, and restoration of racism and sexism as virtues, to the carceral and military industrial complexes, to the destruction of whole communities with pollution, debt-brokering, and infrastructural undermining. Corporations were invented in the public interest and now the public has become enslaved to the corporate interest and market logic in nearly every sphere from politics to culture to law to health care to education.

Moreover, Milken is reconceptualizing education as entertainment, marketing toys as learning tools. By collapsing entertainment into education, Milken suggests that the problem of schooling has to do with students who are bored or technical problems with the delivery of curriculum, again a technical problem rather than an ethical or political issue about how education could contribute to a more just future. Milken's formulation of educational reform envisions children as a target for promoting a popular acceptance of deregulation, the shrinking of state support, and his own globalization initiatives. His forays in the educational field participate in a broad-based, popular valuation of private initiative over state involvement. The critique of the public sphere that Milken wages supports his plans for profiteering globally, opening the world to a corporate culture beyond state controls, national borders, or any sense of public justice. What is in fact a hostile takeover of education as a vital public good is being sold to the public as philanthropy.

EDUCATION, INC.

Education must address corporate needs. Companies face a global economy with increased competition, decreasing product life cycles, more demanding customers and constant technological innovation. In this environment, employees must continuously be retrained to meet the evolving demands of the global marketplace.

—Knowledge Universe Vision Statement

Michael Milken's attack on the public sphere needs to be understood as a part of the broader privatization movement taking place in all aspects of society. Not only schools but also prisons, legal defense, public medical facilities, national and state parks and land, social security, national defense, all are subject to the call to privatize. We are witnessing a sea change in the culture, which the corporate media has actively fostered. The business press is most frank about the successes of corporate culture in making privatization of public goods a matter of common sense and popular morality. *Fortune* magazine writes,

This used to be sacred ground, barred to profit seekers. But people have come to see private enterprise as an antidote to public-sector paralysis. If for-profit hospital chains can squeeze overhead out of the not-for-profit hospitals they've acquired, why can't the same be done for public schools?[4]

No analysis is required to understand who has won and who has lost in the corporatization of the medical industry. Incontrovertibly the corporate media trust is selling the public on privatization through news and entertainment which portrays privatization as the only option, which equates capitalism with democracy and which actively depoliticizes citizens. On the contrary, in a critical democracy, authority needs to be justified in terms of whose interests are served by its exercise. The significance and impact on democracy of corporate media should not be underestimated.

Corporate media is so concentrated that a group of less than ten companies control almost all of American film and television and control major stakes in radio, magazine and book publishing, and the Internet: Time Warner, Viacom CBS, News Corp, Bertellsman/Westinghouse, Disney, ABC. Book and magazine publishing is even more concentrated and intersects with the film and television monopoly. Viacom's recent acquisition of CBS means that one of the largest educational publishers, Simon & Schuster, a Viacom company, now shares financial interests with every commercial sponsor of CBS-TV programming. Michael Milken directly contributed to the rise of the media monopoly by pioneering the use of the junk bond for corporate media mergers.

> Today, the high-yield, high-risk junk bond market is worth an estimated $1 trillion and has helped finance the beginnings of such success stories at Turner Broadcasting and Fox Television.[5]

Milken was instrumental in the growth to monopolistic proportions of Time Warner which included Time's swallowing of Warner Brothers and Turner Broadcasting, and the growth of MCI. Knowledge Universe's board is composed of such major players from the media monopoly as Rupert Murdoch, chairman and CEO of News Corp. Ltd.; Leo J. Hindery Jr., former president and CEO of AT&T Broadband & Internet Services and its predecessor, Tele-Communications Inc. (TCI); and Terry Semel, chairman of Windsor Media and former chairman and CEO, Warner Bros.

The corporate media monopoly's destructive impact on the public relates directly to the rise of the educational conglomerates in that both share the ability to monopolize knowledge production. Private monopolies on the production of knowledge and culture threaten the possibility of democracy because they frame issues and history in the corporate interest, disallow public access to media production and content control, eliminate curriculum or content that challenges structural inequalities, and fail to distinguish public from private interest. For example, *Time* magazine lauded the ethics of Steve Jobs—Apple Computer interim-

CEO-for-life and chairman of the Disney-distributed Pixar production company, creator of both the iMac computer and *Toy Story*—as expressing "his love for the human species in every product he made."[6] *Time* does not at all indicate that Steve Jobs gets to dictate what counts as human value for his own profiteering and career advancing by marketing corporate value as love. Human love is equated to private interest, or rather, love exists only as commodity and faith in the commodity—as Job's biblical name would warrant—while what gets erased is the very idea that love would preferably catalyze communities of solidarity and democratic movements.

In short, both the media monopoly and the education monopoly concern the takeover of information by a corporate culture that places market values over human values. Henry Giroux offers an excellent summation of the danger corporate culture poses to democracy:

> [Corporate culture is] an ensemble of ideological and institutional forces that functions politically and pedagogically to both govern organizational life through senior managerial control and to produce compliant workers, spectatorial consumers, and passive citizens. Within the language and images of corporate culture, citizenship is portrayed as an utterly privatized affair whose aim is to produce competitive self-interested individuals vying for their own material and ideological gain. Reformulating social issues as strictly individual or economic issues, corporate culture functions largely to cancel out the democratic impulses and practices of civil society by either devaluing them or absorbing such impulses within a market logic. No longer a space for political struggle, culture in the corporate model becomes an all-encompassing horizon for producing market identities, values, and practices. The good life, in this discourse, "is construed as in terms of our identities as consumers—we are what we buy." Public spheres are replaced by commercial spheres as the substance of critical democracy is emptied out and replaced by a democracy of goods, consumer lifestyles, shopping malls, and the increasing expansion of the cultural and political power of corporations throughout the world.[7]

The media are producing a culture where public spheres are downgraded and smeared in favor of privatization initiatives that work to derail public involvement in a politics of justice and equality.[8] When *Fortune* magazine refers to public sector paralysis, it is referring to the refusal of some sectors of the public, such as labor unions, and civic and religious groups, to hand over to corporations control of public goods such as education.[9] Private media have a disproportionate amount of public voice. When the popular press issues laudatory proclamations for privatization, it does not merely enjoy its right to free speech. It engages in a form of active, de facto censorship of views that represent the public interest. For example, the very issue of the media monopoly itself and its political consequences does not get aired.

One of the few criticisms of the media monopoly to surface in mainstream content appeared once on General Electric–owned NBC's late night comedy program *Saturday Night Live*. The cartoon by Robert Smiegel, titled "Conspiracy Theory Rocks: Media-opoly," revealed the extent to which corporations such as Westinghouse and GE keep reports such as nuclear accidents and environmental destruction out of their news productions. The political punch of the cartoon was drastically undercut by the fact that it was framed as a conspiracy theory and real media monopoly was interspersed with absurdities and irrelevancies such that someone unfamiliar with the realities of interlocking and synergistic corporate control over communications might assume that the gross environmental abuses of parent companies were no more true than the silly jokes. Nonetheless, within a week of the single broadcast, the *New York Times* reported that the cartoon would never be aired again. Producer Lorne Michaels was quoted to say that this was because the cartoon was not "comedically viable."[10] the *Times* article did not discuss the implications of such corporate censorship for democracy. Of course, this has everything to do with the fact that the *Times* actively eliminates stories and information that challenge government policy and dominant ideology or question the power of corporations.

The Milken brothers also engage in active censorship of book publishing through such underhanded tactics as funding what legal critics consider a seemingly frivolous million dollar lawsuit against publisher Simon & Schuster—a company that the Milkens failed to acquire. Simon & Schuster published James B. Stewart's *Den of Thieves*, a best-selling expose of financial abuses in the eighties. Simon & Schuster has been forced to spend over a million dollars to defend itself. As Doreen Carvajal writes, "Victory or not, cases like the long-running "Den of Thieves" lawsuit cast a certain pall over the publication of other critical investigative books because of the potential costs of dealing with libel lawsuits that could destroy a book's profitability."[11] Former Milken attorney and longtime friend Michael F. Armstrong defended Lowell Milken's funding of the suit on the grounds that it is a "good investment."[12] The case demonstrates the power of big money to control information. If the Milkens cannot buy Simon & Schuster, they can use the courts to make it too expensive for any publisher to print books critical of them.

Through their control of media technology, the corporate elite limit, circumscribe, and control access to the making of public meaning, and they dominate the language in which issues are framed. The political and pedagogical implications of this struggle over the control of knowledge and language are readily apparent in corporatization of school curriculum. Shell Oil's freely distributed video curriculum on the environment concentrates heavily on the virtues of the internal combustion engine, "while offering students pearls of wisdom like, 'You can't get to nature without gasoline or cars.' "[13] In this case, Shell Oil rewrites environmentalism as its diametrical opposite—the plunder, exploitation, and consumption of nature.

Knowledge Universe's (KU) Teacher Universe business exemplifies the transformation of the school by corporate culture.

Using PowerPoint presentation software, Le Whitton puts the finishing touches on a computer "slide show" she has created. The topic: Why teachers at Flanagan (Ill.) Elementary School, where Ms. Whitton is the principal, should take the same technology-training course that she is completing. "I've created one slide show to persuade my school board we need it, and another to convince the teachers," Ms. Whitton says. Creating sharp-looking documents and spreadsheets is among the tasks she mastered in a five-day training institute run by Teacher Universe, a new company that for the time being is focused on helping teachers integrate technology into the classroom. . . . "Administrators have to be as knowledgeable as teachers," says the principal, whose 550-student district in central Illinois paid her travel expenses, plus the $450 tuition, for the institute here.[14]

Clearly, the curriculum at Teacher Universe involves more than the tools involved in transforming any classroom into the image of a corporate boardroom. Administrators learn to use the new tools to market the technology training courses to other administrators. Some glaring questions emerge from this, such as why would five-year-olds need to know how to use a spreadsheet, how in the world does this benefit education, and who will receive this corporate culture and who will not (we know the answer to this because it will be distributed as other educational resources are currently—based on wealth).

What is going on in the transformation of school through corporate culture is about more than an emphasis on slick style over substance (though part of what is happening involves an aesthetic and symbolic makeover of the school in the image of the corporation). Corporate culture in schools involves making politics impossible through an emphasis on aestheticized technicization. In other words, when the problems of public schooling appear as a technical problem (not enough computers) rather than the manifestation of a social system structured in inequality, then solutions can be sought in the corporate sector—a realm of the private largely responsible for causing those social problems in the first place by fostering inequalities of wealth and political exclusion.

Yet, KU's Teacher's Universe does not intend to simply sell computer learning apparatus. They will sell knowledge too.

Teacher Universe instructor Lloyd Spruill focuses on integrating Windows applications into the classroom. (Teacher Universe offers training on a variety of operating systems and applications.) Creating a PowerPoint slide show about the Brazilian rain forest can lead students to use economics, math, language arts, geography, and other subjects, Ms. Spruill says. "If we isolate computer skills, that's like having a pen teacher, or having a pen lab in the school," said Ms. Spruill, who was a school district technology director in Bertie County, N.C., before joining the training firm that preceded Teacher Universe.[15]

And Michael Milken is ready to link his curriculum to his learning technologies through Teacher Universe, KU Interactive Studio, and its subsidiary MindQ Publishing. KU CEO Tom Kalinske intends to use its Nobel private schools to test new curricula to sell to public schools.[16] What can educators seeking learning materials through Teacher Universe's helpful links expect to find in a lesson on, say, Brazil? Mostly issues framed in terms of Western tourism, but some links consider the importance of ecology. However, none of the links discuss the reason that the Brazilian rain forest is being destroyed—corporate profit. Slash and burn methods turn the rain forest into grazing land for cows that will become McDonald's hamburgers. Whoops! Minor omission in the curriculum. The politics links on Teacher Universe are predictably right-leaning, with the left represented by a conspiracy theory link. The only military-related link celebrates the virtues of military spending and glorifies military hardware with graphic images without at all considering the impact of global militarization as a catalyst to global environmental destruction. It does not mention the fact that the world's only superpower continues to invent new enemies and uses for the military to spend record amounts on defense because corporate profit is at stake in the distribution of public money to high-tech firms.[17] It does not consider how U.S. military equipment is being sold to support Colombia's anti-insurgency war, which includes the eradication of subsistence crops of indigenous populations through dumping corporate-produced toxins on rain forest regions.[18] This politics link also fails to mention that Milken's own Milken Family Institute, through the Jerusalem Center for Public Affairs, funds research on militarized policing methods of oppressed Palestinians in Israel, lobbies for the privatization of Israel's public schools, and funded the publication of false, denunciatory, slander of progressive intellectual and Palestinian human-rights spokesperson Edward Said in this country.[19]

This cultural shift, which glorifies all things private and vilifies the public, gets to the most fundamental question of the purpose of schooling in a democracy. The logic of economic rationalism has by far eclipsed any other justification for education. Knowledge Universe makes this demand explicit in their vision statement. "Education must address corporate needs." Sociologist and critical educator Stanley Aronowitz recognizes that the onslaught of educational privatization threatens the development of critical consciousness in students, threatens the development of a democratic citizenry, makes teachers deskilled practitioners, and makes students receptacles for pre-fab units of de-contextualized knowledge. He writes:

> [There is a] new common sense that the highest mission and overriding purpose of schooling was to prepare students, at different levels, to take their places in the corporate order. The banking or transmission theory of school knowledge, which Freire identified more than thirty years ago as the culprit standing in the way of critical consciousness, has returned with a vengeance. Once widely scorned by educators from diverse educational philosophies as a flagrant violation of the democratic educational mission, it has been thrust to the fore of nearly all official pedagogy.[20]

In fact, the potential of Michael Milken's business implies more than the destruction of schooling for critical subject formation and democratic participation. It stands to intensify deeply the reproduction of social inequalities, which include unequal access to knowledge, technology, and resources. It also limits individuals' capacity to produce culture and history. This means that Microsoft's version of history becomes America's history. Michael Milken's idea of democracy as the redistribution of public wealth, control, and knowledge production to corporations becomes American democracy.

In what follows here, we will discuss Michael Milken's education business as a direct continuation of his attack on the public in the financial realm.

REHABILITATION FOR MILKEN'S JUNK HABIT

The 10 May 1999, issue of *Business Week* magazine features a picture of convicted felon Michael Milken on its cover. In the picture, Milken sits cross-legged in a meditation pose, smiling with his hands outstretched. Instead of his fingers joining thumb and first finger to complete the Buddhistic pose, pieces of fruit fly from his hands. Milken is juggling fruit. His lap is filled with vegetables—broccoli, peppers, squash, tomatoes, artichokes. Carrots overflow one pocket and spinach leaves the other pocket of a blue work shirt that looks as if he might have snuck out of the minimum security federal penitentiary, where he served two years on a ten-year sentence for ninety-eight counts of fraud (kind of like keeping the towels from the Holiday Inn). The headline reads, "The Reincarnation of Mike Milken: a close-up look at his life, his education business, and his quest to cure cancer."[21] *Business Week* happens to be owned by McGraw-Hill, the largest educational publisher and one of the biggest investors in

precisely the kinds of for-profit education businesses that Milken is buying up. In a March 1998 article in *Business Week,* regular *Wall Street Journal*
financial reporter Craig Roberts argues that Michael Milken has done
more to help mankind than Mother Teresa.[22]

Business Week and the *Wall Street Journal* are not the only mainstream
publications singing the praises of Michael Milken for his renewal, his
survival, and his good works. The *New York Times* writes of "restoring the
junk bond king"[23] while the *Independent* of London calls Milken's entry
into education and medical research a "resurrection."[24] *The Economist* calls
Milken "The Comeback King."[25] *Time, Newsweek, USA Today,* and a bevy
of mainstream publications join in a chorus of praise for a man that federal prosecutors and the Securities and Exchange Commission allege returned to lawbreaking "the moment he stepped out of prison." Reincarnation, restoration, and resurrection. What could Milken be doing to
transform himself from the figurehead of an era known for vicious greed,
deceit, and predatory behavior? *Den of Thieves* author and financial reporter James B. Stewart described the 1980s scandals of which Milken was
the central figure as "the greatest criminal conspiracy the world has ever
known."[26] What has Milken done to garner such praise, to be celebrated
as a figure of redemption, recovery, health, and promise in mass media?

In addition to investing heavily in public relations schemes and doing
deals for the major players in the media monopoly, the public celebration
of Michael Milken in corporate media has to do with the fact that he has
set his sights on privatizing American public education and transforming
all of American education into a private profit-making venture. Knowledge Universe, Milken's for-profit education corporation, aims to be the
first education conglomerate. Milken makes no distinction between public and private education; they both appear to KU and the other "lifetime
learning companies" as an opportunity for corporate profits. This $600
billion to $800 billion opportunity has been described in the business
press as a bigger take than the defense industry.[27] Using his skills as a fi-
nancier, Milken has quietly built a $1.5 billion company, named Knowl-
edge Universe, by buying up smaller for-profit companies in every conceivable aspect of education. Milken has carried his predatory behavior in
the realm of finance into the realm of education. Just as he broke up businesses for his personal gain and let the public pay for it, now he wants to
destroy public education for his personal profit and have the public finance his destructiveness.

Michael Milken's education endeavors are predatory and destructive to
public education, labor conditions, and any sense of the public good,
community, and solidarity. As well, they are destructive to a democratic
notion of cultural production by transforming knowledge into a commodity and abstracting knowledge from broader political and ethical im-

plications and denying the relationship between knowledge production and power. Milken's "cradle to grave" company is investing in privatizing K–12 public education by running for-profit charter schools (Nobel); he is invested in worker retraining which depends upon weakened job security; he is invested in for-profit welfare-to-work training from which KU is receiving public money, for-profit day care centers that are also being publicly subsidized; he is buying up children's book publishing, educational toy companies, college and executive technology-based distance learning designed to yield profits by replacing teachers with technology and standardizing curriculum, standardized testing centers, standardized test preparation, "outplacement" temporary staffing, consulting, software training, continuing education, and print publishing—and this is only a partial list. KU is poised to enter retail and electronic distribution, the health and medical field, to establish a cable network, a broadcast network, and language training—and this, too, is an incomplete list.

Milken, who served only two of a ten-year federal sentence in a minimum security "country club" prison for ninety-eight counts of insider trading fraud, made his reputation as the Junk Bond King of Wall Street. Milken's fame came not only from his innovative approach to finance and his willingness to profit by breaking the law and breaking up businesses. His notorious temper, shameless displays of wealth, outspoken proclamations about the virtues of greed, and his secrecy also made him legendary. Milken developed the junk bond market with the idea that certain undervalued bonds could be lucrative investments. Milken found three uses for junk bonds:

1. Initially, in the late seventies, he invested in the undervalued bonds himself.
2. In the early eighties he sold the bonds to savings and loans deregulated under the Reagan administration.
3. He also pioneered the use of junk bonds in financing hostile and friendly corporate takeovers and in financing the growth of high-risk companies. The results of Milken's innovation were disastrous on all counts except his personal enrichment and the enrichment of Wall Street's finest.

When the market crashed in the late eighties the investments that Milken had sold the S&Ls lost so much value that a large number of S&Ls collapsed. The federal government was forced to bail out the S&Ls at a cost to the public of billions of dollars. Countless retirees lost their life savings due to deregulatory laws that allowed Wall Street predators such as Milken to sell risky private investment to publicly protected S&Ls. Milken's own crimes involved failing to inform the S&Ls of the full risks of junk investments and also engaging in extensive insider trading. Further widescale disaster resulted from Milken's monster being used to finance corporate takeovers. Often profitable companies were purchased by such corporate raiders as Carl Icahn and T. Boone Pickens to break up the companies and sell off the pieces. Such was the case with Uniroyal Tire. The aftermath included massive firings, destruction of unions, the destruction of productive companies, and the enrichment of investors. Often the junk bond kings would buy a large quantity of a company's stock and then threaten a takeover (the highly confident letter) to drive up stock prices. The junk king would then dump the company's stock for a giant profit, resulting in a lower value for the company. Such speculation resulted in a paranoid state for corporate boards and workers who did not know from one day to the next whether they would be employed. This was the aftermath of the innovations of a man that the *Wall Street Journal* described as "arguably the most important financial thinker of the twentieth century."[28]

The reinvention of Michael Milken as a public hero has been mostly the handiwork of the few massive media conglomerates and Milken's own public relations efforts through his Milken Family Foundation and Milken Institute. The mass media celebration of Michael Milken as a compassionate hero owes much to Milken's friendships and financial dealings with media monopoly tycoons Ted Turner and Rupert Murdoch, who respectively own controlling interests in Time Warner and News Corporation which together control roughly half of incredibly concentrated control over U.S. mass media—television, film, radio, magazine, and book publishing. Hence, don't expect to see reporting critical of Milken or his new education business on CNN, or in *Time* magazine, on HBO, in *Fortune, People,* or *Money,* on Fox News or FX, in the *New York Post,* the *Daily News,* or a hard-hitting book from HarperCollins. Because Milken owns Hoover's Inc. with General Electric's NBC, don't expect to find on NBC or CNBC any hard-hitting journalism about Milken's many recent illegal financial dealings.

Due to the gravity of Milken's financial crimes, he was barred for life from brokering deals. Nonetheless, Milken was found last year to be buying up large quantities of stock in 7th Level, an entertainment software company, driving the stock price up and benefiting enormously as the price inflated. "The New York Securities and Exchange Commission has also investigated three high-level transactions in which Milken is suspected of having played a role."[29] The most serious violation that Milken has been charged with (at least the most serious one that has been discovered) has been proposing and setting up MCI's $2 billion investment in Rupert Murdoch's News Corporation. Milken quickly and quietly settled the violation by paying $47 million to the SEC representing his income on the deal plus interest.[30] Milken's probation has been repeatedly extended as the SEC investigates his role in Time Warner's purchase of Turner Broadcasting, Ronald Perelman's acquisition of New World Entertainment, and other high-level deals. In fact, federal prosecutors alleged that Milken barely stepped out of prison before resuming financial dealings through MC Group, an acquisitions company he formed in 1993.

His financial speculation has carried over into his education business in the way he has been found to inflate stock prices for 7th Level and the fact that he has been buying up company after company for KU. Despite the fact that upon his conviction the SEC barred him from any financial association with brokers for life, Milken's new education business has been built through leveraged buyouts that could not have been accomplished without Milken's financial association with brokers.

What is so disturbing about this very recent (alleged) illegal activity is that not only has Milken's continued lawbreaking gone largely uncriticized in the mass media, but at the same time he is being celebrated as a highly ethical, caring, and compassionate person for his involvement with education. The fact is, in Milken's own words, his involvement in the field of education is not a break with his involvement in the world of junk bonds and finance. Rather, it is a continuation.

JUNK KING EDUCATION

My Own Little Revolution
But old habits die hard. . . . His penchant for secrecy surrounds Knowledge Universe. The firm's ownership structure resembles a set of Russian nesting dolls: Each company opens up to reveal yet another, until at the core one finds the Milken brothers and [Oracle CEO Larry] Ellison. And while the trio have recruited such high-tech players as Larry Geisel, a former Netscape VP who's now Knowledge Universe's CTO, they've also installed longtime lieutenants [from the junk desk at Drexel] in other positions, according to SEC records.[31]

According to Michael Milken himself, his education company is a direct continuation of his financial activities. They are both, he argues, about democratization. Milken has repeated this post-jail narrative in multiple outlets—through the Milken Family Foundation, the Milken Institute, and in press interviews. The story goes like this: Milken says he lived an idyllic life in Southern California until the Watts riots of 1965. After the riots, Milken drove to Watts, where his father, an accountant, had clients. Milken claims to have spoken with a man who had set fire to his own "workplace."

I'm out of this 'Happy Days' family in the San Fernando Valley, and I couldn't understand why people were burning buildings that they were living in or might have worked in. . . . He had no savings and now he had no job. I asked him why and he told me that he wasn't a part of the system. He wasn't living the American Dream.[32]

The story continues that upon returning to Berkeley, where Milken was enrolled as a math major, he changed his major to business with "the vague idea of changing the financial system" to provide investment opportunities for minorities and those excluded from the economic system. If we are to believe Michael Milken, his invention of the junk bond was geared towards economic justice by democratizing access to investments.[33] "Eventually, he came to the conclusion that the system could be opened to more people by providing credit based on a company's potential instead of its past history. Junk bonds became the vehicle."[34] Says Milken, "I viewed that as an opportunity. I viewed that as my own little revolution."[35] According to Milken his junk bond activities of the eighties successfully "democratized capital." What examples does Milken give to support his version of the democratization of capital for the poor, the excluded, and the underclass? A poor, marginalized company called MCI could not compete against AT&T. But the junk bond helped finance its growth from mid-sized corporation to current oligopolistic proportions. The only other example we have been able to locate of Milken's claims of the junk bond's great egalitarian power is his example in an extensive *Fortune* magazine interview of its use in financing media giant Time Warner's purchase of media giant Turner Broadcasting.[36]

If only those other Berkeley radicals had gone to business school, economic injustice and racism could have been conquered. According to Milken, who refers to himself as a social scientist, these injustices *have* been conquered. Despite the realities of a steadily increasing wage gap, growing inequalities in the concentration of wealth, the racial and gendered nature of economic inequality, systematic police brutality, and white supremacist attacks against non-whites and immigrants; despite Rodney King and the L.A. uprising; despite the destructive corporatization of the health care industry, the denial of AIDS medicine to the poor, and rising rates of child poverty and homelessness, Michael Milken claims to have conquered economic injustice in the early 1980s through the "democratization of capital." "I believe that mission succeeded by the early 1980s."[37]

The notion of a predatory bond dealer with a social conscience might seem somewhat unlikely, but evidently Mr. Milken had a higher purpose when he steamed into his Beverly Hills office at 4 a.m. every day, squeezing every last fraction of a yield point out of the deals he made, pushing his staff until they dropped, and hiring top-flight entertainers and stunningly beautiful female escorts for the annual parties [The Predator's Ball] he threw at the Beverly Hills Hotel. Incredibly, too, the apologists still repeat the Milken mantra that junk bonds provide a higher rate of return with no increase in risk, a mantra that proved demonstrably untrue by the end of the Eighties on both counts.[38]

O.K. So the junk bond didn't even turn out to be a good investment for the rich (Milken himself got out of investing in them early on); it didn't really ever finance small business expansion, individual entrepreneurship, or allow workers control and ownership of their workplaces. According to Milken the junk bond financed growth of mid-sized companies in the past three decades, creating jobs while large corporations such as AT&T and IBM were firing people by the thousands. It does not take a business degree to know that big corporate firings were the result of increased economic competition with its imperative for increasing profits for increasing growth to compete. So the mass firings of big corporations had very much to do with increased competition from mid-sized companies that the junk bond financed.

However, the real issue here is not merely the false claim that the junk bond "created jobs." Rather the issue is that Milken's definition of democratic economics translates to corporations' providing jobs in a market economy. In other words, Milken defines *democracy* by the benevolence of those few people in control of markets, people such as himself. In this case, the profit-seeking behavior of the corporate sector is defined as democracy. If this profit-seeking by the rich results in the creation of some jobs, then that is proof of the democratizing potential of profit-seeking behavior and a system designed around maximizing profit for the rich. Milken's vision of democracy excludes citizens not only from control of their own labor and control over their workplaces but also from being involved in decision-making about the kinds of work they will have available in the future. Furthermore, this way of thinking defines democratic action as competition against other citizens for scarce goods and services and defines democratic action as the pursuit of individual interest though such behaviors as consuming private educational services rather than defining democratic action as the pursuit of the public good or common good through the individual and collective behaviors of public service, activism, or civic participation.

Milken's attack on the public sphere in his financial dealings included his defrauding investors and forcing the public to fund the S&L bailout, abusing the public trust by basing junk bonds on companies that were often kept in business by government support, and his contribution to a cultural attack on the virtues of public life, public service, and the public interest by his disgusting promotion of greed and selfishness as public virtues. This cultural attack includes his propagandizing that his bad investments for the rich were really about helping poor and non-white citizens. In reality, Milken's speculation in the eighties worsened the conditions of economic exclusion for poor and minority citizens by contributing to an upward redistribution of wealth, which continues today.

Milken's attack on the public sphere in his educational endeavors are extensive and potentially far more destructive than his anti-public actions in the financial realm. Milken aims to privatize public education and make money from it. He is already doing this with KU's Nobel Learning Communities Inc. As Justin Martin writes in *Fortune* magazine, "private schools represent only a sliver of the K–12 education market. Public schools are the big quarry."[39] Though neither KU's Web site nor Nobel's Web site reveals it, Knowledge Universe has a significant ownership position of 21 percent in what is the largest private school system in the United States, which spans thirteen states and includes 140 schools.[40] Nobel claims it is "currently pursuing plans for further nationwide expansion."[41]

A HEARTLESS GAME

According to Chris Whittle, president of the Edison Project and creator of Channel One, which makes students a captive audience for junk food and clothing commercials, "running schools is the heart of the game."[42] If privatizing public schools is a game, then it might be worth considering who the players are, what the stakes are, and who controls the playing field.

It is, perhaps, no coincidence that the CEO of Knowledge Universe, Tom Kalinske, was previously the CEO of Sega toys, a company that makes and sells games—video games. Actually, the game figures into the education business in multiple ways. Part of KU's focus is on edutainment—the merging of education and entertainment, hence, KU's purchase of Leapfrog, an educational toy maker. KU's technologized learning attempts to sell educational training through merging it with the allure of the video game. Making learning fun is not so much an educational mission as it is a marketing strategy. Edutainment pleasure serves to seduce more potential customers and to trick students into learning what might otherwise be irrelevant knowledge. Making education entertaining replaces the critical concern with issues of what makes knowledge meaningful to students. Meaningful knowledge, in the critical sense, connects knowledge to students' experiences and allows students to question whose interests are served by certain knowledge and to inquire as to their own positionality and relationship to school and culturally transmitted knowledge. Edutainment precludes the possibility of knowledge being made meaningful to be made critical, because the justification for learning as a game is merely visceral pleasure.

Of course, learning games also get the capitalist ethic of competition instilled at a very early age. Whittle's metaphor of the game for what wealthy investors such as himself, Milken, Ellison, and Kalinske are doing accurately represents the way privatization transforms public schools into playing pieces. But who is being toyed with? According to the company, "Nobel Learning Communities' programs are *targeted* towards the working families of America." Why do America's working families need private schools? "Analysts believe the opportunity to build an education company into a significant and profitable business is huge and is fueled by the Nation's need to reform a system that is getting failing grades." Are the nation's schools really in need of reform or are only some of the nation's citizens' schools in need of reform? Certainly Nobel is not targeting the largely white suburban schools populated by the children of the professional class. Nobel schools could not compete with the public schools of professional elites in such places as Lower Montgomery, Pa., outside of Philadelphia; Fairfield County, Conn., and Westchester County, N.Y., outside of New York City; or Montgomery County, Md., outside of D.C. So Nobel's response to the nation's schools getting failing grades is, in fact, a response to a highly unequal system of public allocation of education as a public good. The remedy for such unequal allocation should be the redistribution of educational resources. This redistribution needs to be tied to a broader social redistribution of decision-making about how all social resources are allocated.

Fixing the public schools in a place like Camden, N.J., with an infusion of public investment needs to be tied to the revitalization of that city's infrastructure. The reason the Camden schools are radically underfunded has to do with the fact that the city's tax base has been dismantled by the flight of business and residences. Where did business go? To nearby wealthy, white Cherry Hill and overseas. The loss of local jobs and tax revenue in Camden resulting from corporate flight left an unemployed population with a gutted public sector. Without fixing the economic conditions that result in unemployment, poverty, despair, the resort to drugs and alcohol for consolation and income, and violence, fixing the Camden schools is an empty gesture.

Public schools do need public investment and support so that they can be sites from which citizens can struggle for economic and cultural empowerment and broader social transformation. The public investment in public schools should be based in a broader democratic public transformation, not on the ephemeral promise of competing for scarce and low-paying jobs. Such a rejuvenation should be premised on the development of a critical and compassionate citizenry, the development of a vision for the future in which citizens decide the kind of work they do and the subjugation of the corporate sector for the public good, rather than the subjugation of citizens for corporate profit.

The fact is the corporate sector is complicit in destroying communities in urban areas and now wants to come back and prey on these communities by making them rely on private education.

> Nobel's schools are usually funded and built by outside developers and investors, keeping the Company's investment and start-up costs to a minimum. It will lease a school from its owner from ten to twenty years with minimal up-front costs.[43]

Nobel also claims to be able to make a profit from education as a business by keeping overhead low on labor. Though they claim they do so by having less administration, the fact is the bulk of the savings has to come from paying teachers less than they would earn at public schools. This means that the bottom line dictates who teaches. Obviously the results of this are the use of uncertified, untrained, and inexperienced teachers who are, of course, not unionized. This means teacher job security disappears. Nobel's Web site states,

> In the United States, over $600 billion is spent on education and educational products. It is estimated that $300 billion is K–12 education. Nobel's two areas of concentration, K–8th and preschool expenditures are estimated at $200 billion and $30 billion, respectively, with attractive growth rates. There are also more working mothers with children than any other period in history. Nobel's education staff know that accomplishing their internal mission will guarantee the success of the business mission.[44]

In other words, the justification for education in a democracy is investor profit. The reason that teachers should teach well for Nobel is for investor profit. And, of course, as we see implied here in an ominous way, when investor profit does not increase, teachers can expect to be replaced. Education as a client-based business guarantees a curriculum that is less likely to be critical, which must be geared for promising that education is an economic investment for student-consumers. Such clientism pushes education further in the direction of vocationalization and away from schools as a site of struggle for social emancipation and democracy.

The radical decrease in administration and other staff also means that the school has less infrastructure and hence fewer resources for students. As conservative educator Chester Finn writes in the *Brookings Institute Review* singing the praises of charter schools, these schools often have no transportation, no after-school activities, no lunches, inadequate administration, low-paid teachers, little or no janitorial service, require parental involvement in cleaning the school, and yet, Finn writes inexplicably, these private schools are preferable to public schools.[45] The fact that those who own and run the schools do not use the schools means that the administration has no personal investment in the quality of the education.[46] Often, as in the case of Nobel, many of the owners do not even live in the same state. The fact that they are a business also means that the schools are not accountable to the public and that they can go out of business in mid-year should they be deemed unprofitable for the investors. Because they are a business Nobel does not have to show their financial records to the public. So there is no way to know how much money that should be used to educate children goes to paying for the CEO's new jet.

The business press has described Nobel as the beginnings of a system comparable to the HMO system in medicine.[47] They call Nobel an EMO. As anyone not in the insurance industry knows, the HMO has been destructive to the quality of care by hindering doctors' making decisions based on health rather than money. The HMO did make a few insurance CEOs into billionaires, but their gain has cost doctor autonomy, patient autonomy, and it has cost lives. Of course, the big difference between medicine and education is that education is a public good not a private service. All of these factors mean that when the public schools are replaced by private schools—precisely what the corporate culture wants—there is a loss of quality, accountability, local control, and public involvement, but also a redefining of education in strictly individual terms of consumption rather than social concerns.

MILKEN FAMILY VALUES

The kindness in my father's eyes took nothing away from his serious message. "Never forget," he said sternly, "Businesses are built on trust, and trust starts with the balance sheet."

—Michael Milken

One of Nobel's enticements to investors is, "There are also more working mothers with children than any other period in history." Nobel sells preschool services to working parents. Aside from Nobel's assumption that women are natural caregivers to children, the company recognizes that there is loot to be scored by taking advantage of worsened economic conditions for working class citizens. Due to continually decreasing real wages for working class families, families of four now require two earners as opposed to one.[48] While the economic boom of the late nineties benefited corporate CEOs and the ruling class, it did not materialize for the majority of the population. So Nobel as well as Knowledge Universe's other child-care business benefit financially from worsened economic conditions for working class and largely non-white populations. What must be understood is the extent to which the corporate sector has been instrumental in making families poorer and hence dependent upon the consumption of the corporate child-care industry.

Knowledge Universe owns Children's Discovery Centers of America, for which it paid $80 million.

> As with corporate training, early-childhood services make good sense for KU. These days, 80 percent of families are either dual income or headed by a single parent. But running an on-site day-care center is costly; thus, many corporations outsource this service as well.[49]

Wall Street considers the "early-childhood" market to be a $30 billion opportunity for corporations.[50] The obvious labor issue here involves the ethical question of whether the victims of worsened economic constraints on working class and middle class citizens should be subject to reliance on corporate provision of child-care services. Child-care services should be a universal public good that allows parents the opportunity to participate in the economy. In Milken's world, equal participation in the economy by men and women depends upon the consumption of his private, for-profit child care services.

Leverage buyout masters, junk bond kings, and finance houses are turning to kiddie care in droves. Recent consolidations include: KUs Nobel and Children's Discovery Centers, Kohlberg, Kravis, & Roberts' KinderCare Learning Centers (the nation's biggest chain), Chase Capital Partners' La Petite Academy (number two), Lazard Capital Partners' $16 million equity stake in ChildrenFirst, Inc.

The predators' move into child-care does not stem from altruism. Rather, the corporations are responding to three primary sources of new child-care spending:

1. Then-President Clinton included $600 million in child care in his federal budget proposal in February 1999.
2. Massive tax credits to corporations have been proposed in Congress "toward the cost of setting up, operating or subsidizing on-site child care for their employees."[51]
3. The big haul is "$22 billion in federal money over six years to help subsidize child care for welfare recipients who return to work."[52]

Even as Congress has allocated $4.5 billion for child care to be spread over five years, children eligible for child care vouchers in states like Mississippi are not receiving them, and yet the state's budget for child care remains in the coffers—approximately $25 million in federal allowances and $17 million in state allowances.[53] The difficulties of administering and distributing welfare benefits at the state level—where these functions are now controlled, due to block grant legislation—creates a greater opening for privatization and the move of corporations into the industry to pick up the slack.

The 1996 Republican-led and bipartisan-enacted welfare dismantling was an attack on the idea of a social safety net for those citizens in most need. In this sense, the dismantling of welfare was a part of what Stanley Aronowitz has identified as the gutting of the "compassionate functions of the state."[54] However, it was also fundamentally a redistribution of public resources to the private sector in that direct government provision and non-profit provision largely shifted to for-profit provision. While the people who lost in this attack on social services were the poorest, least enfranchised, and historically most victimized segments of the population forced to "sink or swim," the winners were big corporations such as military contracting giant Lockheed-Martin which had lined up before the law even passed to be rewarded when it did pass with twenty contracts in four states.[55] As William P. Ryan points out in the *Harvard Business Review*, this privatization has resulted in a radically destructive shift in the culture and economics of social service. As Ryan explains, huge capital means for-profits can take over projects more quickly and also quit projects when the bottom line doesn't pan out. They do projects that promise to pay the most. They have a short-term outlook often at odds with individuals or community interests. They force non-profits to compete and operate based on profit and price-competition instead of on a mission of helping people. They remove profit from projects rather than reinvesting them.

What is particularly disturbing is that Knowledge Universe and the other "lifelong learning" companies have a financial interest in the government not providing fundamental social services, including child care, education, welfare, and worker training. As Alex Molnar points out, the endless attacks on the quality of public education from the corporate sector come despite the fact that U.S. corporations spend less on worker training than any other industrialized country.[56] Obviously the "quality" issue that corporate CEOs such as Louis Gerstner of IBM hurl at the public schools does not concern the schools from which IBM will draw employees. Those schools, heavily funded, largely white schools in suburbs are providing IBM with well-educated members of the professional class. So the "failing" schools are not the ones from which IBM intends to benefit by hiring their graduates. However, IBM can certainly benefit from convincing the government that IBM can allow urban schools and their students to compete with wealthy white suburban schools for IBM's shrinking number of jobs if those urban schools buy IBM's many products.

KU's Unext.com and its MindQ are competing for the corporate worker retraining market. The success of these companies depends upon decreased job security. Making corporate retraining an outsourced element of corporations allows big corporations with benefits packages for employees to avoid paying these to in-house trainers. This exploitative practice of outsourcing is apparent as well in the university system. For example, St. Joseph's University subcontracts food services from Aramark so that St. Joseph's, despite its overt mission of ethics, care, and Jesuit concern with social justice, can have an underpaid staff of mostly black women on a wealthy white campus. These women and men are not entitled to free tuition, university benefits, or decent pay, despite the fact that they work on university grounds full-time and live in the mostly black working class neighborhoods surrounding this mostly white professional class school.

Unext is also striving to be an online university.

> Unext.com will push its elite-school connections (would-be partners are said to include the London School of Economics and Columbia, Stanford, Cornell and Carnegie Mellon universities) and multimedia productions linking students and "mentors," simulating classroom exchanges.[57]

Part of the problem with Milken's plan for distance learning is that it defines the quality of instruction in typical market logic fashion—by the prestige carried by brand names. In other words, education as consumer commodity cannot comprehend necessary ethical and political questions such as to what extent this program of learning promotes democratic, equal, free, and just social relations in all social spheres or simply questions of whose interests this knowledge represents and who gets to determine what counts as knowledge. But this online university is more than a high-tech form of instrumentalization and what educational critics have long identified as a form of technocratic rationality. It is also an attack on university labor and academic freedom.

The first fully accredited online university, Jones University, is proving to be a model for future major players in the online learning market.

> Jones University, which became the first online-only university to gain accreditation this spring, already has 600 adult students who pay $4,000 a year, vs. $3,200 at the average state college. Jones has no overhead for dorms or sports fields. And each course is a standard product taught by adjunct instructors instead of costly tenured professors. Still, Jones won't be profitable unless enrollment hits a projected 3,000 in two years—a tall order for a college trying to build a reputation from scratch.[58]

By linking to elite established universities, KU's Unext.com has avoided the credibility problem that Jones University faces. Yet, in order to profit, Unext.com will be forced to use the same destructive tactics of standardized curriculum and extensive if not complete use of adjuncts (an attack on the tenure system). David Levin, director of DePaul University's distance learning project says that online education is the "most rapidly growing area of distance learning. Every day or so, I see some new organization opening up."[59] Many critics in education are proclaiming that this could mean the destruction of higher education. David F. Nobel, a history professor at York University in Toronto says, "Ten years from now we will look at the wired remains of our system and wonder how we let it happen."[60] Online distance learning in its corporate incarnation means more than the attacks on full-time academic labor, tenure, face-to-face instruction, and education as a form of critical dialogue. It implies a radically different educational culture and yet one that continues to structure unequal opportunities based on class position. As higher education continues to be prohibitively expensive for working class students, fewer of the most privileged students will have the opportunity to go to college. Not virtual college. College. Online education will inevitably bring with it a two-tiered system in which workers of the information economy can be trained to do low-paying high-skilled tasks. Recall KU's vision statement,

> We believe that those who have the ability to learn and apply new skills are most likely to achieve career success and personal fulfillment.

As for those not privileged enough and not naturally endowed to consume Milken education or online distance learning . . . well . . . fuck 'em, says the Milken rationale.

Yet, those slated for the ranks of control will not be denied real live education at universities with all that it entails. This is not, in other words, a system that offers more opportunities, but a way for corporations such as KU to attack public education so they can benefit by selling private schooling, then sell worker training and vocational higher education to the students that they deprived of free universal education in the first place.

Despite the fact that conglomerates are scrambling to make the Web into a way to lower educational overhead, critical educators should not underestimate the power and potential of online distance education for being a new counter-public sphere. As a counter-public sphere, online distance education could possibly (depending on how it is configured) provide a space for critical educators and those concerned primarily with social justice to convene with social movements, labor organizers, foreign political parties, and subjugated populations internationally. Criticalists should rush to seize these emerging spaces rather than denouncing them as inherently oppressive. By being involved in the establishment of online distance learning, critical educators increase the possibilities for politicized curricula, a social justice agenda, and the preservation of labor conditions necessary for the maintenance of academic freedom.

CONCLUSION

Michael Milken should be sent back to prison without pardon for his parole-breaking activities in and out of education. Knowledge Universe should be broken up and sold or nationalized. However, these remedies to the problems we have outlined above would not address the fundamental problems of the corporate raid on knowledge production, or the assault on all things public waged by the corporate media in the interests of corporate expansion. There will not be an eruption of a heroic Underground Liberation Force that comes out of the center of the planet to save the world, tearing a hole through The Matrix in order to implode it. Addressing these issues rather requires the institutionalization of a regulatory infrastructure that considers the ethical, political, and social implications of corporate control over knowledge production—corporate media and corporate education. Such an infrastructure would regulate such production according to the interests of the public sphere rather than the corporate. Such a future would have to rethink censorship to realize that corporate monopolies on knowledge production are a form of censorship that must be prevented. Making the conditions for popular and dissenting knowledge and cultural production would involve fostering critical rather than instrumental education while limiting corporate monopolies on knowledge production and producing, instead, more vibrant public schooling that bolsters democratic rather than corporate social relations and values.

NOTES

1. www.milkeninstitute.org/poe.cfm?point=review

2. Securities rated below investment grade by the rating agencies. Using a junk bond, *Forbes* explained, "an acquisitor can almost literally buy a company with its own money." Milken was not the first to recognize the power of junk—academic studies had reached the same conclusion years earlier—but he was the first to popularize it. Then, beginning in the late 1970s, Michael Milken and Drexel Burnham started rewriting all the rules of Wall Street. Drexel volunteered to underwrite for the public market the low-rated bonds of those companies ignored by Wall Street's heavy hitters. The only requirement "was to pay the price: a high yield to investors, and an enormous fee to Drexel." William M. Adler, *Mollie's Job: A Story of Life and Work on the Global Assembly Line* (New York: Scribner, 2000), 238.

3. See Michael W. Apple, *Ideology and Curriculum*, 2d ed. (New York: Routledge, 1990).

4. Justin Martin, "Lifelong Learning Spells Earnings," *Fortune*, 6 July 1998, 197–200.

5. Simon Avery, "Ex-Con Milken a Preacher for Capitalism: Conference in California," *Financial Post* (*National Post*, Canada), 10 March 1999, C1, C4.

6. Michael Krantz, "Steve's Two Jobs," *Time*, 18 October 1999, 68.

7. Henry A. Giroux, *The Mouse That Roared: Disney and the End of Innocence* (New York: Rowman & Littlefield, 1999), 3.

8. "In the state capitalist democracies, the public arena has been extended and enriched by long and bitter popular struggle. Meanwhile concentrated private power has labored to restrict it. These conflicts form a good part of modern history. The most effective way to restrict democracy is to transfer decision making from the public arena to unaccountable institutions: kings and princes, priestly castes, military juntas, party dictatorships, or modern corporations. The decisions reached by the directors of GE affect the general society substantially, but citizens play no role in them, as a matter of principle (we may put aside transparent myth about market and stockholder 'democracy')." Noam Chomsky, *Profit over People: Neoliberalism and the Global Order* (New York: Seven Stories Press, 1999), 131–32.

9. Martin, "Lifelong Learning," 197–200. For a discussion of social movements against corporatization of the public sphere, see Charles Derber, *Corporation Nation: How Corporations are Taking over Our Lives and What We Can Do about It* (New York: St. Martin's Press, 1998).

10. David Corn, "Saturday Night Censored," *The Nation*, 13 July 1998, 6–7.

11. Doreen Carvajal, "Libel Wrangle over Milken Book Drags On," *New York Times*, 28 June 1999, C1.

12. Carvajal, "Libel Wrangle."

13. Steven Manning, "How Corporations Are Buying Their Way into America's Classrooms," *The Nation*, 27 September 1999, 17.

14. Mark Walsh, "Education Firm Charts Growth of Its Universe," *Education Week on the Web*, www.edweek.org/ew/vol-18/43univ.h18, 4 August 1999.

15. Walsh, "Education Firm Charts Growth of Its Universe."

16. David S. Bernstein, "Mister Universe," *Inside Technology* Training, www.ittrain.com/ittrain/98sep_fea2.html, September 1999.

17. Even though the bombing of Kosovo and Serbia certainly created an environmental danger zone filled with floating debris, dead bloated cows, and explosive bombies, the link omits these minor contradictions such as the massive military output on attacking Yugoslavia for "humanitarian interests" (bombs for peace) and then standing by while U.S.-funded, armed, and trained forces commit genocide in East Timor because "we have economic interests there."

18. We discuss this at length in chapter 2.

19. We are referring to the Milken-funded attack on Edward Said by former Israeli security official Justus Weiner in *Commentary*, which turned out to be a series of falsehoods (Justus Reid Weiner, "'My Beautiful Old House' and Other Fabrications by Edward Said," *Commentary*, September 1999, 23–31). The *New York Times* covered the Weiner allegations but never covered their refutations by Said himself. "Defamation, Revisionist Style," *Counterpunch (Online)*, www.counterpunch.org/said2.html, 1999; Alexander Cockburn, "Israel's Torture Ban," *The Nation*, 27 September 1999, 8, and "Wild Justice: Edward Said as Jew," *The New York Press*, 1–7 September 1999, 1; and Christopher Hitchens, "The *Commentary* School of Falsification," *The Nation*, 20 September 1999, 9.

20. Stanley Aronowitz, introduction to *Pedagogy of Freedom: Ethics, Democracy, and Civic Courage*, by Paulo Freire (Lanham, Md.: Rowman & Littlefield, 1998), 4.

21. John Carey, "Money Floods in to Fight a Killer," *Business Week,* 10 May 1999, 104.

22. Paul Craig Roberts, "Who Did More for Mankind, Mother Teresa or Mike Milken?" *Business Week,* 2 March 1998, 28.

23. Andrew Pollack, "Private Sector: Restoring the Junk Bond King," *New York Times,* 14 March 1999, Section 3, 2.

24. Andrew Gumbel, "The Resurrection: Everyone Thought Michael Milken, the Disgraced Junk Bond King, Was Washed Up, But He's Back—and This Time He's Going to Help Save Mankind," *The Independent* (London), 9 June 1999, 1–2.

25. *The Economist,* "Michael Milken, Comeback King," 27 March 1999.

26. Gumbel, "The Resurrection."

27. "Reading, Writing, and Enrichment," *The Economist,* 16 January 1999, 55.

28. Andrew Pollack, "Private Sector; Restoring the Junk Bond King," Section 3, 2.

29. Gumbel, "The Resurrection."

30. Gumbel, "The Resurrection."

31. Todd Woody, "The Riddle of Knowledge Universe," *The Industry* Standard, www.thestandard.com/article/display/0,1151,1021,00.html, 13 July 1998.

32. Michael White, "Former Junk Bond King Rules over New Empire," *The Boston Globe,* 2 May 1999, C15.

33. Reactionary *New York Times* columnist Thomas Friedman actually says this explicitly in all earnestness: "Milken quickly moved from trading those junk bonds that already existed, from fallen grade-A companies, to underwriting a whole new market full of only junk players—risky companies, fallen companies, new companies, entrepreneurs and start-ups who could not get credit from the traditional banks, even financial pirates who wanted to take over other companies but couldn't raise the cash to do it through conventional bank channels. . . . This gave you, me and my Aunt Bev a chance to buy a slice of these deals that had previously been off-limits to the little guy. . . . Soon there was a flourishing junk bond—or 'high-yield'—industry, offering the public a share of all sorts of firms and deals." Thomas L. Friedman, *The Lexus and the Olive Tee: Understanding Globalization* (New York: Farrar, Straus & Giroux, 1999), 48. This is what Friedman calls a "democratization of finance."

34. White, "Former Junk Bond King."

35. White, "Former Junk Bond King."

36. *Fortune,* "Michael Milken," 30 September 1996, 80–96.

37. White, "Former Junk Bond King."

38. Gumbel, "The Resurrection."

39. Martin, "Lifelong Learning."

40. Martin, "Lifelong Learning."

41. www.nobeleducation.com/aboutus.htm

42. Martin, "Lifelong Learning."

43. www.nobeleducation.com/aboutus.htm

44. www.nobeleducation.com/aboutus.htm

45. Chester Finn, Louann Bierlein, and Manno Bruno, "Finding the Right Fit: America's Charter Schools Get Started," *The Brookings Review* 14, no. 3 (Summer 1996): 19.

46. Carol Ascher, Norm Fruchter, and Robert Berne, *Hard Lessons: Public Schools and Privatization* (New York: Twentieth Century Fund, 1996).

47. A standard example can be found in "Reading, Writing, and Enrichment," *The Economist,* 16 January 1999, 55.

48. Edward N. Wolff, "Recent Trends in Wealth Ownership, 1983–1998," Jerome Levy Economics Institute, www.zmag.org/ZNET.htm.

49. Martin, "Lifelong Learning."

50. Martin, "Lifelong Learning."

51. H. J. Cummins, "Kinder Capital," *Star Tribune* (Minneapolis), 11 July 1999, ID.

52. Cummins, "Kinder Capital."

53. Karen Houppert, "You're Not Entitled! Welfare 'Reform' Is Leading Government Lawlessness," *The Nation,* 25 October 1999, 15.

54. Stanley Aronowitz, "The Post-Work Manifesto," in *Post-Work: The Wages of Cybernation,* edited by Stanley Aronwitz and Jonathan Cutler (New York: Routledge, 1997).

55. William Ryan, "The New Landscape for Nonprofits," *Harvard Business Review* (January/February 1999): 127–36.

56. Alex Molnar, *Giving Kids the Business* (Boulder, Colo.: Westview, 1996).

57. Steven Strahler, "Investors Back Online School Like No Other: Nobel Lineup, Star-Studded Financiers," *Crain's Chicago Business,* 29 March 1999, 3.

58. Kathleen Morris, "Wiring the Ivory Tower," *Business Week,* 9 August 1999, 90.

59. Strahler, "Investors Back Online School."

60. Morris, "Wiring the Ivory Tower."

2

Rivers of Fire: Amoco's iMPACT on Education

SLICK!
This is a computer simulation of an oil spill at sea. Students must plan and implement methods of dealing with an oil spill at sea. Designed for use for individuals and groups, having two levels: beginner and expert. This resource incorporates graphics, sound effects and a range of printed materials. . . . L20.00. . . . Add to Shopping Cart.

          —BP Educational Services[1]

From the two sets of three colorful Amoco-branded wall posters to the Amoco-branded curriculum box to the Amoco ads in the videos themselves, Amoco's iMPACT middle school science curriculum provides this massive multinational oil company what advertisers refer to as multiple "impressions" or viewing of the brand logo.[2] The curriculum is clearly designed to promote and advertise Amoco to a "captive audience" in public schools. Brightly mottled posters show Sesame Street–style cartoon characters riding roller coasters to learn physics, a lone cartoon diver encounters a gigantic sea monster to learn biology, and an ominous black mountain explodes with molten magma. These cartoons, with more rainbow colors than an oil slick, include scientific labels with arrows reminding kids that all of this fun is educational. Amoco stamps its corporate logo on fun and excitement, curiosity and exploration, education, nature, science, and work. By rendering its red, white, and blue logo visible in school classrooms, Amoco appears as a "responsible corporate citizen" supporting beleaguered public schools with its corporate philanthropy. Not only does the corporate sector defund the public sector by evading its tax responsibility to such public goods as public schools, but the growing trend towards privatization, for-profit charter schools, magnet schools, commercialization, redefine the public schools as for private profit.[3] In reality, Amoco's use of the innocent-looking aesthetics of children's culture, its appeal to fun and child-like curiosity conceal the fact that this oil company is far from innocent of not only undermining the public sector in this country but of outright human rights violations, widespread environmental devastation, and the uprooting of indigenous communities globally.[4]

Like other corporate curricula, Amoco's sprightly lessons do more than provide entry for corporate advertisements into public space.[5] This curriculum functions as a diversion from what Amoco is actually doing around the world and it functions ideologically to construct a corporate-friendly worldview, define youth identity and citizenship through consumption, define nationality as the corporate interest rather than the public interest. Amoco's curriculum produces ideologies of consumerism that bolster its global corporate agenda and it does so under the guise of disinterested scientific knowledge, benevolent technology, and innocent entertainment.

Separating the pedagogical from the political, Amoco's curriculum conceals how this corporation undermines democratic institutions such as public schooling and participates in the hindering of democracy and perpetration of human rights abuses and environmental destruction abroad. As Wharton economist Edward Herman and ColombiaWatch's Celia Zarate-Laun expose, the largest investor in Colombia, British Petroleum (BP; now BPAmoco), has created its own mercenary forces, but also imported British counterinsurgency professionals to train Colombians. BP gave its own intelligence reports to the Colombian military which was used to track and kill local "subversives": "Amnesty International and Human Rights Watch have documented numerous examples of collaboration between Colombian army units and brutal paramilitaries who are guilty of over 75 percent of the human rights violations that have been committed in Colombia's "civil conflict."[6] The other oil companies in Colombia have also "cultivated the army and police and hired paramilitaries and foreign mercenaries to protect their oil pipelines."[7] BPAmoco's behavior overseas must be understood in the context of the relationship between the U.S. government's foreign policy and its support of the corporate sector.

Though said to be specifically supporting Colombia's "war on drugs" and not its militarized counter-insurgency efforts, U.S. aid to Colombia [third highest amount of foreign military aid after Israel and Egypt] has been earmarked for specific regions of the country such as the Amazon and Orinoco basins and the Putumayo region more largely, regions that happen to be the areas of influence of the rebel Revolutionary Armed Forces of Colombia (FARC), while largely avoiding the northern areas of the country where the drug trade routes are protected by paramilitaries closely allied with drug-traffickers and members of the Colombian army. Exempting and supplying arms to an important segment of the drug trade suggests that, as with anticommunism in the past, the drug war rationale covers over the pursuit of larger objectives, that can be read from what the army and paramilitaries do—remove, kill, and silence the large segments of the rural population that stand in the way of the exploitations of Colombia's resources [by transnational corporations such as BPAmoco].[8]

Under the pretext of the drug war, the U.S. government is funding Colombia's internal war against ideologically dissenting factions such as the FARC (currently 18,000 strong)[9] and the smaller ELN (currently counting 3,000).[10] In June of 2000, the U.S. Congress approved a $1 billion aid package to Colombia, including military training, helicopters, and intelligence.[11] Carla Anne Robbins of the *Wall Street Journal* reports that even though the United States has, for the past ten years, exercised caution in extending developmental aid to Colombia because of widespread allegations of human rights abuses, the Colombian government has managed to reassure Washington that its military equipment will be used only for anti-narcotics maneuvers and not for counterinsurgency. Yet, as Justin Delacour of *Z-Net* has demonstrated, the Clinton administration was "remarkably resistant to conditions placed on the aid that require them to demonstrate that the Colombian government is vigorously rooting out complicity between the army and paramilitaries."[12] In fact, as Marc Cooper of *The Nation* remarks, "Bill Clinton's State Department, with only hours left before the Bush transition, employed a loophole in the U.S. aid package [Plan Colombia] and 'voluntarily' decided to 'skip' having to certify that the Colombian government has complied with U.S. human rights demands attached to Plan Colombia legislation—specifically, suppression of the paramilitary death squads."[13]

The *Journal* admits that unless the close ties between the FARC and the drug trade are loosened, the United States' stated intentions of bringing peace, political reform, and crop substitution to the region will surely fail. José Cuesta of the Citizens' Network for Peace in Colombia alleges, "The coca crops are nothing but a concrete response to the ravages caused by unrestrained free-market policies."[14] Washington has only committed 1 percent of the Plan Colombia aid package to crop substitution, and this means that *campesinos* will not be able to produce even at subsistence level without sustaining coca fields: "In general a kilo of cocaine is sold at 1.5 to 1.7 million pesos (about $6,800–$7,700) and net profit per hectare is 200,000 pesos (about $90). Comparatively speaking a carga, which is about 100 kilos of corn, is sold for 30,000 pesos, and after paying the costs the peasant is left with only 10,000 pesos (about $4.50) per carga."[15] Even as the *Wall Street Journal* professes that the problem in the FARC-controlled regions stems from drug trafficking, however, it also attributes the need for militarization to the FARC's economic reforms, in particular their attempts to tax the corporate sector:

> As conservatives were complaining that Bogota was selling out to the Marxists [because of the Colombian government's agreement to negotiate settlement with guerrillas], New York Stock Exchange Chairman Richard Grasso accepted an invitation to fly to the demilitarized zone to tutor the FARC on the joys of capitalism. . . . [Carlos Antonio] Lozada [one of the FARC's negotiators] . . . explains that instead of indiscriminate kidnapping, the FARC's new Law 002 will levy a tax on anyone with more than $1 million in assets.[16]

The expansion of NAFTA into South America is being accompanied by the expansion of U.S. military presence, not only in Colombia through the provision of military attack helicopters and counter-insurgency equipment for maneuvers nominally against trafficking, but also in Ecuador and El Salvador, where bases are being built. This movement of capital through military expansion illustrates concretely *New York Times* foreign correspondent Thomas Freidman's thesis that "the hidden hand of the market will never work without the hidden fist—McDonald's cannot flourish without McDonnell Douglas, designer of the F-15. And the hidden fist that keeps the world safe for Silicon Valley's technologies is called the United States Army, Air Force, Navy, and Marine Corps."[17] This militarization opens the region to U.S. investment as it destroys the fields and livelihoods of poor peasants, using methods as brutal as those attributed to the FARC. Alongside and contingent to militarization, education can work to open wider reaches for the neoliberal market. Wall Street's journey to the region demonstrates that investors understand how education in the "joys of capitalism" opens the way to corporate infiltration.[18] Clearly, the so-called War on Drugs is in the business of an ideological production partly installed through the very processes of militarization.

This military intervention into the political situation in Colombia owes to the fact that the United States imports more oil from the region than it does from the Middle East (260,000 barrels from Colombia per day). Indeed, the claim can hardly be made that the administration is funding drug containment policies when publicly funded treatment centers have been radically cut from city, state, and federal budgets nationwide. In 1994, the White House commissioned the Rand Institution to research the most effective methods for controlling and reducing drugs. The Rand report found that treatment was 7 percent cheaper and more successful than domestic enforcement, 11 percent more than interdiction, and 23 percent more than source-country eradication policies, the policy which this aid package embraces.[19] Clearly, therefore, the defunding of public support for treatment ultimately benefits the profit-mongering of the private sector. This is why, unlike public advocates like Noam Chomsky and Ralph Nader, private corporations like BPAmoco support the militarization of Colombia's "War on Drugs":

> It's questionable whether or not it even qualifies as a drug policy at all. Several corporations whose interests have nothing to do with drug policy have been pushing the Colombia package from day one. Multinationals and U.S.-based weapons producers who are pushing the package include Occidental Petroleum Corp., Enron Corp., BPAmoco, Colgate-Palmolive Co., United Technologies Corp. and Bell Helicopter Textron Inc. Occidental Petroleum's strong backing of the package derives from the fact that its extensive oil operations in Colombia have been frequently sabotaged by guerrilla groups who object to the terms of the agreement between the Colombian government and multinational oil corporations that operate in the country. Occidental Petroleum's Vice-President Lawrence Meriage was even called to testify before the House Government Reform Subcommittee on Drug Policy, leading observers to wonder how oil executives suddenly qualified as drug policy experts.[20]

Ultimately, then, U.S. taxpayers are paying millions of dollars to protect the oil pipelines of BPAmoco, Occidental Petroleum (a strong backer of Al Gore's political career and presidential campaign), Shell, and Texaco—companies which have spilled 1.7 million barrels of oil onto the soils and rivers in the last twelve years. At the same time, U.S. chemical companies Monsanto and Dow are being enriched by U.S.-assisted spraying of their toxic herbicides (Roundup and Spike) on coca and opium plants in Colombia:

> Monsanto's Roundup, which is the principal chemical being sprayed in Colombia to reduce the coca and poppy crops, contains phosphorus, which upon contact with water captures oxygen and destroys fish in lakes, lagoons, and marshes. Crop spraying affects food crops such as cassava, plantains, corn, and tropical fruits. Likewise, peasants exposed to the spray have reported cases of diarrhea, fever, muscle pain, and headaches attributed to their exposure to the chemical spray.[21]

Not only is this, too, endangering the world's second richest ecosystem (after that of Brazil), but the same drugs evading eradication by the chemical sprays (coca production is in fact on the rise) are being sold to the United States with the profits being used to fund both right wing death squads who work in the interests of the multinationals and the government and to fund the left wing guerrillas fighting against the government and the multinationals.[22]

In short then, the same interests that are supporting drug trafficking are also supporting multinational corporate expansion in the region. This is not just a case of two blood-seeking powers—the government and the insurgency—fighting it out at the expense of the little guy, but rather an imperialist manipulation for economic and ideological control where corporations are winning the conflict on both sides. The entire process of corporate expansion is militarized in combination with the drug trade. However, by omitting any mention of the complex web of murder, pollution, and politics undergirding its quest for profit, Amoco lies to school kids by painting a picture of science and education as innocent and free of their motivating forces—in this case corporate greed. The Amoco curriculum is not simply about hiding the insidious operations of the company abroad under sunny pictures of smiling children playing happy games in pristine parks. The Amoco curriculum also constructs and naturalizes a worldview where public concerns are erased underneath the adventures of corporatism and the thrills of the consumer. Part of educating citizens in the "joys of capitalism" consists of, for instance, making the exploitation of other nations' natural environments, raw materials, and labor forces seem like affective friendships or even love affairs celebrated in joyous pictures of wondering gazes at the triumphs of technological mastery. These kinds of images stage a drama of corporate excellence which overrides any possible apprehension about how exactly such curricula are remaking public schooling itself as training ground for consumer armies:

> At the primary and secondary levels, the spoils of the public school system have long been coveted by "education entrepreneurs," touting the "discipline" of the marketplace over the "inefficiency" of the public realm, and normalizing the rhetoric of corporate management—the public as customer, education as competitive product, learning as efficiency tool. Remember Lamar Alexander's declaration, shortly before becoming secretary of education, that Burger King and Federal Express should set up schools to show how the private sector would run things? . . . While your local high school hasn't yet been bought out by McDonalds, many educators already use teaching aids and packets of materials, "donated" by companies, that are crammed with industry propaganda designed to instill product awareness among young consumers: lessons about the history of the potato chip, sponsored by the Snack Food Association, or literacy programs that reward students who reach monthly reading goals with Pizza Hut slices.[23]

While Amoco seduces school kids with the allures of fun knowledge, it is also actively engaging in practices which directly undermine the public. Domestically, as Amoco was distributing its "Rivers of Fire" curriculum in Chicago, it was creating real rivers of fire in Michigan and Missouri. In River Rouge, Mich., the city was fighting to force Amoco to stop leaking explosive petroleum products into its sewer system.[24] City leaders worried that Amoco was recreating the conditions for an explosion in 1982 that "set off fires and smaller explosions inside nearby sewer lines and blew out windows of buildings and cars."[25] While the "Rivers of Fire" video was being distributed in Chicago, in Sugar Creek, Mo., families were forced to flee their homes as Amoco's cleanup of its decades old ground, water, and air pollution forced contaminated air into the homes of local residents. The Chappell family, advised by the EPA to find alternative lodging, had begun an investigation into unusually high incidence of cancer in their neighborhood.[26] At the same time, BPAmoco pleaded guilty to felony charges in a case of illegal dumping of toxic chemicals.

> Alaska's North Slope is an environmentally sensitive area and BP's Endicott Island-drilling site sits on the Beaufort Sea, home to birds and marine life. Hundreds of 55-gallon barrels containing paint thinners, paints, oil and solvents were dumped, according to federal prosecutors.[27]

The conviction followed a 16-month-long legal battle in which BPAmoco denied knowledge of the dumping, despite the previous conviction of their same contractor on identical dumping charges. This pollution, too, had been going on for years.

Amoco produces this science curriculum in conjunction with Scholastic, Waste Management Inc., and Public Television and freely distributes it to the Chicago Public Schools. The overwhelming corporate interest in investing in this project is far from innocent, philanthropic, or charitable, as the curriculum participates in an overall corporate strategy of producing global corporate citizens and recreating profit motives as moral values, or rather, tutoring the kids in the "joys of capitalism." As Alex Molnar has shown, Scholastic itself is one of the most aggressive and shameless cases of corralling youth into the consumer market:

> [Mark] Evans [a senior vice president of Scholastic, in his 1988 essay in *Advertising Age*] managed to paint a picture of noble purpose and business need combined in perfect harmony to advance the welfare of American students. Perhaps not wishing to seem too self-serving, he failed to mention that at the time he wrote his essay, Scholastic was in the process of establishing its educational marketing division and was looking for corporate clients. Early in his essay, Evans identified a few business-supported educational projects that, in his mind, illustrated how corporations, pursuing profits, and schools, trying to better educate their students, could work in tandem to advance the cause of social progress. Then he dispensed with the good cop fiction and came to the point: "More and more companies see education marketing as the most compelling, memorable and cost-effective way to build share of mind and market into the 21st century." Evans then set aside any pretense of high educational

and social purpose when he chose a model for all to emulate. "Gillette is currently sponsoring a multi-media in-school program designed to introduce teenagers to their safety razors—building brand and product loyalties through classroom-centered, peer-powered lifestyle patterning."[28]

In conjunction with these company goals, the Amoco curriculum certainly shows how profits and market values are replacing social purpose in the education of citizens. The Amoco curriculum demonstrates how corporations are using schools to teach market values and make these values into common sense, even fashioning them as the basis of morality. Oil companies in particular, as David Cromwell points out, are using classroom curricula to spread propaganda that "modern civilization is dependent on the hydrocarbon business"[29] as the popularization of this belief is essential to the survival of the industry. Specifically, as we detail in what follows, Amoco's curriculum envisions nature and knowledge, as well as work, education, and science, through the imaginary of corporate culture.

NATURE

Each of the videos begins and ends with advertisements for Amoco. "Major funding for the New Explorers is provided by Amoco celebrating the adventure of scientific discovery for the year 2000 and beyond." This voice-over accompanies images of pristine nature: the moon, a bald eagle flying over a serene lake. The Amoco logo, in patriotic red-white-and-blue, joins with the bald eagle in suggesting that the trademark could replace the U.S. flag. In the context of public school classrooms (replete with a U.S. flag hanging near the VCR), such merging of these common tropes fashions the idea of national citizenship as corporate branding.

These framing advertisements present serene scenes of idealized yet decontextualized nature, labeled with the oil company logo and suggesting an alignment of ecological health and the Amoco corporation. The ad for Amoco is followed by a connected ad for Waste Management Inc., "Helping the world dispose of its problems." Together these images and assuring voice-over present nature in a state of benevolent corporate management. The pristine horizon punctuated by a range of snow-capped mountains, pure colors, still lake waters, and soaring birds serves to Americanize the natural landscape further by placing the corporate logo in the spacious skies and mountain ranges of the beauty America sings. The pure air and stillness give a sense that time has stopped and that human hands have left nature's sublimity untouched and dazzling. The history of Waste Management reveals, of course, quite another story, and certainly the contention that Waste Management disposes of the world's problems is less credible than would be a contrary claim that it has created new ones. Founder and billionaire Wayne Huizenga, a hero of capitalist consolidation, mergers, and acquisitions, has come time and again under allegations of unethical practices, illegal price-setting, stock bailings, and underworld corruption. Additionally, his profit motivations have proven far from environmentally astute, as he reneged on the waste-hauling industry's practices of breeding pigs to eat edible garbage when his own pigs developed special diseases not evident on the competitors' farms.[30] Though Huizenga has since sold the company, Waste Management has a stake in deregulating capital and finance as well as finding ways to avoid restrictive environmental legislation. The pedagogical intent here is to show nature, indeed, as self-regulating, able to revitalize and reproduce itself without human intervention or investments of any kind. The logo then serves to link the bountiful abundance and cleanliness of nature without controls to the advancement of clean, corporate, healthful capital.

The videos envision nature as not merely best served by corporate management but as an expression of corporate culture. "Rivers of Fire" opens with a drive through the jungle likened to that of a typical suburban commuter on his way to his desk job. "Except for the tropical foliage, [geologist Frank Truesdale's] routine looks like a typical suburban commute, but when he takes the first exit off the paved highway, we get a hint that he's not exactly on his way to a desk job in an office building." Frank's four-wheel-drive jostles down a dirt-paved road flanked on either side by lush vegetation. Corporations themselves thus come to seem part of nature.

Within the imaginary of the videos, nature appears alternately as dangerous and in need of control or as tamed suburban landscape. "If something goes wrong here," warns Bill Kurtis in "Dive into Darkness," "there's no easy escape to the surface. Since cave diving took hold in the 1960s, more than 300 people have died in caves in Florida, Mexico and the Caribbean alone." "Temporary loss of air supply, temporary disorientation, temporary loss of lights—those aren't reasons to die in a cave," admits one of the experts. "The reason people die in those situations is panic, perceived stress. That's what kills people." "But despite these risks," the video concludes, "not one of them [the divers] would turn back. This is not just a job for these divers. It's a mission. Like the original explorers in space. They had to send a person there to really know what's going on." "Rivers of Fire" presents scientists as adventurers, explorers, but also conquistadors driven to control an angry and unpredictable final frontier—namely, the Earth itself about to spew forth burning deadly fluids. Narrator and producer Bill Kurtis kneels before a stream of magma running into the ocean as he explains the danger. "In January of 1983," a voice-over begins, "the skies were just as blue on the big island of Hawaii, the beaches just as inviting as any other day. But thirty miles beneath the crater of Kilauea, molten lava was rising." This narration is accompanied by ominous bassy music, invoking horror movie conventions as in *Jaws* when the monster is about to pounce. Continual video cross cuts intersperse the explosion of this deadly lava with shots of human technology—seismic equipment that Kurtis explains is necessary to watch and hence control the unpredictable earth. Lava flows "threaten homesites and other subdivisions that may be in its way." By framing nature as violent and in need of control by science and technology, "Rivers of Fire" naturalizes the role that the corporation, and here more specifically Amoco, plays in protecting citizens and property from the threat of nature. The technological instruments provide "a way to prevent lava from consuming those who live around the volcanoes."

In this case, the video does more than camouflage the real role that Amoco's science and technology play in threatening citizens and nature. It also denies the history of why the volcano observatory was established in the early twentieth century and by whom. The curriculum fails to mention that the observatory was initially funded by one of the five businesspeople who overthrew the indigenous Hawaiian government and installed a plutocracy. The observatory was designed not merely to study nature but to predict volcanic flows so that other foreign investors could be convinced that their investments in development projects and industry would not be destroyed by lava. In other words, the video presents, as disinterested study of nature, a history of economic and political imperialism. When Amoco and Scholastic describe their lessons as "An Amoco Expedition with the New Explorers," they are actively excluding the history of conquest that paved the way for today's seemingly disinterested measurement of nature. The establishment of the observatory was part of settling the frontier, annexing Hawaii, and continuing the westward expansion that was part of an American history characterized by violence and exploitation and motivated by profit rather than a benevolent protection of citizens from an unruly nature:

> The entire history of this country has been driven by violence. The whole power structure and economic system was based essentially on the extermination of the native populations and the bringing of slaves. The Industrial Revolution was based on cheap cotton, which wasn't kept cheap by market principles but by conquest. It was kept cheap by the use of land stolen from the indigenous populations and then by the cheap labor of those exploited in slavery. The subsequent conquest of the West was also very brutal. After reaching the end of the frontier, we just went on conquering more and more—the Philippines, Hawaii, Latin America, and so on. In fact, there is a continuous strain of violence in U.S. military history from "Indian fighting" right up through the war in Vietnam. The guys who were involved in "In-

dian fighting" are the guys who went to the Philippines, where they carried out a massive slaughter; and the same people who had just been tried for war crimes in the Philippines went on to Haiti, where they carried out another slaughter. This goes right up through Vietnam. If you look at the popular literature on Vietnam, it's full of "We're chasing Indians."[31]

In the Amoco videos, nature, rather than technology, corporations, and the capitalist economic system itself appears to threaten families, consumption, and the innocent pleasures of beachcombing. Additionally, nature functions as an extension of the corporation, becomes plunderable, and substitutes as the workspace. Such an understanding of nature as the worksite serves well oil-drilling sponsor Amoco, who also wants students to see that nature is dangerous to civilization and in need of control, manipulation, and constant measurement by scientists. In "Dive into Darkness" one scientist reminds viewers that nature is being destroyed, "things are disappearing so rapidly we need to document them."

KNOWLEDGE

The Amoco kit includes three videotapes, six colorful wall posters, teachers' guides, and public relations instructions for teachers and gas station owners to place promotional photos and stories about the "partnership" in local newspapers. Amoco's curriculum suggests that education must be fun, exciting, exploratory, and meaningful to students. "I think it's important that students see many things on the way home from school that they saw in the classroom," explains one of the physics teachers. And the success of such meaningful pedagogical practices is proven in the countless testimonies of students who were never interested in science before now. "Any teacher can go to college and get their degree and come in to teach and do all kinds of chalk talk," one student observes. "But Mr. Hicks comes in and makes it all fun. He basically loves every one of us. . . . We're a family and he teaches it with love."

The Amoco curriculum draws on popularized notions of progressive pedagogy to suggest that education should derive from experience, that students be involved in "constructing" knowledge by participating in activities which are meaningful to them, and that learning must not disconnect knowledge from the world. Another middle level pedagogue, Nancy Atwell, in her book *In the Middle*, professes to make learning meaningful by giving kids more power to decide on curriculum and on what happens in the classroom: "Together we'll enter the world of literature, become captivated, make connections to our lives, the world, and the world of other books, and find satisfaction."[32] Atwell, hailed in both

the popular and educational presses as an educational innovator, emphasizes hands-on learning where kids take responsibility in deciding
what the curriculum will be and formulate, in discussions with their
classmates, the kinds of topics they will write about. Atwell contrasts this
new way of teaching middle school with a more traditional teacher-
centered methodology where kids' potentials for imagination and involvement are never tapped or developed. At the same time, however,
she does not talk about how this freedom for educational experimenta-
tion functions to bolster the sense of privilege of her white, private-
school, suburban students, nor does she address how these methods are
meant to train, precisely, those in control of the future means of production. For instance, given the classroom time to write poetry without being assigned specific topics, Atwell's student Joe writes about the emotions he experiences when alone in his bedroom, and Atwell comments,
"When I read Joe's poem, I remembered my bedroom in my parents'
house and the most complicated relationship I ever enjoyed with a physical space."[33] Atwell neglects to mention what kinds of students have
their own bedrooms, what are the politics of real estate that provide for
these kinds of empty spaces, or what kinds of populations enjoy the privileges of solitude. For Atwell, "empowering" students means giving
them a sense of confidence and personal power. Yet, Atwell has no sense
of different levels of power, privilege, agency, and sense of entitlement
experienced by different students in different social, economic, and cultural contexts. Atwell's kids are already in a class position to receive
power. Atwell does not help her privileged students see their privileges
as a part of a broader system that fails to extend basic social services to
students elsewhere. Nor does she offer her students the tools for challenging oppressions, such as the maintenance of a highly unequal structure of educational resource allocation. Atwell, thus, embraces a highly
individualized progressive *methodology* divorced from any social, political referent for more just social transformation. Likewise, Amoco's *Rock
n' Roll Physics* shows conventional classroom physics lessons as the
height of decontextualized, abstract, and boring education which fails by
failing to engage students. A physics teacher drones on spewing formulas as students sleep, doodle, and play with chewing gum. Narrator Bill
Kurtis says, "This is no way to teach physics." Cut to the class riding on
a roller coaster and Kurtis yells from the roller coaster, "Now this is the
way to learn physics." As in Atwell, "Learning is more likely to happen
when students like what they are doing,"[34] but there is no sense given
here about what kinds of students get to experience such pleasures and
under what circumstances, nor what kinds of political values, institutions, and configurations of power are being assumed and supported
through such initiatives. Such pleasure is seldom innocent.[35]

The use of adventure-thrill and high-speed derring-do in the Amoco curriculum keys in to a broader public discourse about the economy which promotes instability, fear, and physical trepidation as the goal of the good life. As the Amoco curriculum redefines the pursuit of knowledge as a dangerous game, *Time* magazine and MTV both juxtapose high-risk sport with day trading and risky stock investment. Quitting jobs, starting businesses, and risky investment in the market are being likened to base jumping, paragliding, mountain climbing, and other adventure sports. MTV shows bungee-jumpers freaking out over whether or not to plunge while an e-trade advertisement contextualizes the situation in the lower right corner of the screen. Clearly, *Time* and MTV construct and romanticize the popular embrace of volatile and uncertain ventures. This could be viewed as simply a ploy to naturalize an increasingly unstable economy as an exciting challenge that the brave can fearlessly negotiate. Job insecurity, an uncertain financial future, and growing inequalities in wealth and income appear as exciting obstacles to brave in the new economy. The economy metaphorizes as nature itself standing there as the tantalizing mountain to climb or jump off of in the Mountain Dew commercial. In other words, adventure sports are being used by corporate mass media to naturalize economic insecurity.[36]

The notion of hands-on learning is indebted to contemporary progressive educational methodologies of constructivism grounded in Piagetian theory as well as the influence of the Deweyan tradition and the wrongful appropriation of Paulo Freire's criticism of banking education. "Education thus becomes," Freire maintains, "an act of depositing, in which the students are the depositories and the teacher is the depositor. Instead of communicating, the teacher issues communiqués and makes deposits which the students patiently receive, memorize, and repeat."[37] These progressive traditions share with the Amoco curriculum an insistence on the centrality of the learner, the need for a de-centering of teacher authority in the classroom, and the importance of knowledge that is meaningful as the basis for further learning. The Amoco curriculum seems progressive by appearing to take seriously the notion that education should be meaningful to students and that the classroom structure should not treat students as depositories for rarefied teacher knowledge. However, like many wrong-headed liberal appropriations of Freire, the Amoco curriculum treats progressive educational ideals instrumentally—that is, strictly as methods to increase the likelihood that students will absorb knowledge of which the justifications for its teaching remain unquestioned.[38] In the case of the Amoco videos, this means that there are no questions raised as to why students should learn physics, whose interests are served by the teaching of this knowledge, what this knowledge is used for in the world, and at whose expense and to whose benefits. Hence, seemingly progressive methodologies are not theoretically justified and end up being just a more efficient delivery system for accepted knowledge about science.

The Amoco videos view nature as a resource. That is, nature appears as needing to be tamed and domesticated, brought within the control of scientific rationality represented in automatic machines drawing lines on graphs, making sense. Nature is out there waiting to be retrieved, transported back to laboratories equipped with state-of-the-art equipment for measurement and storage, named and labeled for future research. "Imagine a place left on earth," says master of ceremonies Bill Kurtis, introducing "Dive into Darkness," "that is virtually unexplored." The underwater cave Sagittarius in Sweetings Cay of the Bahamas is, he continues, an "unstudied world waiting for . . . discovery."

However, the pursuit of knowledge here seems like an alibi. Scattered throughout the surfaces of these environmental niches, scientists find natural holes filled with energy sources: Dr. Jill Yaeger of Antioch University swims across blue holes brimming with blue bubbles. These blue holes, the voice-over explains, give off a strong force which, when reversed by the tides, create twisting fields of force that sweep swimmers into tow without granting any path of escape or release. Searching for knowledge, the scientific exploration team is able to avoid such deep-sea traps. The energy fields themselves are resources to be used in the production of knowledge. The company that sponsors the videos does not think it worth mentioning that it itself is in the business of exploiting energy fields as resources for production. Acquiring knowledge of nature as energy becomes a substitute, even a cover, for exploiting natural sources of energy for company profit. Collecting bits of natural knowledge becomes a safety valve, an antidote to the destruction that natural energy would cause if left unexplored and unexploited, and a compassionate rationale for expanding technocratic controls into foreign territories.

Amoco's view of nature communicates that what is important to know about nature is how it can be used for human progress and profit. "Scientists believe that sharks may hold the secrets to important medical benefits for man," "Dive into Darkness" informs students. "They're animals in need of protection and study." The video neglects to mention that human industry in the form of commercial fishing is the primary cause of the endangerment of sharks. Instead, "humanitarian" concerns serve to justify Dr. Jill Yaeger's dives into darkness on a mission to bring back the newly discovered form of crustacia "remipede" to her research laboratory in Ohio. These animals need to be known about, named, labeled, and catalogued in order to construct a total knowledge of life, the videos suggest, and of evolution. In fact, the sea dives themselves are depicted as travels back through evolution, into the dark origins of life at the bottom of the sea, while the precarious return to the water's surface works as a triumphant enlightenment. However, what made the journey of discovery so successful turns out to be the successful retrieval of the remipede for scientific research, in other words, the collection and acquisition of resources. The videos translate activities of collecting into the ethical entertainment of learning, knowledge acquisition and accumulation. The idea that knowledge of nature needs to be whole and complete means here that mastery of nature leads to a greater variety of products. Also, nature is biding its evolutionary time, waiting to be brought to civilized places where it can be "taught to eat store-bought food," as Dr. Jill Yaeger announces. Amoco does not allude to the ways nature might be destroyed when its products are extracted, nor to how nature and the ecosystem are not designed simply to be exploited for human instrumental use, nor to how all nature is not passively waiting to be turned into products of consumption and objects of display.

EARTHWORMS AND EMPIRES

Public Image: The corporate image of Monsanto as a responsible member of the business world genuinely concerned with the welfare of our environment will be adversely affected with increased publicity.
Sources of Contamination: Although there may be some soil and air contamination involved, by far the most critical problem at present is water contamination. . . . Our manufacturing facilities sewered a sizable quantity of PCBs in a year's time.

—Monsanto committee memo, 1969[39]

Amoco is not the only company using nature to teach kids the values and joys of capitalism. Under these types of curricula, nature is re-made to express and reflect the social relations of capital, and thereby the unequal relations of capital are made to seem part of nature. A 2000–2001 exhibit, titled "Underground Adventure," at Chicago's Field Museum of Natural History, for example, is a spectacular trip underneath the earth's surface to explore the wonders of the soil.[40] "You will never feel the same about the soil again," are the words that welcome you into Monsanto's "fun for the whole family" learning trek. On the other side of the video greeting room called the "base-camp," is Monsanto's magical shrinking machine which make all the critters around the visitors suddenly into towering monsters, gigantic plastic beetles, and bulging roots that would have made Kafka ogle and Gulliver shake his head. What is truly fantastic about the display, however, is not so much that Monsanto is hiding its own destruction of such fertility in the soil through its genetic manipulations or its annihilation of such critters through its production of insecticides such as

Roundup or its own monopolistic stronghold of species' diversity by its horizontal control of agricultural products that create essential needs among farmers for its other exclusive products. Nor is it very surprising, after all, that Monsanto would not acknowledge, in this exhibit, its emissions of PCBs that contaminated much farming and breeding lands in West Anniston, Ala., and caused cancer among much of the population there with the full and documented knowledge of the company itself as to the damage that PCBs cause.[41] Rather, what makes Monsanto's natural history lessons truly magical is precisely how the company manages to exhibit such unethical, unbalanced, and destructive capitalist practices as the way of nature, rather than of multinational corporations.

Monsanto's aims in its exhibit are clear from the moment the visitor enters. The first thing the visitor sees is a series of Plexiglas displays professing the importance of the soil in providing various consumer products. These are not just any consumer products, but rather major corporate trademarks. For example, one case displays an old pair of blue jeans with the glaring "Gap" label, while the sign reads: "Without soil, there would be no jeans. These jeans are made of cotton denim stitched together with cotton thread. Their blue color comes from indigo dye. Cotton and indigo come from plants that need soil to grow. No soil—no jeans." Next comes a basket of Coca-Cola cans piled on top of each other. The sign exclaims, "The aluminum in these cans has been recycled over and over again. But new aluminum starts out locked inside of soil in an ore called bauxite. No soil—no aluminum." The exhibit never admits what Monsanto or the other sponsors have at stake in displaying this particular constellation of goods, for example, Monsanto's production of Nutrasweet artificial sweetener used in Diet Coke. "Without soil there would be no penicillin," the next sign triumphantly declares. The sign does not go on to explain Monsanto's investments in the pharmaceutical industry, nor how the consolidation of large pharmaceutical companies and their lobbying of protections for global intellectual property rights is making medicine less accessible throughout the world to those who need it most, but rather indicates how many lives are being saved because penicillin arises fruitfully from the soil.

Monsanto is clearly telling its young patrons that, just like the mall, the soil is rich in its offerings of fun and diverse things to wear and to buy, as if multinational products emerge straight out of the earth without involving people, labor, or social relations. In other words, Monsanto here seems to literalize the classical Marxist claim that naturalization erases the processes of production from the commodity. Nature is made to seem richly abundant in capitalist output, making invisible the inequalities inherent in the mass manufacturing of cotton or dye, or the injustices practiced in both Third and First World sweatshops where much of, for example, The Gap's merchandise is stitched together (often outsourced) by the poor, the exploited, and the marginalized, or when Coca-Cola's local parent company Minute Maid employs child labor for low wages in Brazil. What is not assessed, too, is how such multinationals are involved in, say, polluting the very soil they are said to enrich by distributing non-biodegradable and non-recyclable litter, or dumping their excesses in Third-World markets to keep prices high, thereby making such items not truly as widely accessible as their spontaneous soil generation would imply.

The first object the visitor sees after having been shrunk is a giant United States penny inscribed with the words, "In Soil We Trust." Indeed, the godhead capital lords over nature here. As well, Lincoln's prominent visage at the entrance invokes the authority of the state and American history to suggest an organic connection to capital growth here in the former prairie-land of Chicago. More simply, first seeing a series of commodities that come from soil and then seeing money itself in the soil, the visitor is being told outright, "There is big money in the soil." To emphasize that the soil is naturally organized by the laws of capital, in the "Root Room," scientific labels mark uniform units of time along the branch of a tree, becoming farther and farther apart to demonstrate that the branch's rate of growth is accelerating. This celebration of unlimited accumulation and growth makes the project of capital seem driven by a natural propensity towards expansion, rather than, as William Greider points out, towards depletion and non-sustainability: "The nettlesome assertion," he writes, "that governing authorities did not wish to grasp [in 1992] was that rising affluence itself, at least as it was presently defined and achieved, faced finite limits. The global system, as it generated new wealth-producing activity, was hurtling toward a wall, an unidentified point in time when economic expansion would collectively collide with the physical capacity of the ecosystem."[42] In real terms, Monsanto's vision of unrelenting growth and monumentalized consumption can only be sacralized by forgetting the social costs of accelerated production, costs usually not accounted for on balance sheets, like "deforestation, desertification, urbanization and other activities that, so to speak, paved over the natural world"[43] as well as other costs attributed to the impoverishment of the places providing the raw materials, or to their domination by outside powers, like weakened institutions for justice, fiscal austerity, starvation wages, and diminished authority for taxing foreign businesses. Making capital bigger does not necessarily make the world better for most people. Moreover, the exhibit does not allude to the fact that Monsanto's own growth did not happen naturally at all. Rather, it resulted in part from a governmental action responding to pressures from big business interests: the passage of the 1996 Freedom to Farm Act which was to phase out federal subsidies to farmers and thereby drive small farmers out of business. The legislation, however, did not work to stabilize prices nor to lessen the surpluses pushing prices up, but rather required an increase in government subsidies to farmers (from $16 billion in 1998 to $32 billion in 1999) as Congress enacted "emergency" relief measures. "Among the consequences," Greider concludes, "the capital-intensive treadmill for farmers sped up, and they became even more eager to embrace whatever innovation promised to boost returns. Just as farm prices were cratering, Monsanto and others began promoting genetically altered seeds for corn and soybeans with cost-cutting promises, and this new technology swept the landscape."[44]

Ideas about bigness and growth presented in the entryway set the standard, throughout the exhibit, for connecting consumption to the expansion of the good life promised by corporate growth. The individual museum-goer is supposed to identify with the bugs and critters and so with corporate greed, wanting to consume enough to fatten corporate bellies. Further down the path of exploration, a section is called, "Recycling Leftovers," where the sign reads: "Partnership or Parasite: Can You Tell Which is Which?" The life-size panorama shows giant worms and bugs feasting on each other in a "feeding frenzy." Across the way stands a vending machine. The first item for selection in this vending machine explains, "millipede: decomposer" while the glass screen displays a package of decaying plants. The vending machine places the viewer into the same position of the feeding critters nearby, proving that nature is but another manifestation of the kind of consumption that vending machines offer when they sell junk food and soda. Critters seem to be selecting their nutrients in the same way that shoppers do, even as some of the selected nutrients cause death and decay to others. Like Amoco, Monsanto is presenting nature as consumer relations under corporate management.

This playful cartoonishness makes violence cute, and even as the bugs chew each other to death, nobody seems to get hurt and everybody seems equally to win organic improvements and benefits. Capital competition appears as a fearless game of destruction through consumption, like Time Warner–promoted Pokémon, making destructive competition fun rather than harmful as it was, for example to Karen McFarlane and her family in West Anniston:

[Karen] has PCBs in her body fat. According to tests done by a local doctor, Ryan's blood has nearly triple the level considered "typical" in the United States; for Tiffany, their six-year-old, it's double. Nathan, eight, has severe developmental problems, and everyone in the family suffers from respiratory problems and the skin rashes associated with PCB exposure. Chris, Karen's eleven-year-old son, who's home from school with an upset stomach and is splayed out on the couch, lifts his Panthers basketball T-shirt to reveal brownish-red blotches up the sides of his chest. "It smells like decaying flesh," Ryan warns. "Like it's rotten."[45]

Certainly for the McFarlanes, the soil where they grow their food and feed their livestock is not abundantly offering consumer items like clothes from The Gap, nor giant smiling pennies, nor the healthy promise of penicillin. Instead, the joyful critters happily participating in Anniston's consuming frenzy are increasing the McFarlanes' exposure to deadly PCBs as the contamination's rate of growth intensifies moving up the food chain. Not only are the McFarlanes and their neighbors now caught up in a litigation suit that will most likely take years before they see results, but also it is clear to them that Monsanto would have been more strictly scrutinized by the government if the contamination were happening in a wealthier and whiter area. As it eats away at the shrunken bugs and worms, Monsanto's drive for unlimited growth and profitability appears no longer as a cute and childish game nor an arcade governed by nature and its laws of free competition, but instead as excessive degradation and costs to powerless citizens with the stakes unfairly and quite unnaturally set against them.

In Monsanto's display of nature, natural organisms are not only consumers but also compose the labor force. Certain critters are presented as looking for jobs, displaying their resumes, classifying their skills like "must work well with others in grazing and/or predatory relationship," "must be energetic and willing to work overtime," or "dis-assembly line worker." In case the point still is not clear, further along there is a tilted tank of soil with water pouring in, demonstrating the way water spreads through the earth. The tank is tagged, "The Trickle-Down Effect." Referencing Reaganomics, conservative pro-corporate economic language seems here to describe relations of nature, showing—as an established fact—how everybody benefits, grows, and is nourished when the top layers get moistened. As Donna Haraway notes about corporate-motivated representations of biotechnology and genetic fusion more generally, "The latent content is the graphic literalism that biology—life itself—is a capital-accumulation strategy in the simultaneously marvelous and ordinary domains of the New World Order, Inc. . . . Specifically, natural kind becomes brand or trademark, a sign protecting intellectual property claims in business transactions."[46] As the visitor leaves the exhibit, famous quotes about the Earth are painted across the wall facing a kaleidoscopic, holographic projection of the world. The globe is constituted by video images of trees and clouds merging into shots of tilled fields which, in turn, merge into housing developments. Consistent with multiple other displays, the video globe suggests a holistic endless cycle of nature within which the actions of clouds, trees, lightning, corporations, and consumers all play roles as redemptive forces of nature. Directly across from this the wall bold letters declare, "Plowed ground smells like earthworms and empires."

Amoco's domination of nature as a resource, which the videos depict as benevolent and fun, clears the way for its domination and exploitation of peoples and nations, its violent bids to control Third-World labor through militarization, and its wiping out of any local and more equitable terms of production. In other words, what the videos show as the healthy curiosity of scientists is, in reality, the violence of colonial conquest for capitalist acquisition, or the reduction of all value to money values and the simultaneous decimation of human values. David Harvey affirms,

> This power asymmetry in social relations [between First and Third World nations] ineluctably connects to the inequities in environmental relations in exactly the same way that the project to dominate nature necessarily entailed a project to dominate people. Excessive environmental degradation and costs, for example, can be visited upon the least powerful individuals or even nation states as environmental hazards in the workplace as well as in the community. Ozone concentrations in large cities in the United States affect the poor and "people of color" disproportionately and exposure to toxins in the workplace is class-conditioned. From this arises a conflation of the environmental and the social justice issues.[47]

Indeed, Amoco's treatment of nature models Amoco's treatment of the people who live in the areas surrounding the sites of exploration. The black people of Sweetings Cay, Bahamas, do not seem to have gainful employment outside of waiting for the explorers to come and put them to work. Like the remipedes, they are sitting around waiting for the white scientists to put them to productive work. As picturesque backdrops, they stand by the boats, seemingly incomprehending as the scientists explain the uses of the equipment to the video viewers. As they start to trek to the lake, the scientists seem overburdened with large and heavy tools for the dive, and Bill Kurtis explains that they have brought two of every piece of equipment in case of failures. The natives are therefore requisitioned to carry the heavy air tanks and gear on their backs, following the scientists through a wooded field in an image reminiscent of a typical colonial scene like the one Michael Taussig describes of Colombian Indians carrying Spaniards across the Andes: "The normal load for a porter was around 100 pounds, while some were known to have carried 200. Even with these weights they were said to climb the mountains with the greatest of ease and seldom to rest."[48] The relationship between the natives and the scientists in the Amoco video seems cordial but non-communicative, as they silently do chores to their benefactors' bidding, expressing no will of their own nor any sense of initiative outside of serving the needs and doing the tasks of the scientists. Though the natives in the Amoco video are indeed laboring, there is no sense here of payment, contracts, organization, conflict, possibilities of worker self-interest or of worker control over work conditions. Instead, the natives are rendered quasi-mechanical, instrumental, objectified, and vitally curious, mirrors of scientific wonder, proving that the scientists' curiosity is natural, primitive, and raw, the kernel of being human. The black men stare out over the waters, and the camera lingers over their profiled tense faces, creating suspense and worry about the scientists' welfare and safety in the dangerous waters. The bravery of the scientists in the pursuit of knowledge is made starkly visible as the natives sit by the waters' edge, not knowing the treasures of discovery which the white establishment, in its superiority, values so highly.

What is the "iMPACT" of such colonialist portrayals being brought into the Chicago public schools, which are disproportionately black and Hispanic? What are the videos teaching to working class students about their relationship to the white establishment and to science? The videos all begin with a message from a light-skinned black woman named Paula Banks who is an Amoco Vice President. Banks, surrounded by countless antique and contemporary Amoco red-white-and-blue filling station signs, explains to young viewers that science should be not only educational but fun and exciting. Distributed to largely non-white students in the Chicago public schools, the video suggests that alignment with the power of the corporation to control nature like the white scientists do, comes through a whitening. Aside from providing Amoco with a few solid minutes of advertising the logo, this prelude establishes the oil company as "multicultural" and hence offering a promise of potential employment to young non-white viewers. Absent here are the historical facts that domestically jobs above the level of service station "jockey" were not available to blacks during the time of the antique Amoco signs and despite the fact that globally the history of oil company exploration and production is the history of white imperialism and enrichment and black subjugation and impoverishment. This is, of course, aside from recent lawsuits against oil giants such as Amoco, Texaco, and others for the maintenance of the corporate glass ceiling on promotions and racist harassment on the job, for their environmental exploitation of jungle lands inhabited by the indigenous people of Ecuador and elsewhere.[49]

More than this, the presence of a light-skinned black woman enters into a racial spectrum manifested in the videos that mirrors that of the skin-tone hierarchy of white supremacy. Race ranges from the dark-skinned primitive natives in the Bahamas to the light-skinned black Paula Banks to the white scientific explorers. The racial representations in the film position blacks as working with nature and a part of nature and whites as controlling, studying, and manipulating nature. Dark-skinned black Frank Truesdale, a federal forestry worker and not an Amoco employee, the only non-white scientist in the videos, who works on the volcano itself, is shown to be in a romantic relationship with a feminized moody earth. "Frank knows his volcano too well to relax," notes the voice-over. "He's seen all her moods. Serene beauty. Wonder. Anger." Unlike the white scientists, Truesdale appears to have an intimate relationship with anthropomorphized nature. "It was the beginning of a beautiful friendship," the voice-over narrates the history of Truesdale's career, "Frank and the volcano." This intimacy establishes him as closer to nature, allied with it. Frank is not the one you see operating the high-tech equipment, the machines, the large needles and measuring rods automatically drawing minute seismic changes on a graph. "These machines," the voice-over explicates, "could hear the volcano's heartbeat." Rather, Truesdale is the one out in the field, discovering and experiencing nature directly with a primitive metal stick that digs up the lava and a barrel of water that cools it for study. Truesdale's work shows him engulfed in nature and so part of it, distanced from technology that facelessly watches over him, overseeing his acquisitions and his labors while processing his collections of data reduced to numbers on a chart.

Neoliberalism envisions a world controlled by corporate power where environmental and human rights as well as democracy are marginalized, if not completely annihilated, in the pursuit of power, profit, and growth. How does such a dystopic idea about the future become widely acceptable, even the only possibility imaginable? Currently, schools are often the ideological mechanisms where the values of international capitalist relations are being diffused. As Henry Giroux notes, "In this scenario, public education is replaced by the call for privately funded educational institutions or for school-business partnerships that can ignore civil rights, exclude students who are class- and race-disenfranchised, and blur the lines between religion and state."[50] In other words, students are learning to see their interests coinciding with those of global capital, even and especially in those places where they are fundamentally at odds. Schools need to become, instead, places where students learn to renegotiate their relationships to corporate-sponsored ideologies and to formulate possibilities for oppositional political agency.

As Amoco and other corporate curricula continue to turn schooling into a propaganda ground for their own destructive interests, one solution is clearly to stop using them. Another is to provide teachers with resources for researching the agendas of the corporations that finance and distribute such products in public schools and museums so that the ideological functions of the curricula can be turned against themselves and the corporations' global agendas will be shown as contextualized and centered within the curricula. In this way, students can be shown how their interests and worldviews actually differ from the way their interests and worldviews are constructed in the curricula. However, in the face of, for example, classroom overcrowding, the growing bureaucratization of teacher tasks and paperwork, and the cutting of public supports, equipment, programs, and infrastructures in schools, teachers are still prone and even sometimes propelled to use the preparation short-cuts that corporate curricula offer free-of-charge. Public actions like the anti-WTO and anti–World-Bank-and-IMF protests in Seattle and Washington, D.C., mainstream information about how corporations are operating against the public interest, are instrumental in perpetuating human rights and environmental abuses, are creating conditions for the exploitation of cheap labor abroad by destroying environmentally sustaining and economic infrastructures in already poor nations, and are weakening the institutions of democracy on a world-level as capital gains power over civil governing. This type of counterhegemonic education of the public serves as a counterpoint to the seamlessly happy world ensconced in the pleasures of pure knowledge promised by Amoco and Monsanto and starts on the difficult up-hill path of demanding that corporations be held responsible for their crimes against nature and humanity. The adoption of global capitalist interests into school curricula cannot be countered simply by teaching students to read critically. Additionally, the school needs to be revitalized as a public power which holds out against private interests. As in South Africa in the 1970s, schools need to be linked to other battlegrounds fighting for democratic values and human liberation as well as to those popular forces now producing counter-scenarios to the lie of disinterested satisfaction in a corporate-controlled public sphere.

NOTES

1. BP Educational Services, www.bpes.com/default.asp.

2. Al Ries and Laura Ries, "The 22 Immutable Laws of Branding," *Harper Business* (1999).

3. John Greenwald, "School for Profit," *Time,* 20 March 2000, 56–57. For example, AOL Time Warner's weekly advertisement for all things corporate, *Time* magazine, informs readers that they should be principally concerned with Wall Street's profit from privatizing public schools rather than even mentioning the implications for democracy of turning over publicly funded institutions to be exploited by the corporate sector. For an extensive discussion of the dangers to democracy posed by public school privatization, see Kenneth J. Saltman, *Collateral Damage: Corporatizing Public Schools—A Threat to Democracy* (Lanham, Md.: Rowman & Littlefield, 2000). See also, Henry A. Giroux, *Stealing Innocence: Youth, Corporate Power and the Politics of Culture* (New York: St. Martin's Press, 2000) and Alex Molnar, *Giving Kids the Business* (Boulder, Colo.: Westview, 1996).

4. For a brilliant discussion of the political use of childhood innocence, see Henry A. Giroux, *The Mouse That Roared: Disney and the End of Innocence* (Lanham, Md.: Rowman & Littlefield, 1999).

5. For an excellent analysis of this phenomenon in relation to the broader privatization of the public sector and of mass media, see Robert McChesney, *Rich Media, Poor Democracy* (Urbana: University of Illinois Press, 1999). David Cromwell

notes that the oil industry, not merely a few companies, are engaged in funding and distributing pro-oil corporate curriculum. "Oil Propaganda Wars," Z magazine, March 2000, 7–8.

6. Justin Delacour, "Human Rights and Military Aid for Colombia: With 'Friends' Like the Senate Democrats, Who Needs Enemies?" www.lbbs.org/ZNETTOPnoanimation.html.

7. Edward Herman and Cecilia Zarate-Laun, "Globalization and Instability: The Case of Colombia," *Z-Net*, www.lbbs.org/ZNETPOProanimation.html.

8. Herman and Zarate-Laun, "Globalization and Instability."

9. Marc Cooper, "Plan Colombia: Wrong Issue, Wrong Enemy, Wrong Country," *The Nation*, 19 March 2001, 14.

10. Cooper, "Plan Colombia."

11. This package also includes aid to Kosovo and Peru, condemned by the Clinton administration for its fraudulent presidential elections.

12. For an in-depth history of how U.S. drug eradication efforts in the region have helped to build up South and Central American intelligence operations that have routinely instituted torture and corruption, see Peter Dale Scott and Jonathan Marshall, *Cocaine Politics: Drugs, Armies, and the CIA in Central America*, 2d ed. (Berkeley: University of California Press, 1991, 1998). The authors here cite as an example the Peruvian agency SIN (National Intelligence Service), which was created by the CIA and whose agents were trained by the CIA. SIN was headed by the now-infamous Vladimiro Montesinos who was revealed as the terrorizing spook behind much of the corruption in Alberto Fujimori's regime. Though Montecino's acceptance of bribes became a mark of his immorality in a spectacle circulated in the international press in 2000, prompting Fujimori's resignation by FAX from Japan, the same sort of outrage was never directed towards what Scott and Marshall have documented as Montecino's undisputed ties to the drug cartels in Colombia and other places (x–xi).

13. Cooper, "Plan Colombia," 14.

14. As cited in Cooper, "Plan Colombia," 16.

15. Cecilia Zarate-Laun, "Introduction to the Putumayo: The U.S.-assisted war in Colombia," *Z-Net*, www.lbbs.org/ZMag/articles/feb01laun.htm, February 2001.

16. Carla Anne Robbins, "How Bogota Wooed Washington to Open New War on Cocaine," *The Wall Street Journal*, 23 June 2000, 1, A12. Not mentioned here is the proportion of now taxable large assets that are associated with the drug trade.

17. Thomas Freidman, *The Lexus and the Olive Tree* (New York: Farrar, Straus & Giroux, 1999), 309.

18. Peter McLaren, *Che Guevara, Paulo Freire, and the Pedagogy of Revolution* (Lanham, Md.: Rowman & Littlefield, 2000), 70. "Raul Reyes, commander of the FARC, met with Richard Grasso, chairman of the New York Stock Exchange, who explained to the guerrilla leader how markets worked. As the two figures embraced in this rebel-controlled area demilitarized by the government, Grasso told Reyes that Colombia would benefit from increased global investment and that he hoped that this meeting would mark the beginning of a new relationship between the FARC and the United States."

19. Delacour, "Human Rights and Military Aid for Colombia."

20. Delacour, "Human Rights and Military Aid for Colombia."

21. Cecilia Zarate-Laun, "Introduction to the Putumayo."

22. Zarate-Laun (*Z-Net* article) "Crossroads of War and Biodiversity: CIA, Cocaine, and Death Squads" by the Eco-Solidarity Working Group in *Covert Action Quarterly* (Fall–Winter, 1999), 16–17.

23. Andrew Ross, "The Mental Labor Problem," *Social Text* 63 (Summer 2000), 1–31.

24. William M. Adler, *Molly's Job: A Story of Life and Work on the Global Assembly Line* (New York: Scribner, 2000), 104–05. This wasn't the first time this particular river was made into a polluted site by oil-related industries. There's a history here. "Virulently antiunion employers, epitomized by Henry Ford, retained their own strikebreaking 'security forces.' During the Communist-led Ford Hunger March of unemployed workers in March 1932, Ford's men shot to death four workers at the gates of the huge River Rouge complex. After more than seventy thousand sympathizers attended the funeral march, Ford and other employers responded by purging and blacklisting thousands of suspected radicals from their plants."

25. Steve Pardo, "River Rouge Fears Explosion: City Sues BP/Amoco in Effort to Clean Up Sewers and Avoid Repeat of 1988 Blast," *The Detroit News*, 30 November 1999, D3.

26. Pardo, "River Rouge Fears Explosion."

27. Pardo, "River Rouge Fears Explosion."

28. Alex Molnar, *Giving Kids the Bu$iness: The Commercialization of America's School* (Boulder, Colo.: Westview, 1996), 30–31.

29. David Cromwell, "Oil Propaganda Wars," Z magazine, March 2000, 8.

30. Martin S. Fridson, *How to Be a Billionaire: Proven Strategies from the Titans of Wealth* (New York: John Wiley & Sons, 2000), 148–50. "Subpoenas and fines for harassment of competitors and price-fixing dogged Waste Management during its spectacular growth period. . . . Regulators and prosecutors relentlessly investigated Waste Management, inspired by previous revelations of organized crime's control of commercial waste hauling in southern New York and northern New Jersey. . . . Not only his business strategies, but also his financial practices generated criticism. Observers objected to the prices he paid in certain acquisitions, arguing that they exceeded industry norms. . . . Huizenga also had to endure the accusation that the companies he created through consolidation fared poorly after he left the scene. . . . Finally, critics lambasted Huizenga's practice of acquiring businesses for stock," etc.

31. Noam Chomsky, "Breaking Free: The Transformative Power of Critical Pedagogy," in *Harvard Educational Review,* edited by Pepi Leistyna and Stephen Sherblom, 1996, 111.

32. Margaret Atwell, *In the Middle: New Understandings About Writing, Reading, and Learning* (Portsmouth, N.H.: Heinemann, 1998), 35.

33. Atwell, *In the Middle,* 52.

34. Atwell, *In the Middle,* 69.

35. See chapter 6, in which we discuss at length the politics of youth innocence.

36. In chapter 6 we discuss the way rising insecurity about uncertain labor conditions is channeled into private concerns with family, thereby undermining collective action to address the causes of insecurity.

37. Paulo Freire, *Pedagogy of the Oppressed*, translated by Myra Bergman Ramos (New York: Continuum, 1970, 1993), 53.

38. Amoco is hardly the first corporation to appropriate progressive methodology in a way that jettisons critical social transformation as an underlying ideal. Disney's Celebration, Florida, schools exemplify this corruption: see Henry A. Giroux, *The Mouse That Roared*. As Donald Lazere has argued, "Many . . . Freireans . . . have failed to perceive that the political right has coopted their ideas to depict its own social camp, even in its most powerful, privileged, and prejudiced sectors, as meriting the same level of pluralistic encouragement of self-esteem and expression of feelings accorded the least privileged groups. Some such students expect teachers to make them feel good about being bigots, like Rush Limbaugh does—and some teachers . . . gladly comply." Donald Lazere. "Spellmeyer's Naive Populism," *CCC* 48 (May 1997): 291.

39. Nancy Beiles, "What Monsanto Knew," *The Nation*, 20 May 2000, 18–22.

40. Monsanto is the main sponsor of this exhibit. Other sponsors include ConAgra Foundation, National Science Foundation, the Fort James Foundation, Chicago Park District, Abbott Laboratories, Pfizer Foundation, Prince Charitable Trusts, ServiceMaster Company, Marion S. Searle/Searle Family Trust, and the Chicago Board of Trade Foundation.

41. Beiles, "What Monsanto Knew," 19. "'PCB is a persistent chemical which builds up in the environment. It, therefore, should not be allowed to escape. . . .' —Monsanto, 1972."

42. William Greider, *One World, Ready or Not: The Manic Logic of Global Capitalism* (New York: Touchstone, 1997), 455.

43. Greider, *One World, Ready or Not*, 456.

44. William Greider, "The Last Farm Crisis," *The Nation*, 20 November 2000, 15.

45. Beiles, "What Monsanto Knew," 19–20.

46. Donna J. Haraway, *Modest_Witness@Second_Millennium.FemaleMan_Meeets_OncoMouse: Feminism and Technsoscience* (New York: Routledge, 1997), 65–66.

47. David Harvey, *Justice, Nature and the Geography of Difference* (Malden, Mass.: Blackwell, 1996), 155.

48. Michael Taussig, *Shamanism, Colonialism, and the Wild Man: A Study in Terror and Healing* (Chicago: University of Chicago Press, 1987), 298.

49. Eyal Press, "Texaco on Trial," *The Nation*, 31 May 1999, 11–16.

50. Henry A. Giroux, "Cultural Studies and the Culture of Politics: Beyond Polemics and Cynicism" (forthcoming).

3

A Time for Flying Horses: Oil Education and the Future of Literature

A LEARNING COMPANY

In 1984, Keri Hulme's Maori novel *The Bone People* won the Pegasus Prize for Literature established by Mobil Corporation.[1] Since then, *The Bone People* has been frequently read in college courses on postcolonial and/or multicultural literature, and its appeal in the classroom and in lists of required reading for doctoral qualification is seconded only by its promotion, even today, in major bookstores, where, for example, a multiplex Barnes & Noble in Manhattan's Union Square included it in its recommended readings for Christmas 2000. Started in 1977, the Pegasus Prize is awarded, the publishers remark on the back cover, "to distinguished works from countries whose literature too rarely receives international recognition," and is chosen by a group of scholars, reportedly outside of Mobil's oversight, in a country first selected by elite members of the U.S. literary establishment like Paul Engle (then-director of the celebrated Iowa Writers' Workshop) and William Jay Smith (former chair of Columbia University's writers' program), among others.[2]

Mobil's stated cause here is to promote multiculturalism on a global scale. "Mobil has long been interested in celebrating the art and cultures of many countries where it does business," announced Joel H. Maness, President of Mobil de Venezuela, host of the 1998 Pegasus Prize granted to Ana Teresa Torres for the novel *Doña Inés Vs. Oblivion*, the first woman writer to receive the prize since Keri Hulme.[3] As Mobil's promotion states,

[The Pegasus Prize] was designed . . . to make sure all voices are heard in the global chorus of ideas. . . . Mobil strives to demonstrate that business can enrich international understanding by helping to illuminate and communicate the best values of the world's cultures. . . . "We created and support the Pegasus Prize because as a global company with operations in more than 125 nations, Mobil's interest lies in bringing people together—culturally as well as economically," says Lucio A. Noto, Chairman and Chief Executive Officer of Mobil Corporation. "And the Prize helps us demonstrate to foreign leaders and publics that we're a unique kind of business partner."[4]

In the eyes of its corporate promoters, *The Bone People* presents an opportunity for English-speaking readers to learn what is valuable about Maori culture and what Maori culture can contribute to a universal human spirit, in order to "recognize" and give dignity to a historically marginalized and, indeed, colonized ethnic population.[5] Mobil has become, as *New York Times* correspondent Thomas Friedman has said of Chevron in his widely acclaimed best-seller about globalism, "not an oil company, it's a learning company."[6]

Praising Mobil as the third largest corporate sponsor of the arts and humanities (probably ascending on this list after its merger with Exxon, which is also a major contributor), the Taft group documents that "Mobil Corp. and the Mobil Foundation disbursed grants totaling $9,879,000 in grants to arts and cultural organizations."[7] Corporate involvement in education certainly reforms curricular content as corporate intent, as when an "environmental curriculum video was produced by Shell Oil . . . offering students pearls of wisdom like, 'You can't get to nature without gasoline or cars'"[8] or when an Exxon-produced video "praises the company's role in restoring the ecology of Prince William Sound while avoiding any discussion of what (or who) caused the Alaska oil spill in the first place."[9] Large investments in education and culture by large corporations in general—and oil, communications, transportation, and aerodynamic firms in particular—indicate that consolidation is backed by massive distributions of ideological messages that advance and sell capitalist worldviews as a whole. Fredric Jameson has argued that the GATT and NAFTA agreements have been necessarily accompanied by innovative types of cultural production and consumable forms of cultural diversity where "freedom of ideas is important because the ideas are private property and designed to be sold in great and profitable quantities."[10]

BRAND MAORI

The Bone People is the story of Kerewin, an independently wealthy artist (she won the lottery, and then invested the surplus) who isolated herself in a tower, cutting off connections with both family and friends in order to pursue freely her creative work. When the novel opens, her creative spirit is blocked. Enter Simon. Simon is a mute boy, an angelic prodigy, who suddenly and mysteriously appears in the tower and ends up winning over her heart. Kerewin next meets Joe, who is Simon's ostensible father (it is only later that Joe tells of how Simon was washed up on the beach after a shipwreck and how Joe and his wife adopt him before his wife and child die of the flu). As the story develops in a series of fishing trips and nights of drinking, these three characters play out a cycle of violence and forgiveness. Kerewin soon discovers that Joe is beating Simon and tries to stop the abuse but only ends up identifying with Joe's frustrations and hitting Simon herself. The three are split up when Joe bashes Simon's head in, causing a serious concussion and permanent cerebral damage which land Simon in the hospital. But because of his love and devotion to his adopted family, Simon only dreams of bringing the three of them back together, defying both doctors' orders and the better judgment of state social workers who intend, most maliciously, to keep Simon away from his tormentors forever. In the last section of the novel, all three characters, broken, go on pilgrimages, encountering figures of Maori foundational mythology. Joe becomes the keeper of the lost Maori canoe, which brought the Maori people to the island of New Zealand; Kerewin has her stomach cancer healed through the interventions of an ancestral Maori phantasm; and at last the three happily meet again as the guardians of the sacred canoe, reuniting for a harmonious feast in a moment of renewal preordained in the Maori mythical return to the homeland.

While a text such as *The Bone People* is open to different interpretive frameworks, interpretations are hardly endlessly open-ended. Rather, they are shaped and limited by broader discourses in the cultural field that are historically and materially struggled over. *The Bone People* needs to be read in a way that shows how it affirms rather than challenges the activities of multinational oil companies such as Mobil-Exxon that make corporate values into human values. So why would Mobil Corporation want to promote this version of Maori culture under their own trademark? Setting aside for now the hard-to-swallow idea of benevolent and forgivable child abusers, one might remark, to start, on the novel's constant invocations of a pristine and unsullied environment on both land and sea, on the complete absence of any kind of labor problems or organizations, even though Joe works in a factory, and on the elimination of any state role except for the rather stupid and ineffectual social workers who treat Simon, the useless schools which are not able to discipline his eruptive spirit, and the healthcare system, which is neglectful, in, for example, the case of Joe's wife and child, of preventing death from a perfectly treatable disease.

"COMPASSIONATE" CORPORATISM

The Maori certainly do have just cause to criticize and even vilify the state, not only because of the state's role in implementing a colonial government which, among other abuses, took away much of their territory, but also as the current state continues to cause deprivation among the Maori. However, the curtailment of state powers in New Zealand, as capital is deregulated and consolidated, has not effectively brought equality and justice to the Maori, but rather the opposite. Underfunding of Maori education and health care, welfare cuts, and assimilation policies have caused, according to Donna Awatere, decreased birth-rates among the Maori, increasing poverty and a growing culture of white supremacy affecting hiring practices, justice claims, salaries, and incarceration rates. "Any Maori child is four times more likely than a white child to appear before a Children's Court."[11] "In 1976 and '81. . . , there were three-and-a-half times more Maoris unemployed than whites."[12] "In 1976, . . . six more whites earned $10,000 and over compared to Maoris, yet every Maori wage had to support 2.2 people (compared to 1.5 for whites)."[13]

As the governing power of nation-states declines, the growth of corporate power has meant, for many people around the world, the literal annihilation of democratic possibilities and civil protections. At the time that *The Bone People* was published in New Zealand, New Zealand was considering new laws for transportation, commerce, licensing, and energy that would seriously affect Mobil's operations on the North Island, where the events in the novel take place. In the 1930s, New Zealand's labor laws restricted the distance goods could be transported away from the railway lines to thirty miles, favoring the interests of domestic workers and state-supported infrastructure. In the 1980s, new legislation would be passed that would ease Mobil's abilities to exploit oil for export by lifting these restrictions and deregulating transportation. Additionally, in the late seventies, after years of oil companies' vying for the rights, New Zealand's Liquid Fuels Trust Board approved Mobil's controversial methanol-to-gas processing plant projected for construction on the North Island in 1985.

The Bone People's publication happens simultaneously, then, with a concerted effort by corporations—and by oil and transportation in particular—to transform public power into private power and to introduce new neoliberalist policies oriented against the protection of labor and domestic production and towards a globalist focus for the economy. A reading of *The Bone People* must therefore consider how the very act of dismantling these corporate values requires a revitalized notion of civil society, public life, and public institutions to offset corporate controls and the consequent end of democratic citizenship. As Gayatri Spivak elaborates,

Some commonly understood arenas such as health, education, welfare, and social security, and the civil as opposed to penal or criminal legal code, fall within the purview of civil society. . . . When increasingly privatized, as in the New World Order, the priorities of the civil society are shifted from services to the citizen to capital maximization. . . . Transnationality is shrinking the possibility of an operative civil society in developing nations.[14]

The shrinking of civil societies throughout the world has led to a severe diminution of a politics of the public, reducing most oppositional political action to motivations defined by narrowly defined private interests or identity-based claims to rights. Among other institutional supports of the public, education needs to counter such imaging of corporate citizenship as depicted in *The Bone People* in order to establish itself as a viable public sphere for democratic deliberation, learning, thinking, and action.

The New Zealand governments of the 1970s and 1980s were instrumental in furthering the interests of international capital at the expense of the public. New Zealand's 1984 election responded to a critique of the welfare state starting, under a Conservative administration, in the 1970s and ushered in a period of austerity, cuts in social spending, deregulated exchange rates, tariff cuts, incentives for foreign investment, and anti-labor policies. Such a reconfiguration of economic relations, of course, eased Mobil's position within the New Zealand economy on the one hand, but, on the other hand, spurred economic trouble in New Zealand as the external debt quadrupled, rates of productivity growth for the next eight years fell to 0.9 percent, while rates of unemployment and poverty increased.[15]

Even as new legislation was limiting federal democratizing interventions into the economy, the government itself was spinning tales of new democratic openings. A 1997 report from New Zealand's Ministry of Commerce, for instance, evaluated the deregulation initiatives of the mid-eighties as advancing democratic access to the economy by removing barriers to entry. Because of the reduction of environmental protectionist laws and the agencies to enforce them, the report claims, it is less costly for smaller companies to compete in the industry, resulting in more services available to consumers even if they are at higher prices.

Lowering these unnecessary costs . . . would at least make it easier and more profitable to undertake investments which might otherwise be inhibited. . . . Because there are no barriers to entry into the New Zealand petrol market, government action to facilitate entry is not required. . . . Any intervention to facilitate entry would therefore introduce inefficiencies into the market. For example, policies designed to break down horizontal arrangements or force participation in horizontal arrangements by incumbents . . . could be expected to increase costs of supplying petrol in New Zealand.[16]

Omitted from this analysis are the ways that the current consolidation of capital has resulted in mergers, buyouts, and takeovers, allowing large companies to price out small companies by outsourcing parts of the production process to satellites, or to control markets by becoming the only buyers of a particular stage of the production process. Unmentioned as well is the history of oil which, as William Greider has shown, has never been on a free-market course, but rather managed by governments.[17] In other words, the oil industry's consolidation has led to oligopolization touted as democratic freedom, while democratic freedom is being refashioned as the "unfettering" of markets in the name of profits and consumer rights, even if labor, environmental, and democratic decision-making and access get thwarted, and even if "unfettering" is exactly what such deregulation policies are not accomplishing. As in *The Bone People*, the good citizen appears as the independent investor, free of labor and controls, unconcerned about human connections, living in an unworrisome environment, surrounded by a mythically crystalline sea.[18]

Like the government's own self-reporting, *The Bone People* provides a benevolent image of a deregulated society.[19] It also develops a sense of autonomous individuals who are completely free, sovereign masters of their own choice in a landscape open and available to their wanderings even as it falls under a system of private ownership: Simon is a trespasser in Kerewin's tower, for instance: "In case no-one ever told you before, people's houses are private and sacrosanct,"[20] she tells him, but he makes himself welcome and Kerewin would never restrict his access. Contingently, all public institutions are demonized because they restrict this freedom: Simon is scared of doctors and panics in hospitals, and at school (which he frequently avoids, to nobody's real consternation) he comes in for a lot of "petty bullying and shitslinging . . . because he's a bit of an outlaw,"[21] where school confines Simon's self-expression by restricting his wayward explorations in the wild. *The Bone People* operates within a certain logic where (1) reading produces identifications with capitalist power and capitalist values; and (2) relations of power and human values that support capitalist expansions and appropriations are made to seem natural and common sense.

THE PEGASUS NOVELS

In general, the Pegasus novels do not overtly pontificate the values of corporatism nor expound on the benefits of oil-based energy. Rather, they create and sell a social vision in which globalization seems logical, natural, wholesome, necessary, and good, while the faultlines and destructive capacities of capitalist growth and greed become illogical, invisible, and

even unthinkable. As a whole, the novels share certain ideas about the relationship between characters and their social environments:

1. The novels are primarily psychological, introspective, and sometimes existential, emphasizing the individual, psychological subject.
2. The characters are wanderers, often using the globe itself as plane on
   which to explore and discover the psychological self. "A Person born
   of honest Folk who in foreign Lands doth wander, findeth that [in] his
   Travel . . . many a time against his own Will is he beset by unforeseen
   Hardship and Misfortune and doth require Money and other Necessities of Life, and so he desireth, and in Truth he hath but this Choice,
   to set out upon Land and Sea," begins, for example, *Dollar Road*.[22]
3. The novels are experimental, dressing themselves up as "the new"
   without ever invoking newness or change in terms of the social relations of production.
4. The novels often present multicultural encounters, as in *And the War
   Is Over*, recipient of the 1984 prize, which tells of Dutch prisoners of
   war in an Indonesian camp during the Japanese occupation, or *Rituals*, which concludes in a Japanese tea ceremony taking place in the
   Netherlands.
5. Labor is considered an affront to the humanity of the subject as well
   as an oppression forced by the state, whereas investment indicates
   freedom of thought and expression.
6. There is a natural movement of history towards capitalist progress,
   so large-scale capitalist production is never at fault for destruction,
   alienation, or hardship, but rather destruction, alienation, and hardship figure as just a natural, though sad refuse to a much grander,
   even inevitable historical project. "On the day that Inni Wintrop
   committed suicide," begins, for example, Cees Nooteboom's *Rituals*,
   a Dutch novel and winner of the 1982 Pegasus Prize, "Philips shares
   stood at 149.60. The Amsterdam Bank closing rate was 375, and Shipping Union had slipped to 141.50."[23] In this novel, the main character Inni, expelled from school, works in an office (he does not say
   what he does) until he receives an inheritance from a long-lost aunt.
   Though, until now, "he had never become anything. . . . There was
   no central thought, such as a career, an ambition. He simply existed.
   . . . ,"[24] he received the inheritance because "that job of yours is point-
   less, that is obvious. You should spend a year reading or traveling.
   You are not suited to be a subordinate."[25] In fact, Inni's psychological search is so tied up with finance and investment that desire operates only through the free-flow of money: sex with his wife is described as "the squaring of accounts,"[26] as they "play prostitute" and
   exchange cash in foreplay.

Travel continues as an important motif in the Pegasus novels, linking the journeys of capital to the free movement of the consuming, desiring subject. For example, the 1992 Pegasus Prize winner, Martin M. Simecka's Slovakian novel *The Year of the Frog*—introduced by former playwright, political theorist, and president of the Czech Republic, Václav Havel—tells the story of a former prize-winning runner who is searching for the meaning of existence during the waning years of the Communist regime in Prague. When the Communist police track him down and threaten arrest, he is forced to work in various state-run enterprises: first a cancer ward, then a hardware store, and finally a birthing clinic that does just as many messy, grotesque, even tragic abortions. The pressures put on him by the police and by his work schedule severely limit his wanderings through the city, his running, his love, his home-life, and his art (he is also a writer). Describing how globalization creates new class hierarchies based on relations of space, Zygmunt Bauman has explained how movement indicates consumption on the one hand and, on the other, a lack of responsibility for local communities as capital freely relocates. In contrast, the state is seen as restricting, constraining, and policing movement: "Today's existence," he forewarns, "is stretched along the hierarchy of the global and the local, with global freedom of movement signalling social promotion, advancement and success, and immobility exuding the repugnant odour of defeat, failed life and being left behind. . . . Life ambitions are more often than not expressed in terms of mobility, the free choice of place, travelling, seeing the world; life fears, on the contrary, are talked about in terms of confinement, lack of change, being barred from places which others traverse easily, explore and enjoy."[27] This ideological configuration of globalization underlies the logic of *The Year of the Frog*, as freedom of movement is associated with Western consumption: "How beautiful life is when you can just walk into a store and buy a pair of Marathon running shoes the first time you go in,"[28] In the places where the protagonist works, however, he confronts only graphic scenes of death, sickness, desperation, corruption, and shortage. In fact, the novel begins with a condemnation of, precisely, a state-run refinery which is condemned first for ill-treating labor ("I've lost thirty pounds in the last three months," says the old man the protagonist meets at the payroll office[29]) and then for polluting ("It's the gas, my boy, the gas that's leaking from the pipes"[30]). Death and disease, the stopping-up of thought and expression, are linked to the stagnancy of a state-controlled heavy-industry and production-oriented capital that cannot move. This is opposed to speculation or investment capital which runs unrestrictedly across natural borders like the rugged terrain, the bridges, tree roots, and icy passages crossed by the narrator.

The movements of capital do not control just consciousness, desire, and freedom in the Pegasus novels, but also politics, nature, happiness, and history. "In a plain, indisputable way," writes Kjartan Fløgstad in the Norwegian novel *Dollar Road*, winner of the 1988 Pegasus Prize, "Selmer Høysand sensed the mysterious power that finds its statistical expression in the capitalistic logic of daily stock-market prices."[31] *Dollar Road* chronicles the family history of a father, his son, and his nephew as a Scandinavian region passes from agriculture to industry and then to global entrepreneurship, shipping, militarism, adventurism, and the like. Though industrialization is clearly ruining the landscape, even ruining traditional ways of life as it forces people away from their homes, there is no sense of any alternative to the factory that offers the only possibility of lucrative work for the failing farmers. Neither is there any sense of connection between the coming of the factory and the laying waste of the fields, except that the factory absorbs the surplus labor as the farms become economically unviable. Just as politics does not seem to matter except as it registers the historical rhythms of change in the stock market,[32] so pollution seems to touch only surfaces and then wash away, its victims moving from industrial smoke-inhalation to global environmental catastrophes. "The oil tank exploded!" Rasmus Høysand, the nephew, woke up one night to discover. "The oil tank!! . . . Oil was thick in his mouth, black before his eyes, plugging his ears. Everywhere. Now for a match! A spark! Now for the Apocalypse!"[33] The spill was caused by a natural disaster, a tropical hurricane, rather than by corporate mismanagement or faulty equipment, and the rig itself seems to belong to no one in particular. The next day, he woke up on a raft, floating on the sea, with "oil stains over his entire bare body,"[34] only to be rescued by a friendly ship bringing raw aluminum from Jamaica back to Europe. Here, there is no outside, no respite or rescue from the tragedies of capital, and capital is not, the text suggests, wreaking as much havoc as you would think. The oil is no sooner spilled than forgotten as new and profitable adventures await.

In fact, the progress of capitalism brings justice by allowing for multicultural kinship, but what kind of justice is it, who gets to define it, and who benefits from its outcomes? *Doña Inés vs. Oblivion* narrates the story of a land dispute starting in colonial Venezuela and resolved in the present. The plantation-owner Alejandro Martínez de Villegas y Blanco promised a portion of his land to his illegitimate mulatto son, Juan del Rosario Villegas, borne by one of his slaves. When Juan del Rosario formed a community of runaway and freed slaves on the fallow plantation lands, Alejandro's surviving wife, Doña Inés Villegas y Solórzano, initiated a series of legal claims questioning her former houseboy's titles, escalating it to the point where the ex-slaves even petition and win an audience with the King of Spain. Throughout the next four hundred years of Venezuelan history, Doña Inés's dead voice tells of governments and their laws that rise and fall, wars that are waged, new political philosophies that gain prominence, waves of migrants that overtake the cities, and technology that changes the ways people live on the land and the types of production they perform. Yet, in the end, the authenticity of the original title is "justly" reinstated as Doña Inés's descendants, in trusting partnership with the community of inheritors of Juan del Rosario's tract, turn the plantation into a multinational tourist haven by the sea. In a manner of speaking, property itself takes on the role of "character" in the novel as different propertied positions enter into conflict and then resolve their differences, while Doña Inés's "voice" is developed through her various claims to ownership.[35] Furthermore, this image of a new, peaceful future of a Venezuela full of multicultural camaraderie (in the name of business) is guaranteed in Venezuela's redemption as an oil-producing nation: "this is a poor, backward country," says Salbic the jeweler, a small-business owner who eventually gets run out by the multiplex businesses that arise on all sides, "but you'll see, the oil business will change it completely. Keep in mind what I'm telling you; a few years from now, everything's going to be different."[36]

The novels are not, therefore, simply promotional materials exhibiting a brand-name on an uplifting cultural product, but rather they provide an image of capitalist logic that determines the ways economic, cultural, and social relations can be thought. For example, as a laborer, Joe accepts without dissenting, organizing, or resisting his "being a puppet in someone else's play. Not having any say."[37] *The Bone People* depicts labor as, succinctly, non-political, using his position as laborer to define Joe as a citizen without political opinions. Though this might have provided an opening for considering Joe's child abuse in relation to alienation and economic oppression, Joe's resolution to labor dissatisfaction is, instead, to go on vacation: "I'd dearly like to take a decent holiday," he says,[38] cutting off any suggestion that political action or change would be the necessary antidote, not a few days off. Joe, Kerewin, and Simon then go to Kerewin's ancestral home for fishing, feasting, and quiet healing. Like the novel's project of cultural retrieval, the implication here is that a culturalist escape will soothe the pain of economic hardships and exploitation rather than providing a way of thinking of cultural discrimination in the workplace as imbricated in systematic economic injustices or in the reason that Joe's working conditions are so egregious. In other words, *The Bone People* constructs Maori culture as a way of avoiding confrontation and finding therapeutic solace within an oppressive system, rather than to ask the important questions that Nancy Fraser has asked: "Under what circumstances can a politics of recognition help support a politics of redistribution? And when is it more likely to undermine it? Which of the many varieties of identity politics best synergize with struggles for social equality? And which tend to interfere with the latter?"[39]

EXPRESSIONS OF DIFFERENCE: GENDER ROLES

The criticism of *The Bone People* focuses on two major ways the novel supposedly succeeds in its political project and its empowering expressions
of difference: one, in its feminist statement; and two, in its multicultural-
ist support of cultural recognition, diversity, and inclusion. *The Bone People* gets interpreted as feminist because it supposedly dismantles traditional ways of thinking about gender and family. As Chris Prentice
writes, "In *The Bone People* . . . Hulme has created physically and, from a
traditional perspective, behaviourally ambiguous characters. . . . Stereo-
typical literary portrayals of femininity are rejected. . . . Kerewin, Simon
and Joe are all unstable mixtures of passivity and activity, control and aggression, nurturance and selfishness."[40] While Joe is not aggressively
male and is content to wait patiently for Kerewin's attentions to turn towards him, Kerewin is asexual, androgynous, and can fight. "All right,
woman, you think you can fight a man?" Hulme begins her description
of Kerewin's "manly" warrior skills, "and strikes for Kerewin's face. . . .
Kerewin kicks him [Joe] in the side and dances around Simon. . . . She
slips past the flailing hands and hits him on the mouth with the side of
her hand. It feels like being hit with a board. He staggers, is spun round
and kicked viciously in the back. . . . She whacks his face again and then
steps sideways and drives her knuckles across his midriff."[41] This form
of androgyny, an identification with power and violence, is what these
feminist critics have indicated as a feminist answer to oppressive gender
typing. In addition to being liberated through these physical traits of
masculinity, Kerewin is independent both financially and emotionally,
and her independence is frequently interpreted as evidence of the novel's
emancipatory intentions.

As Keri Hulme describes the publication process in the introduction, a
feminist collective saved the novel from falling into relative obscurity.
Three other publishers that considered the novel first rejected it. However, the Spiral Collective noticed the talents that these other companies
failed to see, and appreciated the novel for the very eccentricities for
which it had been faulted. Here is a story of an independently thinking
artist working in isolation, an artist whose genius is innovation and who,
because of her innovations, almost ends up as a beleaguered pariah.
Despite the attacks from institutions of power, however, this genius-artist
persisted in her individualistic idiosyncrasies until a small upstart, revolutionary, and entrepreneurial group recognized her virtues, and by this
miraculous stroke of luck, her talents were finally recognized and she single-handedly, by sheer force of endurance, managed to work her way
from rags to riches, hitting the limelight.

What is left out of this glorious story, however, is that the other three publishers that Hulme solicited with *The Bone People* had, actually, a much more radical agenda than the Spiral Collective's. As C. K. Stead remarks,

> For the record let it be said first that of the three who were offered the novel before Spiral saw it, one was a feminist publisher who thought it insufficiently feminist for her list. . . . It should also be said that Spiral received a government grant which made the publication possible, and that this was on the recommendation of the Literary Fund Advisory Committee, consisting at that time of five men and one woman.[42]

Perhaps what makes so many critics see *The Bone People* as feminist has to do with how it exposes that a female who challenges gender roles in her androgyny and independence is still relegated to a maternal role through the inevitable closure of the family cycle and, despite herself, falls under the sway of her maternal instinct. This is why, for instance, Suzette Henke, who can see that "Keri Hulme deliberately reconstructs and redistributes traditional sex-roles,"[43] concludes that, "Who but a female hero could rescue this battered goblin-soul [Simon]?"[44] *The Bone People* conforms to what Edward Herman and Robert McChesney have portrayed as the narrowing of media and ideological content resulting from the increasing alliance and centralization of corporate interests in what they call "oligopolistic markets . . . [and] loosely knit cartels"[45] all but locking out dissent and public debate: "A supportive environment [for selling goods] does not challenge materialistic values and is not set in grim circumstances; it shows people who spend and gain status by acquisition and consumption, displayed in surroundings of wealth . . . , favoring consumption as the solution to human happiness. . . . Plots regularly honor the family-oriented."[46] As Nancy Fraser and others have pointed out, the ideal of the nuclear family is the main avenue through which contemporary capitalism justifies its policies of unequal economic distributions, including cuts in social welfare spending,[47] as responsibility for social hardships and inequalities is transferred from public institutions to the private family or, more particularly, to the mother. What *The Bone People* does is to repeat the status quo, to use Kerewin as proof of the entrenchability of gender, class, and the naturalness of the nuclear family, and then to gloss it over by labeling this reactionary attitude as a subversive gesture.

Nancy Fraser has argued that celebrating women's sexual and economic independence as an emancipatory project is tantamount to equating human worth with wage-labor. For Fraser, the critique of women's dependence currently shapes popular dismissals of the welfare state: "The condition of poor women with children who maintain their families with neither a male breadwinner nor an adequate wage and who rely for economic support on a stingy and politically unpopular government program."[48] Taking the next step, *The Bone People* upholds speculation as the basis for conceiving the liberated, autonomous subject. Kerewin's propensity to resist the role of reproduction to which women in the nuclear family are often reduced is therefore set in place by a nonproductive economic structure, an idea of wealth promising low-growth and low social investiture while historically assuring high profits for highly corporatized economic sectors like telecommunications and oil.[49] The idea of "feminism" in the novel serves as a back-handed critique of government's redistributive interventions in the economy, claiming that freedom arises only through economic self-motivation and regulatory autonomy. The connotation here is that oppositional feminism can appear only as material comfort.

EXPRESSIONS OF DIFFERENCE: AUTHENTICITY

The second major concern of the criticism is about whether or not Hulme's novel is an adequate or authentic representation of Maori culture, especially, such critics assert, when Hulme herself is only one-eighth Maori and is writing in English.[50] Much criticism on *The Bone People* insists that the novel's intent is to revive community "and make human beings one family."[51] Indeed, the coming together of the threesome and their respective families in the final feast is definitely a feel-good, even salvational moment after the hardship of their separation. For example, Christine Hamelin says, "despite Kerewin's remarkable self-sufficiency, the concept of individualism is subverted and replaced with the notion of commensalism. . . . Kerewin's new view of the artist is linked to the gradual replacement of her controlling voice with the polyphonous voices which rise up at the end."[52] In *The Bone People*, therefore, the overconsumption of alcohol and related violence appear as a recognition (for multiculturalists outside of New Zealand) of the Maori[53] and, particularly, of the Maori rituals of commensalism. Alienation and alcoholism are reframed as positive values—cultural expression, rituals, family bonding events, and customary practices fill the novel with constant excuses for prideful drunkenness: "knots of happy people, chattering people, singing-tired and weeping-drunk people."[54] Even bringing kids into bars is lauded as a type of family bonding: "Nobody minds a kiddie being in the bar," asserts the bartender, "provided someone's looking after it. Better that than leave them at home uncared for, or stuck out by themselves in a car, isn't it?"[55] Here, the narration assumes that drinking is necessary and inevitable for the building of cultural community, so kids must be accommodated around it, rather than the parents participating in events that would benefit, educate, or simply amuse the kids. Meanwhile, Hulme depicts the carpenter who

opposes Simon's presence in the bar as brutish, threatening, and mean, jus-
tifying Kerewin's drunken show of force. The family ritual of Maori commensalism reframes negative effects of addictive consumption into cultural assets: affective bonding and parental protection.

Yet, for the most part, criticism of *The Bone People* uncritically celebrates
the novel as subversive in its compassionate embrace of "Otherness"
and/or cultural "hybridity." Graham Huggan, for example, claims, as he
explores the implications of Hulme's Modernist influences, "[Hulme]
hints at the emergence of an emancipated post-colonial voice containing
within it the contradictions of and hybrid elements in post-colonial cultures which perceive their creolized status in terms other than those of
self-deprecatory assimilation or self-glorifying recuperations."[56] *The Bone
People* creates a feel-good sentiment around globalization. Like the other
Pegasus novels, it uses images of multicultural love to sweeten globalization even as it seems to recognize cultures of difference. Omitted here is
any possibility of recognition for ethnicities in places where Mobil might
not do business.

Many advocates for multiculturalism profess that the mere recognition
of other cultures outside the West is a counterhegemonic action, undermining the reification of identities and representations, denaturalizing
racist categories, and radically challenging presuppositions of power
granted, institutionally, to some over others. For example, Maryanne Dever contends that *The Bone People* "offers an alternative voice, one that en-
franchises multiplicity and undermines the authority of imperialism's
homogenizing linguistic imperative."[57] Suzette Henke professes that "in
the utopian dream of 'commensalism' that concludes this allegorical tale,
Keri Hulme suggests that New Zealand's future lies neither in Maori sep-
aratism nor in Pakeha [New Zealand's white settlers] dominance, but in
the celebration of a rich multi-cultural heritage amalgamating the best of
Maori, Pakeha and European traditions in a finely tempered community
of human fellowship."[58] By simply adding on more differences and more
features, such inclusionists claim, more equality can be achieved, so that
justice becomes merely a matter of refining realist methods with a greater
and more abundant attention to empirical form and detail, and a clearer
and more precise focus on the way things get named. Culture becomes a
matter of aesthetics, and therefore immaterial, leaving aside issues of economic redistribution or equitable reorganization.

Such views also uncritically celebrate love—and in particular family
love—as the basis for getting along across cultural borders. However,
they are not able to consider at the same time how this vision of multicultural love supports power, and that this power is not necessarily going
to allow an optimistic or utopian future for everybody, where, as in the
dénouement, everybody has their "arms round each other's necks all

good cheers and covered tears and matey friendship."[59] Not only do these assertions of multiculturalism tend to romanticize Maori culture, but they also tend to force Maori culture to express the ideals of peace and love that are lost and needed for the redemption of a poetically beleaguered West too much immersed in commerce and technology. Such a recreation of Maori culture only offers an easy, symbolic redemption. As Donaldo Macedo and Lilia I. Bartolomé acknowledge, "Many white liberals willingly call and work for cultural tolerance but are reluctant to confront issues of inequality, power, ethics, race, and ethnicity in a way that could actually lead to social transformation that would make society more democratic and humane and less racist and discriminatory."[60] C. K. Stead's contention against Mobil's granting of the Pegasus Prize to Hulme was that the novel allows Maori culture to be recreated through its identification with white culture, allowing for such "affirmative action" initiatives by multinational corporations to seem as though they are helping oppressed cultures. *The Bone People* gives a sense of liberal benevolence, inclusion, and tolerance, excluding an analysis of how some parties dominate the terms for this mutual harmonizing.

In *The Bone People,* a Maori "cultural authenticity" appears as a type of artistic expression, but such expression is not just a pure surge of ancestral spirit emanating from a connection with the Maori community and landscape, as the criticism would have it. Christine Hamelin, for example, writes, "Kerewin's notion of the artist shifts as she becomes an active individual, involved in the community, open to emotions, prepared to accept the fragmentation of life and to lend an unencumbering pattern to it. The artist must also be joined to the land."[61] The image of Maori "cultural authenticity" and expression which the novel gives does not, however, talk about how the Maori myth of the canoe was drawn from several European colonialist and settler accounts and has tended, in recent land reform movements, to give favor to the most powerful and influential among the Maori tribes. Anne Maxwell has discussed how in 1985 the Labour Government in New Zealand instituted an official policy of biculturalism to enforce original land contracts, made under Queen Victoria, between the Maoris and the British Crown. There was subsequently an upsurge in interest in university Maori studies as well as in Maori literature and Maori language, and this interest served to create a binary concept of New Zealand culture, which excluded those Maoris who did not fit under the homogenizing definition offered in these official versions. These official and exclusionary versions, like *The Bone People,* concentrated on the Maori canoe mythologies.[62] "The White Nation has offered the concept of 'multiculturalism' to Pacific Island people," Donna Awatere adds. "The hidden agenda of this offer is to align Pacific Peoples to the White Nation. . . . However the 'multiculturalism' offered to Pacific peoples is not decision-making power, it is another lizard's trick, a continuation of white power dressed up in tapa cloth. True multiculturalism would mean that Pacific Island people must be part of the economic, political and philosophical policy making systems. This will *never* occur under white sovereignty."[63] Kerewin's version of Maori "cultural authenticity" allows for the making of art, the autonomy of the artist, and most importantly, the freedom from productive labor.

This is not to say that all multiculturalism must therefore be dismissed as just another phase of imperialism or racism. Clearly, multiculturalism does not always feed cultural differences into a corporate, colonialist mill, but still, it is worth both noting that multiculturalism sits comfortably as a product of globalization and it is worth thinking about the reasons why.[64] Contingently, multiculturalism can only provide a counterhegemonic imperative if it contributes a sharp critique of the way contemporary global power works as well as ideas about ways to organize against it. One needs to ask of *The Bone People* how and when multiculturalism actually supports the growth of market cultures around the globe, not only by commodifying exotic goods and spectacles, but also by producing a sense that there can be no alternative to the authority of the market and global capital, and that the values of capitalism are being expressed as human values and expressions of love.

THE ENVIRONMENT

In its rhapsodic celebrations of the Maori experience of nature, *The Bone People* is unable to envision history, context, politics, ethics, or economic distributions in terms of the ways these forces already affect nature's possibilities. For Kerewin to rejuvenate her creative spirit, she needs to reintegrate herself aesthetically and emotionally within the Maori culture from which she has become alienated. What is left out here is any kind of consideration that systems of capital flow are what have alienated her from Maori culture in the first place. *The Bone People*'s "Maori culture" includes ritualistic practices, family relations, and diet, but also a sensibility and respect towards nature, an emotional and even religious connection to both land and sea. "Tears come to my eyes whenever I hear a gull keen," Kerewin laments, "or watch a shag pass on whistling wings. O land, you're too deep in my heart and mind. O sea, you're the blood of me."[65] Kerewin cannot bear to see living creatures get hurt, so she throws fish that are not good to eat back into the crystalline waters. These images of nature reveal Maori "cultural authenticity" as proof of an idyllic natural abundance and environmental sustainability. In *The Bone People*, cancer is a product of a loss of faith rather than of noxious industrial emissions. There is no mention here of industrial pollutants, contaminants, environmental destruction. There are no plants or animals sickly or dying from exposure to poisons and toxins. There is no sense that Maori ways of life have been seriously threatened by oil spills, nor that the reason that the fish might not survive has to do more with waste products of multinational manufacturing than with individual fisherpeople making catches with fishing rods and canoes. There is no description here that relates to other testimonies of regions where multinationals have excavated oil, as in the Oriente of the Ecuadorian Amazon where Texaco has extracted 1.4 billion gallons of crude oil since the 1970s while disregarding international laws protecting the environment and human rights. There, as a correspondent from *The Nation* writes, "everything was eerily still, the fish and birds nowhere in sight and the vegetation stained black with petroleum residue."[66] The extreme environmental devastation in this region has caused death and disease among indigenous peoples, revealing that oil companies are not in the service of defending human values but rather, like Chevron, in systematically rooting out obstacles to production. "The poisoning of streams and rivers has amounted to . . . nothing short of ethnocide."[67] Yet, the benevolent way which Kerewin, through her Maori-ness, has learned to treat nature makes invisible the processes through which capitalism has already changed the terrain, how increased corporatism promises even more widespread damage, and that everything might not appear quite so green upon Kerewin's arrival the next time, through no fault of her own. Kerewin and her "authentic Maori culture" might not have such complete control over maintaining nature in a state of purity, cleanliness, health, and abundance as the novel wants to suggest.[68]

SPECULATION

By focusing on Maori "authentic culture" as a spirit-force necessary for the production of art, Hulme is able to erase the way both culture and nature are configured through power struggles while disallowing any sincere and engaged critique about how the construction of "authentic Maori culture" serves class interests. Indeed, *The Bone People*'s realization of Maori "authentic culture" is provisioned on support from Kerewin's international investments. "Once," she admits,

> I had to work at horrible jobs to earn enough money to buy food to eat it in order to live to work at horrible jobs to earn enough. . . . I hated that life. . . . So I quit. I did what my heart told me and painted for my living. . . . Money was the only problem . . . then it all changed. I won a lottery. I invested it. I earned a fortune by fast talking.[69]

Not only has stock ownership been concentrated among an ever narrowing circle of the very rich,[70] but, too, as Gayatri Spivak has noted, the rise of multiculturalism in pedagogical practice happened simultaneously with the opening up of financial and currency markets to transnationalism in the early seventies.[71] Thomas Friedman attributes what he calls the democratization of financial and investment markets solely to junk-bond felon Michael Milken's ideas, implemented in the seventies and eighties, about selling bailout blue-chip stocks "to the little guy" who had formerly been locked out of credit from traditional banks.[72] Kerewin's story shows how this same process was then internationalized so that individuals, even in developing countries, could buy bonds on foreign state debt, ensuring themselves that private efforts can reduce losses due to public failings like the depletion of social security or commitments like requiring the provision of employee benefits.[73]

VIOLENCE AND THE POLITICS OF RECOGNITION

The most wrenching, difficult, and appalling feature of what *The Bone People* counts as Maori "cultural authenticity" is, however, purely and simply the acceptability of extreme violence. Joe's treatment of Simon is defined as quite simply a casualty of love. Simon is impetuous, does not attend school when he should, does not follow Joe's directives all the time, sometimes steals, and is strong-willed, stubborn, mischievous, and at times destructive. During the last beating, he even attacks and seriously wounds Joe by cutting into his stomach with a piece of jaded glass. So, as Kerewin herself observes, Simon deserves it, and even benefits from it: "It all shows you cared deeply. In a negative way, so does the fact that you beat him. At least, you worried enough about what you considered was his wrongdoing to try and correct it."[74] In the logic of *The Bone People*, causing severe pain is what people do when they care.

The critics concur. Elizabeth Webby, for example, writes, "The horror of Keri Hulme's portrait of the child as victim, of well-meaning even more than not well-meaning adults, would be unbearable if she had not created in Simon such a tough little nut of a character."[75] Georges-Goulven Le Cam even goes so far as to say that the abuse turns Simon into a Christ-figure on which the redemption of the world depends: "Right till the end, the boy shows amazing *forgiveness* for Joe, his 'torturer,' and keeps loving the man with a vengeance. His 'sacrifice'—the ultimate bashing-cum-crucifixion that sends him into a coma—is necessary to *redeem* the threesome, and beyond the threesome, to redeem New Zealand. The Kingdom has come and things can start healing again."[76] Yet, the brutality of Joe's attacks on Simon is not easily dismissable as good parenting or the prerogative of a father to punish severely a wayward child:

He is aching, he is breaking apart with pain. The agony is everywhere, hands, body, legs, head. He is shaking so badly he cannot stand. The hard wood keeps grinding past him. . . . The first punch hit his head. His head slammed back into the door frame. The punches keep coming. Again. Again. And again. . . . The blood pours from everywhere. He can feel it spilling from his mouth, his ears, his eyes, and his nose.[77]

The culmination of a long series of similar outbursts, this time Simon loses his eyesight and the doctors speculate that the brain damage will be permanent. *The Bone People* presents Maori "cultural authenticity" as naturally violent, violent in the blood, inheriting a legacy of cannibalism and precolonial warfare, which resurfaces as the core of identity.[78] Pain and injustice are redefined as cultural recognition. Unexplainable acts of aggression on the part of power lead to peace, understanding, empowerment, learning, and love. Multiculturalism's politics of inclusion and Maori "cultural authenticity" are here being used as an alibi, an excuse for a politics of violence.[79]

Charles Taylor defines *multiculturalism* as the "politics of recognition," in other words, an acknowledgment that "cultures that have provided the horizon of meaning for large numbers of human beings . . . are almost certain to have something that deserves our admiration and respect."[80] Yet, in commending the obviously beneficial values that multiculturalism contributes to education, to the Enlightenment's values of universal humanity and universal human freedom, critics like Taylor must also consider what it means that one compelling example of multicultural recognition and inclusion was when, for example, from one week to the next, most Americans learned and recognized that there was a place called Kosovo— one providing "the horizon of meaning for large numbers of human beings"—because bombers were being sent to wreck it. The violence in *The Bone People* must be read as not simply a study in the multiple meanings of violence nor as a complex look at violence from different points of view nor as a nuanced analysis of psychological motivation nor as a tableau of human sentiment revealing a deeper comprehension of human action and suffering. Instead, it must be read alongside the other ways that understandings of violence, and particularly corporate violence, influence meaning, power, and justice within geopolitical and ideological struggles. Just as the news coverage on Kosovo produced identifications with U.S. military power, *The Bone People* allows an "understanding" of the psychology of child abusers and a resultant sympathy with the traumas and frustrations that might have caused their recourse to extreme brutality, thus incapacitating either a critique or an outright condemnation of violence against the less powerful. One must distinguish between the multiculturalism that has been successful in disrupting and decentering the power structure of canon, allowing for a greater equality and justice, and another multiculturalism which has been

successful in strengthening the power of capital to exploit the globe, supporting a racist corporate agenda and, ultimately, establishing canonical
Western values as undeniably right in their very mighty genocidal abilities to eradicate others.

THE FUTURE OF LITERATURE

There is nothing new in power's use of culture for the purposes of domination of the less powerful. As various theorists of colonialism—from
Franz Fanon to Paulo Freire, Edward Said, Homi Bhabha, and so on—
have demonstrated, colonialism is a pedagogical practice because it
teaches meanings, assigns values, relegates consciousness, redirects social
signification, and consolidates hierarchies of oppression. In fact, education has historically supported the enforcement of colonial regulation and
production. As Gauri Viswanathan has shown in the case of nineteenth-
century India,

> The history of education in British India shows that certain humanistic func-
> tions traditionally associated with literature—for example, the shaping of
> character or the development of the aesthetic sense or the disciplines of eth-
> ical thinking—were considered essential to the processes of sociopolitical
> control by the guardians of the same tradition. . . . Indeed, once such impor-
> tance is conceded to the educational function, it is easier to see that values as-
> signed to literature—such as the proper development of character or the
> shaping of critical thought or the formation of aesthetic judgment—are only
> problematically located there and are more obviously serviceable to the dy-
> namic of power relations between the educator and those who are to be ed-
> ucated.[81]

Viswanathan discusses how, in colonial India, literature replaced military
power as the primary enforcer of morality and respect for the law, as the
Indians were taught that assimilation into the ranks of the colonial administration required the ability to absorb the lessons of literary eclecti-
cism. Jacqui Alexander and Chandra Mohanty have pointed out that, in
colonialist situations, the ruling classes propagate "'myths' . . . to preserve
the capitalist status-quo." These myths "are . . . propositions about 'Democracy' within a liberal, capitalist culture."[82] "Together," Alexander and
Monhanty continue, "these myths constitute a rhetoric of freedom and
equality that consolidates the very oppressive practices and values of capitalist domination."[83]

The values and lessons propagated in the service of power and private
profit, however, are not fixed in meaning, but rather are negotiated. The
myths that Alexander and Mohanty have identified as furthering colo-

nialist expansion can and must therefore be unlearned for new emancipatory social relations and governing systems to form: "Decolonization has a fundamentally pedagogical dimension—an imperative to understand, to reflect, and to transform relations of objectification and dehumanization, and to pass this knowledge along to future generations."[84] Indeed, as corporations and corporate messages infiltrate school curricula, it is more important than ever to revitalize a notion of education as vital to the expansion of public knowledge and public power and the consequent production of meaning in the service of civil society and democracy for citizens rather than only for corporations.

Mobil's support of *The Bone People* makes indelibly clear the role that literary studies must play in dismantling a popular imagination geared more and more into a corporate mantle, setting up, in its stead, the possibility of alternatives. However, in her 1998 presidential address to the Modern Language Association, Elaine Showalter actually concedes that literary scholarship is too far removed from the economic-assimilation aims to which higher education has been reduced. The downsizing of the university, the diminishing importance of the humanities in general and, particularly, the shrinking of literary departments in higher education—all these tendencies seem to Showalter an invitation to encourage graduate students to use their literary knowledge to pursue corporate careers:

> Another way to increase the commodity value of humanities Ph.D.s is to give them mobility and choices. As Bob Weisbuch writes, . . . "On the day when the year's most gifted graduate in, say, comparative literature decides to forego an assistant professorship at Stanford for a beginning position with the *Washington Post* or the Ford Foundation or the McDonald's Corporation, the status of the Humanities is revolutionized." . . . I would add that the humanities will be even more revolutionized when a mid-level graduate student can choose among teaching at a college perhaps very different from the sort of place he or she originally aspired to, going into academic administration, or joining the corporate world. . . . As Paula Backscheider asserted as long ago as 1981, "Should we not be as proud of the Ph.D. who begins as *a "communications manager" at Gulf Oil* as we are of the one who starts out as an assistant professor?"[85] (emphasis ours)

Showalter admits to a crisis in the academic job market but does not admit that part of this crisis is due to corporate infiltration in higher education in the form of long-distance learning and other curriculum restructuring, the turning of university administrations into investment portfolio management systems, the attack on tenure, and the like. She also does not admit that constructing literary training as corporate training would inevitably lead to an emptying out of the public value of education as well as a curtailment of the possibilities of imagining social relations differently than in corporate models. Like the kaumatua, Joe's spirit guide, Showalter seems to think that "all we can do is look after the precious matters which are our heritage, and wait, and hope,"[86] accepting passively the overwhelming cultural domination of "development schemes" that are creating such a "mess."[87] She does not, rather, identify the current humanities crisis as a sign of a much larger crisis in economic distribution and as a call to take action. Reducing all career options as well as ethics to the lowest common denominator of universal exchangeability, Showalter does not argue the need for literary studies to discuss how they got to seem marginal or even negligible to the management of the contemporary economy, the ideological configuration of global capital, and the deification of corporate culture. In her view, what is important is solely determined by students' free consumer choice: unfettered fashion trends, pleasures, and taste rather than by questions of power, ideological manipulation, and funding. Showalter should know from her renowned contributions to feminist literary studies that denying the politics of literature, pedagogy, and other cultural work, affirms power, oppression, and the credibility of violence and hinders the possibilities for constructing a democratic, global civil society for the future.

NOTES

1. Taft Group, "Top 10 Givers in the Top 9 Categories—1999," www.taftgroup. com/taft/. Praising Mobil as the third largest corporate sponsor of the arts and humanities (probably ascending on this list after its merger with Exxon, which is also a major contributor), the Taft group states, "Mobil Corp. and the Mobil Foundation disbursed grants totaling $9,879,000 in grants to arts and cultural organizations. Supporting a variety of arts disciplines, Mobil encourages mixing cultures, customs, and ideas through sponsorship of painting, theater, music, literature, sculpture, weaving, and numerous other cultural activities: PBS for Mobil Masterpiece Theatre, the Mobil Pegasus Prize for Literature, and art exhibitions are some of the programs being sponsored by Mobil."

2. Keri Hulme has also acknowledged the support of other institutions, such as the New Zealand Literary Fund, ICI, Otago University, the Maori Trust, Auckland University Press, and the literary journal *Islands*.

3. Business Wire, "Venezuelan Author Ana Teresa Tores Wins the 1998 Mobil Pegasus Prize for Literature," 15 October 1998, www.businesswire.com/webbox/ bw.101598/839033.htm. "Mobil de Venezuela, an affiliate of Mobil Corporation, was established in 1994. It is involved in all aspects of the Venezuelan petroleum industry, from a joint venture with PDVSA and Veba Oel to produce 120,000 barrels a day of heavy oil from the Cerro Negro field in the Orinoco tar belt by 2001 to exploration on the La Ceiba block on the southeastern shore of Lake Maracaibo. The company has also begun Phase 1 engineering for a new olefins plant in Jose in a 50/50 joint venture with Pequiven. Mobil is also the leading brand among private lubes marketing companies and recently entered the Venezuelan fuels market with plans to brand over 200 service stations in the next three years."

4. Mobil, "Pegasus Prize: Background," n.d., www.magnolia.com/pegasus_prize/background.html.

5. *The Bone People* is, to date, the only Pegasus novel originally written in English. Mobil's promotion explicitly states that part of its purpose is to counter "the one-way flow of translated fiction in the U.S."

6. Thomas L. Friedman, *The Lexus and the Olive Tree: Understanding Globalization* (New York: Farrar, Straus & Giroux, 1999), 176.

7. Taft Group, "Top 10 Givers in the Top 9 Categories—1999."

8. Steven Manning, "The Corporate Curriculum," *The Nation*, 27 September 1999, 17.

9. Manning, "The Corporate Curriculum."

10. Fredric Jameson, "Notes on Globalization as Philosophical Issue," in *The Cultures of Globalization*, edited by Frederic Jameson and Masao Miyoshi (Durham, N.C.: Duke University Press, 1998), 61.

11. Donna Awatere, *Maori Sovereignty* (Auckland, New Zealand: Broadsheet, 1984), 23.

12. Awatere, *Maori Sovereignty*, 15.

13. Awatere, *Maori Sovereignty*, 15.

14. Gayatri Spivak, "Diasporas Old and New: Women in the Transnational World," in *Revolutionary Pedagogies: Cultural Politics, Instituting Education, and the Discourse of Theory*, edited by Peter Pericles Tirfonas (New York: RoutledgeFalmer, 2000), 5–6.

15. Edward S. Herman and Robert W. McChesney, *The Global Media: The New Missionaries of Corporate Capitalism* (London: Cassell, 1997), 179.

16. ACIL Economics, Policy and Strategy Consultants, "Barriers to Entry to the New Zealand Downstream Oil Market: A Report to New Zealand Ministry of Commerce" (Canberra, Australia: Crown, 1997), 9–10.

17. William Greider, "Oil on Political Waters," www.thenation.com/greider, 23 October 2000. "For the past thirty years, the world price of oil has been 'managed' by governments, albeit with haphazard results. The price was maintained by the OPEC cartel of oil-producing nations, with discreet consultations from the United States and other industrial powers. Before OPEC, the world price of oil had been managed since the thirties by the fabled Seven Sisters, global oil corporations that still have an influential voice in the conversations. Oil-price diplomacy, for obvious reasons, is mostly done in deep privacy."

18. This is most likely related to the oil industry's most pressing promotional and customer relations problem: how to dull public fears over oil spills.

19. This is not to say that Keri Hulme is to blame, or that she intentionally supported a promotional campaign where she single-handedly built exploitative practices into the economy, or that her aim is to advertise oil. Neither is the argument here about how Hulme should be condemned or castigated for not drawing attention to how multinational corporations are destroying environments in other countries, unjustly bypassing local laws and ethical considerations about local land tenure systems and economic rights, or making life conditions more and more miserable for larger numbers of people, particularly indigenous peoples, by deregulating labor and environmental protections. The purpose here is not to target individuals but rather to show how corporations and the institutions that support them—the system of global capitalism itself—have succeeded in limiting

possibilities for what can be expressed, configuring human value as conceivable only within neoliberal productive relations.

20. Keri Hulme, *The Bone People* (New York: Penguin Books, 1983), 20.

21. Hulme, *The Bone People*, 49.

22. Kjartan Fløgstad, *Dollar Road*, translated by Nadi Christensen (Baton Rouge: Louisiana State University Press, 1989).

23. Cees Nooteboom, *Rituals*, translated by Adrienne Dixon (San Diego, Calif.: Harcourt Brace, 1983), 1.

24. Nooteboom, *Rituals*, 32–33.

25. Nooteboom, *Rituals*, 34.

26. Nooteboom, *Rituals*, 15.

27. Zygmunt Bauman, *Globalization: The Human Consequences* (New York: Columbia University Press, 1998), 121.

28. Martin M. Simecka, *The Year of the Frog*, translated by Peter Petro (Baton Rouge: Louisiana State University Press, 1993), 6.

29. Simecka, *The Year of the Frog*, 1.

30. Simecka, *The Year of the Frog*, 1.

31. Fløgstad, *Dollar Road*, 8.

32. As history creeps forward towards increasing technologization and increasing centralized control of capital, politics goes from Social Democracy to Labour to Socialism and the factory replaces the fields in a flash without distinction, as though it made no difference who the faces were as long as the historical currents of capitalist transformation eked on in their mysterious way.

33. Fløgstad, *Dollar Road*, 159.

34. Fløgstad, *Dollar Road*, 160.

35. Ana Teresa Torres, *Doña Inés vs. Oblivion*, translated by Gregory Rabassa (New York: Grove Press, 1999), 200. In fact, the voice of property is the promise of democracy, which, in turn, is the promise to do business: "What it's all about is the fact that the land has no rightful heirs. Who are the owners? The occupants are a few peasants who till their plots with no titles of ownership that give them anything; that's why I don't believe in democracy."

36. Torres, *Doña Inés vs. Oblivion*, 149.

37. Hulme, *The Bone People*, 89.

38. Hulme, *The Bone People*, 89.

39. Nancy Fraser, *Justice Interruptus: Critical Reflections on the "Postsocialist" Condition* (New York: Routledge, 1997), 12.

40. Chris Prentice, "Re-writing their Stories, Renaming Themselves: Postcolonialism and Feminism in the Fictions of Keri Hulme and Audrey Thomas," *Span* 23 (September 1986): 71.

41. Hulme, *The Bone People*, 191.

42. C. K. Stead, "Keri Hulme's 'The Bone People,' and the Pegasus Award for Maori Literature," *Ariel: A Review of International English Literature* 16, no. 4 (October 1985): 102.

43. Suzette Henke, "Keri Hulme's *The Bone People* and *Te Kaihau:* Postmodern Heteroglossia and Pretextual Play," in *New Zealand Literture Today*, edited by R. K. Dhawan and William Tonetto (New Delhi: Indian Society for Commonwealth Studies, 1993), 136.

44. Henke, "Keri Hulme's *The Bone People*," 140.

45. Herman and McChesney, *The Global Media*, 187.

46. Herman and McChesney, *The Global Media*, 140.

47. "If marriage still too often resembles a master/subject relation, this is due in large measure to its social embeddedness in relation to sex-segmented labor markets, gender-structured social-welfare policy regimes, and the gender division of unpaid labor" (Nancy Fraser, 228).

48. Fraser, *Justice Interruptus*, 123.

49. Noam Chomsky, *Profit over People: Neoliberalism and Global Order* (New York: Seven Stories Press, 1999), 24. "In 1971, 90 percent of international financial transactions were related to the real economy—trade or long-term investment—and 10 percent were speculative. By 1990 the percentages were reversed, and by 1995 about 95 percent of the vastly greater sums were speculative, with daily flows regularly exceeding the combined foreign exchange reserves of the seven biggest industrial powers, over $1 trillion a day, and very short-term: about 80 percent with round trips of a week or less. Prominent economists warned over 20 years ago that the process would lead to a low-growth, low-wage economy, and suggested fairly simple measures that might prevent these consequences. But the principal architects of the Washington consensus preferred the predictable effects, including very high profits. These effects were augmented by the (short-term) sharp rise in oil prices and the telecommunications revolution."

50. The point here is not to argue that Keri Hulme is or is not authentically Maori, or that *The Bone People* is or is not an authentically Maori text. Rather, the point here is to ask under what political conditions the very question of cultural authenticity gets mobilized, and towards what ends.

51. Hulme, *The Bone People*, 199.

52. Christine Hamelin, "'Fitted to His Own Web of Music': Art as Renaming in *The Bone People*," *Australian & New Zealand Studies in Canada* 10 (December 1993): 110.

53. Hulme, *The Bone People*, 338. "As a race, we *like* fighting" (original emphasis).

54. Hulme, *The Bone People*, 441.

55. Hulme, *The Bone People*, 245.

56. Graham Huggan, "Opting out of the (Critical) Common Market: Creolization and the Post-Colonial Text," *Kunapipi* 11, no. 1 (1989): 35.

57. Maryanne Dever, "Violence as *Lingua Franca*: Keri Hulme's *The Bone People*," *World Literature Written in English* 29, no. 2 (1989): 25.

58. Henke, "Keri Hulme's *The Bone People*," 146–47.

59. Hulme, *The Bone People*, 443.

60. Donaldo Macedo and Lilia I. Bartolomé, *Dancing With Bigotry: Beyond the Politics of Tolerance* (New York: St. Martin's Press, 1999), 14.

61. Hamelin, "'Fitted to His Own Web of Music,'" 117.

62. "Ethnicity and Education: Biculturalism in New Zealand," in *Multicultural States: Rethinking Difference and Identity*, edited by David Bennett (London: Routledge, 1998), 197. "The state's upholding of these . . . narratives of identity has meant that small tribes . . . have been forced to bury their historical traditions and tribal identities and adopt those of larger, more powerful tribes if they are to compete for resources," concludes Maxwell.

63. Awatere, *Maori Sovereignty*, 37–40.

64. Chicago Cultural Studies Group, "Critical Multiculturalism," in *Multiculturalism: A Critical Reader,* edited by David Theo Goldberg (Oxford: Blackwell, 1994, 115). The Chicago Cultural Studies Group has convincingly pointed out that "it is far from clear whether a multicultural emphasis in education will result in a more democratically critical society or rather in one with more subtle international administrative abilities."

65. Hulme, *The Bone People,* 166.

66. Eyal Press, "Texaco on Trial," *The Nation,* 31 May 1999, 11.

67. Press, "Texaco on Trial," 12.

68. David Cromwell, "Local Energy, Local Democracy," www.zmag.org/ Zsustainers/Zdaily/2000-8/15cromwell.htm, 15 August 2000. Advocates for environmental reform have pointed out that the oil industry as a whole is in the business of expanding hegemonic, neo-colonial controls through expanding the areas of extraction. "According to the San Francisco–based Transnational Resource and Action Center (TRAC), 'Big Oil's long-term strategy is still dictated by the urge to explore.' New exploration as well as oil or gas pipelines threaten the survival of peoples in the Amazon basin, Southeast Asia, and North America. BPAmoco, the world's largest solar company, is committed to spending $5 billion in the next 5 years on oil exploration and production in the sensitive environment of Alaska alone. This dwarfs the trifling sum of $45 million recently spent on its solar business division. . . . Other companies such as the combined Exxon-Mobil, the world's largest oil corporation, are doing even less to develop renewables. In the global economy, the unsustainable expansion of corporate activities into ever-larger markets means that there is an almost irresistible force driving the formation of mega-companies of all types. . . . At Exxon and Mobil, job losses will exceed 9,000. As TRAC notes, Exxon had already been cutting jobs at the rate of 4 percent every year for over a decade."

69. Hulme, *The Bone People,* 28.

70. Edward N. Wolff, "Recent Trends in Wealth Ownership, 1983–1998, table 6, www.evy.org/docs/wrkpap/papers/300.html, April 2000. In 1998, the richest 1 percent of the population owned 42.1 percent of stocks, mutual funds, and retirement accounts. The bottom 90 percent owned 36.6 percent.

71. Gayatri Spivak, "Who Claims Alterity?" in *Remaking History,* edited by Barbara Kruger and Phil Mariani (Seattle: Bay Press, 1989), 275–76. "Thrown into this chiastic field a phenomenon I invoke often: the shift into transnationalism in the early seventies through the computerization of the big stock exchanges. Of course, changes in the mode of production of value do not bring about matching changes in the constitution of the subject. But one is often surprised to notice how neatly the ruses change in that arena that engages in coding subject-production: cultural politics. And the universities, the journals, the institutes, the exhibitions, the publishers' series are rather overly involved here. Keeping the banal predictability of the cultural apparatus in transnational society firmly in mind, it can be said that the shift into transnationalism brought a softer and more benevolent Third Worldism into the Euramerican academy. . . . It is in this newer context that the postcolonial diasporic can have the role of an ideologue. This 'person' . . . belonging to a basically collaborative elite, can be uneasy for different kinds of reasons with being made the object of unquestioning benevolence as an inhabitant

of the new Third World. . . . This produces a comfortable 'other' for transnational postmodernity. . . . In fact, most postcolonial areas have a class-specific access to the society of information-command telematics inscribed by microelectronic transnationalism. And indeed, the discourse of cultural specificity and difference, packaged for transnational consumption along the lines sketched above, is often deployed by this specific class." Spivak cites as evidence the National Governors' Report issued in Washington on 24 February 1989, which "calls for more language learning and culture learning, because otherwise the U.S. will be 'outcompeted'" (290).

72. Friedman, *The Lexus and the Olive Tree*, 48.

73. Friedman, *The Lexus and the Olive Tree*, 51. "America is moving from a country in which companies guaranteed an employee's pension through a defined "set of benefits" to a country in which many companies now just guarantee a defined "contribution," and the individual manages his or her own money and shifts it around, according to where he or she can get the best return. And with people now living longer, and wondering whether social security will be there when they want to retire, they are not only turning to these mutual funds and pension funds in an aggressive manner but also managing them very aggressively for higher returns."

74. Hulme, *The Bone People*, 325.

75. Elizabeth Webby, "Keri Hulme: Spiralling to Success," *Meanjin* 44, no. 1 (March 1985): 20.

76. Georges-Goulven Le Cam, "The Quest for Archetypal Self-Truth in Keri Hulme's *The Bone People*: Towards a Western Re-Definition of Maori Culture?" *Commonwealth* 15, no. 2 (Spring 1993): 74.

77. Hulme, *The Bone People*, 308–09.

78. Hulme, *The Bone People*, 335. "He could never imagine his great-grandfather, who had taken part in several feasts of people, as a cannibal. He remembered the old man only as a picture of a silver-haired fiercely dignified chief. He'd always imagined cannibals to be little wizened people, with pointy teeth. 'We're meat, same as anything else,' his grandmother had said."

79. Michel Feher, *Powerless By Design: The Age of the International Community* (Durham, N.C.: Duke University Press, 2000), 40; E. Ike Udogu, "The Allurement of Ethnonationalism in Nigerian Politics: The Contemporary Debate," *Journal of Asian and African Studies* 29, nos. 3–4 (July–October 1994): 159–72. Frequently, blockages to democracy are exhibited in the press, by the national or international spin-weavers, and/or through culture, as resulting from unbridgeable gulfs between ethnic groups, or, as post–Cold War cultural logic suggests, from the resurgence of ancient ethnic rivalries or incompatible cultural practices. As Michel Feher has shown, throughout the nineties, the masters of the international community continually claimed that all post–Cold War world conflicts "were about 'tribal' disputes–over land, resources, ethnic or religious supremacy, and so forth—rather than rival ideologies and adverse political projects." Yet, as E. Ike Udogu has argued, "a focus on ethnicity obscures the fact that . . . ethnic movements may be encouraged and incited to action by the political 'princes' who accede to power and use it to further their individual and group interests. In a way, therefore, ethnicity becomes a mask for class privileges."

80. Charles Taylor, "The Politics of Recognition," in *Multiculturalism: A Critical Reader,* edited by David Theo Goldberg (Oxford: Blackwell, 1994), 101.

81. Gauri Viswanathan, *Masks of Conquest: Literary Study and British Rule in India* (Delhi: Oxford University Press, 1998), 3–4.

82. M. Jacqui Alexander and Chandra Talpade Mohanty, "Introduction: Genealogies, Legacies, Movements," in *Feminist Genealogies, Colonial Legacies, Democratic Futures,* edited by M. Jacqui Alexander and Chandra Talpade Mohanty (New York: Routledge, 1997), xxxiii.

83. Alexander and Mohanty, "Introduction: Genealogies, Legacies, Movements," xxxiii.

84. Alexander and Mohanty, "Introduction: Genealogies, Legacies, Movements," xxviii–xxix.

85. Elaine Showalter, "Presidential Address 1998: Regeneration," *PMLA* 114 (May 1999): 325.

86. Hulme, *The Bone People,* 371.

87. Hulme, *The Bone People,* 371.

4

The Mayor's Madness:
So Far from God

I think this is the highest form of compassion and love—to help people to help themselves, to get them to the point where they can take care of themselves, to ask them to do something in return for the help that they are being given by the city, state and the Federal Government.

—Rudolph Giuliani[1]

PRIVATIZING RESPONSIBILITY

In the fall of 1999, New York City mayor Rudolph Giuliani announced that homeless people would have to go to work to be allowed to stay in shelters. Many of these homeless people were, additionally, suffering from mental illnesses, particularly schizophrenia.[2] Giuliani's act was in blatant defiance of a 1979 New York State Supreme Court ruling in the landmark case *Callahan v. Carey* that said the New York State constitution guaranteed the right to shelter for homeless New Yorkers, as well as of a 1979 federal law which created "federal preferences" for public and Section 8 housing assistance based on income, thus setting up housing, health care, and job programs for the homeless.[3] Nevertheless, Giuliani went even further, declaring that the children of these homeless people would be put in foster homes. He did not mention the New York City welfare surplus. Some of this surplus is meant to be allocated to the development of day-care centers that would serve the public better than would taking people's kids away from them, but child-care facilities and programs have not been implemented and so those affected by welfare-to-work imperatives have not been able to access such mandated provisions: City councilperson Stephen DiBrienza said that "forcing parents to work would overburden the city's day care system. He estimated that 40,000 poor and working families were already awaiting openings in subsidized day care programs and that the policy would add 5,000 more families to that list."[4]

The next crunch came when the administration decided to arrest people who set up beds on the sidewalk. "Streets do not exist in civilized societies for the purpose of people sleeping there," Giuliani said.[5] This comment comes in the wake of a pitiful housing policy performance on the part of the city administration. In this time of budgetary surplus, Giuliani has slashed the housing budget to 5.6 percent of the capital budget, while it was 10.7 percent and 12.5 percent under the Dinkins and Koch administrations in times of severe budgetary constraints. Giuliani has also slashed the number of shelters built from 2,000 in 1995 to 523 in 1999, while the number of people in shelters has grown. Even as, in the summer of 2000, Giuliani's political career seemed to be coming to a screeching close, his real political crimes—that is, his attack on the helpless and destitute and, ironically, his anti-family initiatives justified as ensuring the safety and security of families and private businesses (called "quality of life" policies)—were not the grounds for the type of public scrutiny, outcry, and political critique they deserved, nor did they ever serve as a reason to reduce his hold on power. Instead, the failure of his marriage in the face of, supposedly, his overwhelming, uncontrollable passion and love for women led to his demise in the 2000 senatorial race. This event thus witnesses an eclipse of the political, where the privacy of subjectivity—of passions and sentiment—and of family life has taken center stage as a glaring public concern and as the focus of all possible public contention over the politics and ethics of an unprincipled administration.

The homeless and the mentally ill represent the bottom-line testing ground where the limits to government power are being drawn, but the way people perceive the limits to government power in this instance will also serve to substantiate the cutting of other governmental supports of public life like welfare, health care, public schooling, and so on. Giuliani's attack on the homeless is part of a much broader redefinition of the relationship between public and private responsibility in the creation of a new global citizen, a redefinition that is shaping cultural visions of political possibility and effective agency. In this chapter, we discuss how Ana Castillo's *So Far from God* (1993) understands Chicana feminist empowerment as necessarily outside of government's reach.

Castillo's ideas about political community and activism envision oppositional politics squarely and succinctly as individual initiative and personal responsibility. As Kamala Platt remarks, "Castillo underscores the importance of personal responsibility for lifestyle in reducing the global vulnerability of environmental destruction."[6] This is tantamount to saying that if individuals try really hard, they can offset the widespread environmental damage produced by First World industrial emissions, and that private citizens themselves can accomplish such grand oppositional actions without the aid of governmental checks, legislated and enforced regulations on corporations, and international standards, without, that is, turning government enforcement towards the regulation of capital growth rather than towards disciplinary control of the public. Contradictorily, this way of thinking about radical action conforms to and feeds a popular anti-government critique (such as Giuliani's), which eases globalist agendas into place by erasing the possibilities for action in the strengthening of a public sphere, proclaiming that homelessness is an individual rather than a social problem and so needs to be solved through individual efforts. This is not to say that Castillo does not identify important issues to address. After all, with the passing of anti-immigrant legislation, English-only initiatives, barriers to access to childcare and schooling and health care, welfare curtailments, unequal geographical distributions of ecological sustainability, the deskilling of labor, and enforced sterilization programs, for instance, the Chicano community certainly does have ample reason to criticize the state and its treatment of its populations both currently and historically. In their criticisms of power, however, cultural critics and cultural producers need also to reconceive possibilities for the state to intervene compassionately, benevolently, and productively in public life, rather than dismissing the government altogether as simply the repressive opponent of freedom and the private citizen, because maligning the state as contrary to personal interests fuels a popular anti-federalist sentiment that is currently driving globalization. As Robert Kuttner explains, "The quest for a viable mixed economy necessarily leads back to government and politics, for the democratic state remains the prime counterweight to the market. . . . Government has less popular legitimacy, and fewer resources with which to treat escalating problems. The less government is able to achieve, the more it seems a bad bargain."[7]

The case of the homeless and mentally ill in New York City as well as the way the Chicano community confronts social crises in *So Far from God* both demonstrate how the new global configuration of power is privatizing responsibility, making individuals responsible for misfortunes that were formerly public, state concerns. This follows on the weakening of public institutions to the point where, as Zygmunt Bauman has shown, there is an "increasing gap between power and politics," and where "the orthodox centres of economic, military and cultural powers once condensed in the nation-state [have been] now sapped and eroded,"[8] undermining possibilities of public institutions for the promotion of public agency. The ideology behind Giuliani's move on the homeless and Ana Castillo's critique of racism and sexism both posit individual freedom as endangered by a predatory state, whereas in reality it is the growth in transnational corporate power that tends to weaken the individual's power and political influence precisely by weakening the state's supports of public and community life. As Edward S. Herman and Robert W. McChesney point out, the global growth in corporate power has witnessed a simultaneous diminishment in the power of the public to make political choices, to participate in political processes, as well as a catastrophic unraveling of a public sphere and communities for democratic involvement.[9] Henry Giroux insightfully adds, "'The requirements of citizenship necessitate vigilance in public affairs, criticism of public officials (and corporate interests), and participation in political decision making in the interests of expanding equality of opportunity, justice, and the public good. Such activity resists the privatizing impulses of corporations, which attempt to overshadow the demands of citizenship with the demands of commerce."[10] Growth in corporate power has been the foremost threat to democracy. When private corporations gain power over the state, ordinary citizens no longer have access to deliberative processes, critical challenges, and interventions in the public sphere. The increasing domination of corporate ideology and corporate interests means that public culture is severely crippled.

The demonization of state supports therefore goes hand-in-hand with the derailing of national government regulations at all levels except for enforcement in order to allow for multinational interests to override national laws.[11] The replacement of public supports by public discipline is clear in, for example, Giuliani's absurd defense of the police despite their murderous rampages against the public, increasing police presence throughout the city in the name of "quality of life" (that is, making the streets safe for retail), profiling, growing incarceration even for nonviolent crimes, and the militarization of surveillance, patrolling, and apprehension. The corporate undermining of the public functions of the state has, further, led to increasing concentrations of wealth and the increasing production of pockets of misery on a global scale. "The rhetoric of free trade insists that government step out of the way of economic activity. . . . Barriers to new investment need to be eliminated by pressing changes on other governments, and wealth has to be detached from those specific places where it had been generated. Indeed, two-fifths of the world's nations are experiencing negative growth rates. Russia has witnessed a net population loss of nearly a million people per year as life expectancy for men has fallen from 64 to 58 in ten years. For every three of the world's workers with a job, another can't find one, an estimated one billion unemployed."[12] Neoliberal market reform has instigated global crackdowns on labor and environmentalism as well as an economic squeezing out of cultural, racial, and ethnic differences.

It is imperative at this moment to imagine a different purpose for state government, a different way for it to contribute to the bolstering, rather than the annihilation, of the public. While Chomsky has so clearly and compellingly pointed out that state intervention has a history filled with atrocities, greedy invasions, human rights abuses, and the seeking of geopolitical leverage at the expense of the less powerful, the struggle for equality and social justice demands that a state that is not purely in the service of capital can be built, a state that can support, protect, and guarantee basic freedoms, as it does at least ideally in the universal provision of education. Discourses of empowerment, however, often repeat Giuliani's gestures in making individuals' political salvation and heroism depend on their concerted opposition to and freedom from the state.[13] Individuals themselves, this logic goes, must take full responsibility for creating a better life. This view is based on an idea of the state as purely negative and repressive in its function, an idea of the state that justifies the neoliberal demand for limits to state power in the name of freedom and that precludes the possibility of the state as productive power.

SO FAR FROM GOD

So Far from God is the story of a Chicano matrilineal family in New Mexico who, in the face of the growing power of corporations and the narrowing of possibilities for citizen action, chooses to create an identity-based community, ostracizing Anglo foreigners with different economic practices like breeding peacocks, and subsidizes it with cooperative weaving and grazing. Sofi brings up her children on her own, supporting them with a meat butchering business, and then becomes mayor of their town, Tome; of her children, Esmeralda goes to college, gets involved with a radical Chicano La Raza social movement because of a love affair, abandons it to become a journalist, and eventually gets killed as a hostage in the Gulf War; Fe's ambitions to assimilate into a middle-class culture as a banker get thwarted, and she becomes a factory-worker, contracting cancer because of the poisonous toxins emitted in the worksite; as a result of a rape, Caridad becomes a clairvoyant and spirit channeler, disappears on a pilgrimage until she is found praying in a cave and sanctified, eventually falls in love with a lesbian, and mystically transcends in a joyous leap over a cliff while holding her lover's hand; La Loca stays at home, caring for her family until she dies of AIDS despite the attentions of a psychic surgeon. *So Far from God* is the telling of their heartbreaks and failings and ghostly returns; their persistence against all odds; the strength of their family-love-and-devotion in the face of atrocities, disasters, abuses, and the crunch of corporate capital; their campaign to resist poverty, encroachment, assimilation, and marginality by reinvigorating their cultural heritage, community-bonding, religion, custom, and ritual; and, finally, their spiritual renewal.

So Far from God places the idea of freedom within a self-sufficient, identity-based, economically productive (though not, when all is told, profit-motivated) Chicano/a community devoid of politics and separated from the broader national or international field. "He [Mr. Charles, the peacock breeder] was an outsider and there were a lot of outsiders moving in, buying up land that had belonged to original families, who were being forced to give it up because they just couldn't live off of it no more, and the taxes were too high, and the children went off to Albuquerque or even farther away to work, or out of state to college, or out of the country with the Army, instead of staying at home to work on the rancherías."[14] The tendency—on the part of postmodern movements—to isolate particular identities and to suggest that ethnic, racial, sexual, and gender differences represent self-enclosed, segregated interests and needs is currently serving to displace blame for political injustices. Instead of directing criticism towards the general assault on democracy and the institutions that allow this to happen, such identity-based movements advocate privatizing subjective and experiential awareness, relegating it to the outside of politics and declaring politics as irrelevant and, actually, contrary to goals of survival. "In the ultimate account," Zygmunt Bauman asserts, "'multicommunitarianism' cannot, without falling into contradiction, recognize the citizen as the principal public agent (or perhaps even as, simply, a public agent). Community is the only legitimate public agency. The realm of law meant to regulate the cohabitation of communities is viewed as an aggregate of community-oriented privileges."[15] Bauman goes further to suggest that this identity-based communitarianism contributes to the growing separation of power from politics presently fueling globalization. Such movements indicate how citizens have become more and more isolated from public communication around interests and issues oriented around the construction of a more universally focused common good. Additionally, the sacred purity of the identity-based community closes off the possibility of an outside critique, redefining the questioning of the present and the contingent posing of alternatives as quite simply the products of racism. In contrast to the non-communication of what he calls "multicommunitarianism," Bauman offers a multicultural ideal, where cultural ascriptions and affiliations and the maintaining of cultural differences in beliefs and practices do not bar cultural exchange across enclosed communities nor inhibit participation in common public life. Indeed, even if the circumscription of identities as the basis for political action seems to follow the same logic as corporate privatization, public fragmentation, and political disenfranchisement, one would be hard put to reject the political and theoretical advances made by much identity-based work in the name of feminism, the civil rights movement, gay and lesbian activism, Latino liberation movements, and the like, especially when it is so compellingly clear that the wretched of the earth still suffer under the persistent oppression of such ideological and institutional forces as racism and sexism. The irony is that the strongest levers of political opposition also feed the corporate enemy. The challenge is to build a public ethics in which feminism, Latino/a struggles, and other identity-based movements can be articulated as antithetical to social relations under capitalism, because capitalism in its current global form puts women, blacks, Latinos/as, immigrants, and other marginalized groups on the losing side, making them increasingly subject to unequal wages and work conditions, less stable labor, increased exposure to pollution, police repression, and the like.

What is at stake here is the very definition of multiculturalism and its new curricula, how multiculturalism is used pedagogically, and what kinds of issues it can and must address. The mere knowledge of cultural plurality does not necessarily rectify political injustices. What needs to be asked is in what form does the recognition of diverse cultures allow for social change and in what form does it just repeat and extend the politics of domination and capitalist exploitation. Readings of cultural recognition often serve to hide the ways that a novel might be espousing a political vision that is actually contrary to the interests of the culture supposed to be recognized. For example, Roland Walter sees Castillo's novel as a "symbolic act with an ideological utopian function intent on finding imaginary solutions to existing social conflicts" by posing a "'renunciation of authority' and a narrative that connotes '*free choice* and *otherness*.'"[16] However, this critique tends to stop at the level of language, celebrating the text's overturning and disordering of binary oppositions and linguistic codes. Theresa Delgadillo sees *So Far from God* as challenging realism in order to "recognize women as agents of social change" and recover a "hybrid spirituality" in the "india/mestiza voice," which "becomes one with political action."[17] This view tends to see that including more voices in what counts as knowledge is itself disruptive of the powers of domination as well as the subordination of women and minorities: *So Far from God*, Delgadillo suggests, "fueled by a woman-centered spirituality emerges to challenge subjugation of women within and without Chicana/o cultures, the marginalization of other sectors of U.S. society, and the destruction of the environment. . . . It highlights the centrality of hybrid spirituality in the lives of characters engaged in cultural and political resistance."[18] It is, however, surely not enough simply to add other cultures onto the palette of canonical knowledge without considering the political changes and economic redistributions necessary to allow cultures to survive in an era of globalization. Multiculturalism should not be just about broadening aesthetic possibilities in the name of diversity and paternalistic practices of inclusion and tolerance. What is missing here is how such literature and criticism can be appropriated as propaganda to enhance projects of globalization and corporate control. If globalization is omitted from consideration when talking about literature and multiculturalism, there is no way of discussing how it is very much in the interests of global capital to recognize diversity, how such recognition helps to spread markets, sell goods, and to bring marginal cultures under hegemonic control and not necessarily to foster emancipatory movements nor to empower marginal communities. What needs to be developed is a way of thinking a literature which might participate in imagining more equitable and just futures and in working to produce new social relations and to transform the world towards this vision.

CORPORATE CARE

A clear example of how Ana Castillo's anti-government politics inadvertently supports a politics of globalization can be found in her earlier novel *Sapogonia* (1990). This novel is about a community of expatriated artists from a mythic Spanish-speaking nation called Sapogonia, which has been forcibly taken over by the military. Fleeing the ensuing repressions, these global migrants come to resettle in Chicago. Representing the indigenous Mexican goddess Coatlicue and capable of magical enchantments, the female protagonist Pastora, the famous singer, becomes gradually politicized transporting illegal immigrants to refuges and even goes to jail for it. Released from prison, she appears at a mayoral press-conference as an advocate for Latino rights. There, directing herself towards the public, Pastora speaks of the necessity of child care programs to help women working outside the home. However, her ideas about what needs to be done to fix this problem place private responsibility on the political agenda above the strengthening of the public. "Funding didn't have to come from the government. In the case of private industry, it should come from the company's profits."[19] The conversation that ensues then must focus on whether or not a private company should be so obligated, situating private corporations as the central decision-maker of how public functions should be administered and what courses of action should be ethically pursued in the interests of the public. However, if corporations are solely responsible for providing child care for their workers, citizens' roles are limited and corporate power is augmented in deciding what types of facilities and programs to implement. Contingently, the bottom line will always be the primary justification as cutting costs becomes more essential than providing for the public good. Additionally, women working for smaller companies would most likely not be able to benefit from such programs, while corporate values would enter the socialization process at an ever earlier age of a child's development. Castillo's understanding of political action would energize the corporate sector, making children into just another commodity to be traded on company profit and showing the government as unsuitable, if not ineffectual, in the care of its citizens. In other words, Castillo's anti-government vision is similar to Giuliani's in that she sees private and business control as more vital than public interventions in working for social change. As such, her work tends to clear space for a corporate expansion into people's everyday lives, an expansion that serves the interests of global capital, commercialism, and privatization at the expense of building a politics of the public good.

By relegating the care of citizens to the corporate sector, Castillo empties the public of the possibility for viable action. The public becomes then just another site for corporate profit. Likewise, by removing the homeless from city streets, Giuliani was making it impossible for the homeless to occupy any public space whatsoever while, at the same time, forcing the poor to justify their existence through work as the only valid measurement of human value. "'We're not going to be separating children from parents,' says deputy mayor Joe Lhota, 'We're asking able-bodied people to work 20 hours a week for their shelter. What's wrong with that?'"[20] The idea that labor productivity and human value can be equated certainly makes even the most marginal into replicants of corporate ideology (on the other hand, Giuliani himself does not have to justify his own occupation of a shelter paid for by tax-payer dollars, nor does he need to justify such non-productive activities as waging useless legal battles against, for example, publicly funded museums). Giuliani's requirement that the homeless in shelters be made useful reinvigorates a cultural confining of madness, which Foucault has identified as a "police matter," a way of controlling labor, or "the totality of measures which make work possible and necessary for all those who could not live without it."[21] For Foucault, madness threatens modernity with spectres of freedom, the return of the absolute liberties of animality, the outside of the determinism of a laboring order: "It was no longer merely a question," writes Foucault, "of confining those out of work, but of giving work to those who had been confined and thus making them contribute to the prosperity of all. The alternation is clear: cheap manpower in the periods of full employment and high salaries; and in periods of unemployment, reabsorption of the idle and social protection against agitation and uprisings."[22] In Giuliani's New York, the care of the homeless will be in the hands of the police whose practices Giuliani has defended even to the point of murder. Giuliani's "quality of life" policies have targeted, as Christian Parenti has shown, squeegee operators, youth truants, street vendors, sex shop owners, jaywalkers, recreational bikers and bike messengers, and African-American and other ethnic neighborhoods, cleaning up the city streets in order to make New York City safe and orderly for capital, investments, relocated service labor, and tourism and thereby to attract retail businesses in the form of Disney's conquest of Times Square and urban shopping malls. Public spaces like parks, schools, and the streets themselves fall increasingly under state surveillance, bans to entry, curfews, and drug and loitering laws while citizens are increasingly harassed by police for activities such as walking dogs without leashes, blocking sidewalks with beach chairs, or simply walking in public spaces at the wrong hour. Meanwhile, "complaints of police brutality have jumped by 62 percent since Rudolph Giuliani took office in 1994, while in the same period the city has paid out more than $100 million in damages arising from police violence."[23] As Giuliani increased police presence in the city, public funds shifted from providing safe refuges to clamping down on the public and enforcing law-and-order, from people to policing.

Moreover, Giuliani was claiming that this decision benefited the homeless by bolstering their self-esteem, self-respect, and self-worth. "I think this is the highest form of compassion and love," Giuliani announced, "to help people to help themselves, to get them to the point where they can take care of themselves, to ask them to do something in return for the help that they are being given by the city, state and the Federal Government."[24] For Giuliani, wage labor is the only measure of human value, the only activity that makes parents into exemplars of the laboring process for the benefit and healthy socialization of their children. Giuliani's earlier clampdown on taxi drivers for not accepting fares from minorities and his public denunciation of a pathetically attended Ku Klux Klan march both serve to evade, to obscure, if not to erase the utter and absolute racism of his decision to target the homeless and kick them out of the shelters just as winter set in. Moreover, Giuliani's proposition to remove children forcibly from their parents' care indicates that the discussion about homelessness also participates in a general scapegoating of mothers in particular, rather than government negligence or social policy, as the principal causes of social ills. Basically, by bringing up issues of parenting and child care, Giuliani reconceives the social problem of homelessness, as well as the debasement of public responsibility, as poor women's problem is with poor parenting.

So Far from God places the entire responsibility for the well-being of its characters in the development of a matriarchal Chicano community. What makes the novel feminist, according to critic Roland Walter, is the "strong images of . . . earthy women"[25] which produce an "implicit de-construction of the patriarchal order."[26] This paternalistic position, how-ever, by assuming that strong women are a rarity, implies that individual strength in women alone is enough to overturn the patriarchal order (as if this idea alone could challenge some sort of norm) without necessary schemes of economic redistribution which would give more than just emotional fortitude. Additionally, the main character Sofi learns to value herself through laboring, even though, contrary to Giuliani's initiatives, she works towards acquiring control over the means of production and the conditions of the workplace. Sofi's husband Domingo abandoned the family without saying where he was going or sending much money and only came back twenty years later once the four daughters had grown. Though Sofi brings up the four girls on her own, there is no insinuation here that there should be public assistance programs, aid to children, or child-care provisions. Sofi's heroism depends on her ability to do it on her own. "At least neither Sofi nor la doña Rita were on food stamps."[27] Any kind of government support stigmatizes while all oppositional ac-tion is directed against the state, in defense of the private: "And of course, la Caridad . . . was having long discussions . . . with Esperanza about the war, about the president's misguided policies, about how the public was being fooled about a lot of things that were going on behind the whole war business, how people could get some results by taking such measures as refusing to pay taxes."[28] Instead of being seen as a means of economic redistribution, providing social services and protec-tion from injustice, taxes hinder the citizen's freedom, federal action de-ceives, the state itself simply lies to and cheats the public, and the only avenue for contestation would be keeping funds intended for public sup-port under private control.

LA LOCURA

Ana Castillo's So Far from God is an example of a professedly feminist text that envisions mental illness as contrary to and even destructive of insti-tutional forces of power like religion, language, medicine, and patriarchy. The novel positions the mentally ill La Loca as a representative case of governmental failings, the weakness of public institutions, the insuffi-ciency of public interventions, and the absolute necessity of private citi-zens' taking responsibility for their own hardships. Castillo's vision of the mentally ill, as well as of the other social problems addressed in the novel (e.g., AIDS, rape, industrial toxins), is very similar to the neoliberalist ver-sion of the homeless and the mentally ill given by Giuliani. For Castillo as well as for Giuliani, the only two roles for the government are policing and the military. Unlike Giuliani, though, Castillo has a point and is legitimately criticizing the government for its racist practices and social injustices. In the face of wide-scale discrimination, anti-immigrant legislation, worker exploitation, educational exclusivity, and the like, Chicanos/as certainly have plenty of reason to criticize, resist, and revolt. As Castillo herself says in her work on Chicana feminism:

> When we profess a vision of a world where a woman is *not* raped somewhere in the United States every three minutes, where one of every female children do *not* experience sexual molestation, where the Mexican female is *not* the lowest paid worker in the United States—we are not male bashing or hating whites because overall they live a healthier life than we do, we are trying to change the facts of *our* conditions.[29]

Though fully in support of this project, we would still want to ask if there were any way to conceive of a government as other than either repressive and punitive or simply absent, a government that could actually address and amend issues of economic inequality, racial injustice, and violence proactively, a government that is instrumental in building up rather than in destroying public institutions of solidarity and alliance. As Ellen Willis observes, "American conservatives' success in weakening the federal government and starving it of funds will not lead to a democratic dispersal of power to local governments closer to the people; it will merely accelerate the process of consolidating corporate economic power on the transnational level. What can "American democracy" mean when no one even bothers to hide the fact that economic policy is made, not by elected officials accountable to their constituencies, but by the croupiers of global capital's floating crap game?"[30] Even though, as Willis later points out, historically "the modern state came into being to serve the needs of capital,"[31] dismissing state politics as therefore inimical to the interests of human freedom and equality might be a strategy which cuts off a politics of public possibility. Instead of writing off the welfare policies of the twentieth century as defeated or only set up in the interests of controlling labor and the underclasses and therefore defunct as a politics of social and democratic change, it is worthwhile to think of the state and the public as sites where the struggle for meaning, control, power, resources, and identities takes place. Instead of defining state institutions such as schools and medical services as contrary to human dignity and the good life, such publicly minded programs as multiculturalism, entering into debates about access to public schooling, should open up discussions about the relations between history, culture, and power, providing mechanisms and models for how citizens can use public knowledge in fighting oppressions.

This maligning of the public function of government has implications beyond the novel itself. Giuliani's attack on the homeless participates in a national debate over the role of government in providing health care. The status of Medicaid and Medicare, pharmaceutical plans for children and the elderly, infant vaccination campaigns, as well as debates over national health care have, since Clinton took office, all been undermined by the hard-core lobbying of private companies, the insurance industry, and their Congressional proponents. As well, Giuliani's measures against the homeless do not only extend the administration's commitment to ending welfare, but also grow out of an earlier attempt on the part of the city administration to cut back the social net supporting the care of the mentally ill in particular. In January 1999, a schizophrenic homeless man pushed a woman onto the subway tracks and killed her. A debate ensued about the status of funding for the treatment of the mentally ill. New York State governor George Pataki was advocating increased support of $125 million for hospitals, managers, housing, and treatment centers rather than dropping off the mentally ill, after brief hospital stays, under the Williamsburg Bridge with two subway tokens and $1.50 and letting them fend for themselves. Giuliani was opposed to the plan, even as hospitals had been depopulated (from 93,000 patients to 6,000, according to the *Daily News)* and outpatient services were clearly inadequate.[32] Subsequently, in November, a woman was bludgeoned with a brick and ended up in critical condition in a coma. The police were instructed to look for a suspect who was mentally ill and homeless even before ample evidence or substantial witness reports had been collected. The media decried the homeless as dangerous to the general public. *The New York Times,* for example, writes, "The mayor's pledge of renewed enforcement efforts came as there has been a widespread public outcry, including an unusual front-page editorial in the *Daily News* calling on the city to 'Get the Violent Crazies Off Our Streets.'"[33] Eventually a mentally ill homeless man was arrested as the attacker. Both the media and the city administration were assuming that the public posed a threat, and that the homeless, rather than social policy, were the source of this danger. As well, the supposed lawlessness and violent freedom of the mentally ill, in this case, serve the administration as a justification for augmenting the power of the police and of disciplining the public. Such a message encourages distrustfulness and scapegoating of the poor, undermining any possibility of alliances or community and creating antagonisms, apprehension, and even panic in the public sphere.

As in Giuliani's New York, Castillo shows madness as delimiting the no-go zone of governmental policy. *So Far from God* opens when a three-year-old girl dies in a seizure and, during her funeral, is resurrected and, defying the orders of the presiding priest, floats to the top of the church's roof. From then on she is known as La Loca. She is medically diagnosed as epileptic even as her mother continually is driven to convince the rest of the community that she is not, in fact, crazy. She lives in quasi-seclusion, refusing to associate with humans outside of the family because they smell bad. La Loca's feelings of disgust for other humans instill a sense throughout the novel that the public at large is both offensive and threatening: "This was only the beginning of the child's long life's phobia of people. . . . For the rest of her life . . . , she was to be repulsed by the smell of humans. She claimed that all humans bore an odor akin to that which she smelled in the places she had passed through when she was dead."[34] Castillo does not acknowledge here that La Loca's disgust at others' hygienics falls within a current popular rationale for distrusting the public and for cutting public services. For example, in 1992, New York City was hysterical over cases of tuberculosis because of the appearance of new strains resistant to old cures. Tuberculosis is an AIDS-related bacterium which can be transported through the air, so any kind of close physical contact with a carrier could cause an infection. "Kindled by the AIDS epidemic, and fueled powerfully by urban crowding, homelessness, immigration, drug abuse and the rapid disappearance of preventive-medicine health clinics in cities from New York to Los Angeles, . . . tuberculosis," reports *The New York Times*, "is spread in tiny droplets through the air. It moves with grim efficiency in places like poorly ventilated homeless shelters, overcrowded clinic waiting rooms and prisons."[35] Public spaces are being invaded by invisible death-carriers, black poisons, noxious death-dealing viruses, and body snatchers. The *Times* is using disease to create a paranoia about public spaces, about the homeless, immigrants, and prisoners, and a general sense that neighborliness, community, and publicly supported institutions promise only fatality and should therefore be distrusted. This distrust and vilification of all-things-public, in turn, produces an ideological support for the private powers coming to imminence through globalization: the body's immune system is an economic gateway separating domestic health from contaminant economically draining cultures: different races, disease, affliction, political turmoil, and their concomitant bad smells. As a recent *Newsweek* update on tuberculosis adds, "In a world without fences, our neighbors' health becomes our own worry."[36]

As a result of La Loca's disgust for other human beings, she never attends school, learns incredible lessons (like how to heal and play the fiddle) through isolated inspirations, and she refuses to visit public hospitals. Yet, she communicates mystically with animals and possesses healing powers, even curing her sisters of, for example, the despair of rape in the case of Caridad, of abandonment in the case of Fe, and performing abortions on Esperanza. La Loca's healing powers demonstrate that individuals and families on their own initiatives are more successful in curing or attending to the sick and helpless than are public health institutions, presenting the family as safe and nurturing precisely because it is free from politics. La Loca's situation sets up a sense developed in many of the novel's story lines that public institutions are ineffectual, uninformed, and generally unfavorable to the safety, security, well-being, and health of their clients. Private businesses work better. "Once the baby was able to receive medical attention," writes Castillo about the aftermath of the resurrection, "(although Sofi took her child this time to a hospital in Albuquerque rather than to rely on the young doctor at the Valencia County clinic who had so rashly declared her child dead), it was diagnosed that she was in all probability an epileptic."[37] As government is proven untrustworthy and the public shows itself as too smelly and repellant for compassion, La Loca takes up the mantle. It is now her responsibility alone to care for the afflicted in her family. La Loca's madness shows how individual talents can fix affliction when freed from government. Instead of offering ideas about how to re-establish the effectual protection and strengthening of the public through transforming and funding public institutions, *So Far from God* suggests that public problems need to be addressed as private concerns, giving up altogether on possibilities for public intervention.

Mental illness is a charged social category, full of implications for reinforcing social identities, helplessness, and hierarchies in a class structure. And yet, because mental illness seems in itself to break through the restrictions of a rationalized culture, it also often indicates a break or disruption in the rationalization of daily life and particularly in its institutions. As such, cultural theoreticians have recreated mental illness as a sign of resistance to dominant paradigms of grammar, sense, logic, and comprehension. For example, Hélène Cixous:

> In the front line was Dora, who fascinated me, because here was an eighteen-year-old girl caught in a world where you say to yourself, she is going to break—a captive, but with such strength! I could not keep from laughing from one end to the other, because, despite her powerlessness and with (thanks to) that powerlessness, here is a kid who successfully jams all the little adulterous wheels that are turning around her and, one after the other, they break down. She manages to say what she doesn't say, so intensely that the men drop like flies. We can very well see how—at what moment, in what scenes, by which meaning—she has cut through.[38]

Particularly in feminism, mental illness has served as an indication of difference, principally because of the history of women's sexuality being medicalized as a hysterical symptom and the ways in which psychoanalysis developed as a response. The argument that dementia challenges or even overthrows regimes of rationality follows from a feminist appropriation of the Lacanian pre-Symbolic. According to such feminist positions, the time before language is the time of identification with the mother, a time when the grammar and logic of language can be transformed along with all the social institutions which support it.

Julia Kristeva, explaining the "semiotic chora," the poetics of modernity, writes:

> By exploding the phonetic, lexical, and syntactic object of linguistics, this practice not only escapes the attempted hold of all anthropomorphic sciences. . . . Ultimately, it exhausts the ever tenacious ideological institutions and apparatuses. . . . This signifying practice . . . attests to a "crisis" of social structures and their ideological, coercive, and necrophilic manifestations. . . . There emerge, in retrospect, fragmentary phenomena which have been kept in the background or rapidly integrated into more communal signifying systems but point to the very process of significance. Magic, shamanism, esoterism, the carnival, and "incomprehensible" poetry all underscore the limits of socially useful discourse and attest to what it represses. . . . Under what conditions does this "esoterism," in displacing the boundaries of socially established signifying practices, correspond to socioeconomic change, and, ultimately, even to revolution?[39]

One of the problems of such an argument is that it assumes that social change happens first at the level of language, and certainly, if changing, reforming, or revolutionizing language could alter or uproot the oppressive systems that support it, mental illness could be the big, bad wolf that blows the straw off of the structures of power. This infers that a crisis of cultural intelligibility would cause the system's breakdown, even when it has become obvious that mass culture knows precisely how to absorb such unintelligibilities and breakdowns in meaning, as it does with such phenomena as the Jerry Springer show. Additionally, depictions of psychic strife as revolutionary tend to privatize resistance, containing it within the dysfunctions of the psyche rather than dispersing it throughout the social. However, Giuliani's attack on the mentally ill serves to bolster his anti-federalist policies and neoliberal ideologies which are more than just linguistic edifices, proving that power cannot be overturned simply by undoing systems of signification. In this instance, the powerlessness of the mentally ill cannot be idealized as dismantling the system but is, instead, part of what greases the wheels of systematic oppression. Stopping the bloodbath of the poor will hardly result from non-sense, baby-talk, and poetry. This is not to deny the fact that there is a psychic life of power, and that there do exist certain psychological/linguistic edifices upon which the social order hangs, and certainly there can be no criticism of power without accounting for how power operates through language and representation. However, a feminism which uses psychoanalytic theory to individualize power and responsibility simply repeats and defends neoliberal doctrine, hiding it under diagnostic and culturalist metaphors, and thereby contributes to the global impoverishment of women. This type of feminism needs to be revamped if not discarded in order to reconfigure the political in ways that reduce violence, further popular justice, allow collective action, and increase democracy.

Chicana feminism has often understood mental illness as a form of thinking difference and counterhegemonic challenge. This motif follows from a Latin American and particularly Mexican literary tradition which Jean Franco has identified as the voice of the *mystérique*, seventeenth-century nuns who went into epileptic rapture in communicating with God and whose language—"halting, disjointed, or apparently irrational babble" (3)—was transcribed as mystical, a vehicle for truth: "'Mysticism' was a language of the self and the body that women could speak and, if they were fortunate, could legitimately speak. . . . [Yet,] mysticism was too close to the practices of the heretical *alumbrados* whose satanic pride was fueled by their intoxicating visions."[40] Empowered on the margins, fragmentary, contradictory, complex and multiple, the Chicana feminist voice claims itself as a defiance of white, male, privileged authority, power, normality, and meaning production. As Gloria Anzaldúa writes:

> The Third World woman revolts: *We revoke, we erase your white male imprint. When you come knocking on our doors with your rubber stamps to brand our faces with DUMB, HYSTERICAL, PASSIVE PUTA, PERVERT, when you come with your branding irons to burn MY PROPERTY on our bottocks, we will vomit the guilt, self-denial and race-hatred you have force-fed into us right back into your mouth.*[41] (original italics)

As in Schreber, schizophrenic language, in its multiple interrupting voices, changes reality: "The order of the World reveals its grandeur and magnificence by denying even God Himself in so irregular a case as mine the means of achieving a purpose contrary to the Order of the World."[42] The shift between different voices and different languages in Chicano/a literature, evident in frequent splatterings of Spanish as well as in idiomatized and vernacular typified speech, is meant to decode the binaries of domination and reverse or transcend hierarchical orders in schizophrenic transformations.

PRIVATE PROPERTY AND THE ABSENCE OF COMMUNITY

Sofi's self-sufficiency, however, is reliant on her own property holdings which, unlike for the homeless in New York City, guarantee La Loca and her family shelter until the end. When Domingo loses the house in a gamble and Sofi has to start paying rent, Sofi talks about how her rights to ownership—not only of the house but also of the butcher shop business—are part of her Chicana legacy, going back to the land grant from the Spanish crown. In other words, private property is her rightful heritage, the underpinnings of both her identity and her empowerment, her protection. Granted, New Mexican land has been continually taken from Chicanos as they lose competitive edge to consolidated capital and large-scale, technologized producers. However, Castillo does not consider those Chicanos who are not privileged enough to acquire deeds from kings, nor does she give any sense at all that though housing should be an entitlement, for many it never is, even if they can pay rent. The limitation of considering "the primacy of domesticity as a site for subversion,"[43] as bell hooks recommends, is that, in the case of *So Far from God*, domesticity so easily substitutes for the privilege of property which is not available to all. To say that "the home space in Castillo's novel is infused with political resistance"[44] is really to circumscribe potential activism within a community with rights to deeds and titles. What is more, Sofi loses the house "to a *judge,* a servant of the people, for heaven's sake!"[45] Again, it is the vile and corrupt government with its tainted systems of justice—in the colonialist tradition of "the gringos [who] took most of our land away when they took over the territory from Mexico"[46]—that gets in the way of the natural rights of people to take care of themselves by, in this case, owning private property. Redistribution can only serve the rich to get richer: the state official, the representative of justice is interested only in private acquisitions rather than in building municipal holdings for public housing. Following in the tradition of liberalism, *So Far from God* upholds private property as the basis for self-sufficiency and political empowerment.

Sofi starts a political movement to get the community to keep the land and businesses as communal property, defending them from outsiders who are buying up the properties of original families to breed peacocks instead of sheep. Sofi's conception of politics consists of a self-help program of community uplift, a personal effort to take the place of ineffectual and absent government programs. "The only way things are going to get better around here," she says, "is if *we,* all of us together, try to do something about it."[47] Sofi's activism involves establishing a cooperative and then running for mayor in the town of Tome in order to improve living conditions for its inhabitants. The cooperative would start a sheep-grazing and a wool-weaving enterprise (complete with child care and college credit) in order to establish "economic self-sufficiency . . . [because] the government had no money to lend them, so they were on their own."[48] Tome had never had a mayor and, indeed, most of the residents hardly ever voted. Absent are any viable possibilities for governmental aid or institutional supports for basic public freedoms. Only without government can economic innovations be practiced and vitalized and new types of organized production tested. There is no suggestion here that government could be instrumental in fostering ideas and building institutions in order to counter mainstream economic exclusivity. Responsibility for change or for any organized political challenge is completely transferred into the hands of individuals in segregated communities.

Indeed, the only real functions for government in *So Far from God* (as in Giuliani's New York) are militaries and policing, and these functions override completely the will and consideration of the public. The oldest sister, Esperanza, dies when she becomes prisoner of the Saudis while reporting on a war. The federal government was negligent in ensuring her safety, searching for her whereabouts, committing to save her, or, in the end, retrieving her body: "Sofi and Domingo wrote letters and made telephone calls to congressmen and senators and were even invited by one big shot to Washington, but nobody had yet found out anything about what happened to Esperanza and her crew."[49] When Caridad is raped, the police investigation drops off rather quickly due to a heartless police morality and its disregard for public safety: "But there are still those for whom there is no kindness in their hearts for a young woman who has enjoyed life, so to speak. . . . And as the months went by, little by little, the scandal and shock of Caridad's assault were forgotten, by the news media, the police, the neighbors, and the church people. She was left in the hands of her family, a nightmare incarnated."[50] Most egregiously, when Fe was unknowingly contaminated by industrial toxins at Acme International—a firm subcontracted by the Pentagon to build parts for high-tech weapons—the FBI investigators blamed her, rather than her employers, for the spill.

In not one of these crises is there ever any kind of prior public organization or political group working for change. Fe dies without a union or an environmentalist lobby to defend her rights, alone before an unfriendly legal bureaucracy as she quickly develops fatal skin sores, lesions, bad breath, and internal organ disintegration. Likewise, when the lesbian couple gets chased by an armed vigilante on a country road, there is no sense that this is not an isolated or aberrant incident performed by a madman, a country bumpkin, or an "asshole" (126), but instead part of a vast and systematic campaign of hatred, intolerance, homophobia, and violence operating on both a social and discursive level to police sexualities, and that gays and lesbians have been organizing, consciousness raising, and building social movements of pride and awareness to combat it, especially in the past thirty years since Stonewall. Then La Loca contracts AIDS. Nobody knows quite how she contracts it, as she refuses all human contact. Nevertheless, the novel presents no solidarity networks or political associations working to increase funding for AIDS research, to legislate checks against discrimination, to offer hospice to the sick and suffering and human compassion to their families. There is no sense here that home-care workers have been unionizing to provide better and more affordable services to the sick and disabled.[51] Instead, the public is devoid of any politics. *So Far from God* treats diseases and epidemics as an individual rather than a social problem, relegating responsibility for caring and curing to the isolated family unit. In the comfort of her own home, which she refuses to leave, La Loca is visited by a curandero, Dr. Tolentino, who advises faith, prayer, votive candles, herbs, kerosene, boiling water, and offerings of cookies to the saints. Gone is any consideration of those AIDS victims who are without homes and family, for example, the "hundreds of people in the last two years [who] have had to stay on the streets or with friends when the city did not have room for them" in New York. According to *The New York Times,* there are an estimated 2,000 homeless people with AIDS in New York City. The current law in New York says that the city must provide housing for homeless AIDS victims within twenty-four hours. With low immune defenses, such people are put at major risk from even a night on the streets. Yet, lawyers for the city have said that "it's not in any way a widespread problem" if clients had to wait even longer than the specified twenty-four-hour period for shelter.[52] In its intense advocacy of personal politics and empowerment as the solution to such social crises, *So Far from God* is not able to envision the obvious need for government and public policy to be redesigned with the intention of constructing a better "quality of life," enfranchisement, and political possibility for the public at large, one, for example, not uniformly in line with a middle-class or commercial desire for safety, security, law, order, profit-crunching, family privacy, and the image of cleanliness.

For Castillo, politics and political vision need to focus on reconstructing indigenous spiritualism, which has been crushed under Western imperial expansion. Working together with institutionalized religion, capitalism's eradication of spiritualism goes hand-in-hand with the repression of the feminine, of sexuality, of Mother worship, the goddess principle, and the body. "Here is the juncture in our story where I believe Xicanisma is formed," she says of her feminism:

> In the acknowledgement of the historical crossroad where the creative power of woman became deliberately appropriated by male society. And woman in the flesh, thereafter, was subordinated. It is our task as Xicanistas, to not only reclaim our indigenismo—but also to reinsert the forsaken feminine into our consciousness. . . . The very act of self-definition is a rejection of colonization.[53]

This implies that only through extreme individualism can political freedom be achieved. What is more, this kind of individualism—this spiritual alternative to politics—makes mothering responsible for public order and improvement: "If we believe in a value system that seeks the common good of members of society," she writes, "by applying the very qualities and expectations we have placed on motherhood to our legislature and our social system—to care selflessly for her young, to be responsible for her children's material, spiritual and emotional needs—we are providing for the future."[54] Symbolizing touchy-feely tenderness and the sentimental in human relationships, a personalized, individualized motherhood, instead of social institutions and working systems of justice, is supposed to, as in Giuliani's New York, take up responsibility for the failings of the political.

What Castillo misses is that spiritual practices or relationships of motherhood are not going to restitute a public torn asunder by current day imperialist forces and the new corporatisms. What she does not consider is what kind of politics is necessary at *both* the state and community levels to offset, obstruct, and even end the role of corporations in gouging the public, polluting public spaces, causing diseases, abandoning the helpless, restricting economic access, denying services, impoverishing families, and driving desperate people away from their homes. When Domingo loses her house in a gamble, Sofi is still allowed to live there, albeit the insult is that now she has to pay rent for what was formerly her right to own. Contingently, Castillo characterizes corporate injuries to citizens as personal, and citizens' responses carried out as familial, affective obligations. For example, at one point Sofi notices that La Loca is wearing a pair of blue jeans with the label torn off. When asked why, La Loca responds, "I saw on T.V. that some people in a factory are boycotting the company that makes these jeans. . . . You know. Mom. Una factory that is unfair to its workers, just like where le Fe worked at."[55] The political is here so far reduced to the personal—to the family—that there is no room to discuss exactly how the manufacturer is engaging in unfair labor practices and in what ways the global capitalist system as a whole is promoting such practices as child labor, unprotected work spaces, sweatshops, lack of adequate insurance provisions, insufficient environmental regulations, and the like, while hiding—not exposing—its atrocities beneath the corporate screening of television news programming.

The novel's resolution occurs as, when all the daughters have died, Sofi founds a spiritual group of mothers called M.O.M.A.S. (Mothers of Martyrs and Saints), which congregates to call back the spirits of their dead children. Though certainly concerned with political issues like uranium contamination on Navajo reservations, pesticides, nuclear power plants, radioactive waste dumps, and the lowering poverty level of Native and Hispanic families, M.O.M.A.S.'s annual conference became a spectacle and a commercial fairground triumphantly compared to Disney World. In Castillo's resolution, activism gets corporatized. Castillo does not, however, show M.O.M.A.S.'s connection to other organizations of mothers calling back dead children, like the Mothers of the Disappeared in the

Plaza de Mayo movement in Argentina, where the disappearance of children was and still is linked to the harsh measures of a military government in the service of neoliberalization. Rather, the ghosts that M.O.M.A.S. calls back gossip with their families and friends and this in itself arouses skepticism in public officials, "which, I guess," Castillo concludes, "is the nature of politics."[56] Castillo's recourse to a feminist spiritualism as *the* agenda for political action only sees politics as an expression of transcendent individual autonomy and personal empowerment, feelings, and care for friends and family, and inhibits imagining public institutions or movements which could, alternatively, reduce corporate power and strengthen the public cause of democracy.

DARK DAYS

This personalizing of poverty and hardship means that the political and social causes of poverty can be whitewashed, and the homeless themselves can be envisioned as people who are being punished for stepping off the path of righteousness rather than as the inevitable result of capitalism's need for labor surpluses and the imperative towards growth and accumulation. Another example of this pervasive view that poverty results from personal failings can be found in Marc Singer's film *Dark Days*. Winner of three prizes at the year 2000 Sundance Film Festival (Cinematography, Freedom of Expression, and the Audience Award), *Dark Days* is a black-and-white documentary about a community of homeless people living in the Amtrak tunnel under New York City. The film is replete with images of the homeless sleeping, cooking, eating, cleaning, shaving, cutting hair, decorating their cardboard dwellings, taking care of pets—in other words, performing the mundane rituals of everyday life that emphasize their humanness. Their confessions tell of harmful mistakes that landed them in their current positions, whether doing drugs or abandoning their children or doing petty crimes.

While focusing obsessively on the human universality of their fears and compassions, the film never shows the homeless interacting with people who are not homeless, nor does it show the world above, that is, the world of capital exchange and labor markets, as though these social elements are somehow irrelevant to this story. In fact, at one point, one of the informants tells of his desire to get an entertainment center for his TV along with a set of couches, and yet the film never explains the corporate media's creation of these types of consumers, commercial images of the "perfect home" which are so influential in ideologically, politically, and materially marginalizing the homeless. What saves this particular homeless man from the misery and alienation of the tunnels is his assimilation into a consumer market, just as one of his neighbors is saved as he confesses his profuse appreciation for a low-level service-sector job of which he promises never to miss a day. The message is clear: the life of consumption offered by these cookie-cutter apartments and cookie-cutter jobs is the personal antidote to hell. The film never suggests that the homeless could want anything but this atomized life of banal accumulation and lack-luster consumer dreams, for instance, that they might want access to education or living conditions that promoted, rather than fractured, the possibilities for continuing the community organization they had already established.

Instead of exposing or criticizing the politics of homelessness in New York City, the filmmaker himself admits, "I never wanted to go on a mission with this film. I never wanted to convert anyone into helping the homeless."[57] Why make a film about the homeless without wanting change? For the *Village Voice,* indeed, the reduction of social problems to aesthetic images is what constitutes the film's beauty and humanity: "Singer's portrait of two years in the life of New York's underground dwellers is wrenchingly beautiful. It shows the crack addicts, the rat roasters, and the scavengers."[58] The film constructs beauty out of homelessness because, the *Voice* continues, the filmmaker loves his subjects: "I never felt more accepted in my whole life than I did down there," Singer explains. "They were my best friends, my family."[59] Helping the homeless would therefore be a sentimental and personal concern rather than a public commitment.

In the end, both Amtrak and the city administration combine forces to get apartments for the film's subjects, suggesting that the homeless have atoned for their human sins and, as a result, have been rewarded, emerging out of the dark tunnels into light and airy suburban New Jersey. A private corporation emerges as the story's hero. The film insinuates that the tragedy ends there, that the problem of homelessness has been resolved. There is never any sense that homelessness persists because the social system that produced it still exists. Instead, a private and public partnership is formed to save the desperate, rather than, as the Giuliani administration has amply demonstrated, to defeat them. Screened at New York City's Film Forum, the film sold out over Labor Day weekend and was greeted with enthusiastic audience applause. *Dark Days,* indeed, does not convert. Instead of inspiring its viewers to change the conditions that create homelessness, the film confirms that all is well in the state of Denmark and that the homeless are loveable. The film arouses more sympathetic laughter, acceptance, and identifications with the all-too-human homeless than discomfort or angry indignation.

MARKETING INTELLIGENCE

In *So Far from God* , the non-recognition of a history of public culture and social movements demonstrates that the debate about the status of the New York City homeless participates in a broader cultural logic whereby responsibility for public order is firmly placed in the hands of private power rather than in the jurisdiction of public institutions. Giuliani's reason for pulling public services for the homeless and the mentally ill is that the social effects of mental illness can be counteracted in the self-determinism of a deregulated marketplace allowing for, even requiring the expression of free will. In other words, Giuliani argues that economic misery, oppressive social conditions, and the marginalization of identities are all subject to change, but change wholly contingent on the market, while the market itself is the only cure for social sicknesses, the only way out of incapacitating stagnancy, the only possibility for agency.[60]

Giuliani's contention that the market, free of government regulations (meaning, social services), will counteract the negative social effects of mental illness comes out of a slew of mass-mediated projections about the future of intelligence and its construction as a commodity. Dietary supplements that improve memory—e.g., Bayer's new Consumer Care vitamin pills labeled "Memory and Concentration Formula" made $8,000 in profits—and the not-so-futuristic genetic enhancers for memory and intelligence will soon become purchasable if they are not already, promising an intelligence based on market rationality and the rationality of property. As *Time* magazine envisions, "If you suffer from MCI ["mild cognitive impairment"], you might consistently come out of the mall and not remember where you parked your car (with dementia, you'd forget that you even owned one in the first place)."[61] In the mainstream media, intelligence is consistently measured as the ability to maneuver in the market and own property while rationality itself consists in the cunning to outwit and cheat competitors in struggles to acquire products and profits. *Time* uses the evidence of tricky profit-seeking to prove the evolution of intelligence in animals:

> Consider the time that Charlene Jendry was in her office at the Columbus Zoo and word came to her that a male gorilla named Colo was clutching a suspicious object. Arriving on the scene, Charlene offered Colo some peanuts, only to be met with a blank stare. Realizing that they were negotiating, Charlene upped the ante and offered a piece of pineapple. At this point, without making eye contact with Charlene, Colo opened his hand and revealed that he was holding a key chain, much in the manner that a fence might furtively show a potential customer stolen goods on the street. Relieved that it was not anything dangerous or valuable, Charlene gave Colo the piece of pineapple. Astute bargainer that he was, Colo then broke the key

chain and gave Charlene a link, perhaps figuring, "Why give her the whole thing if I can get a bit of pineapple for each piece?" If an animal can show some skill in the barter business, why not in handling money?[62]

In equating intelligence to rational performance in the market, *Time* does not mention that, indeed, intelligence and memory are produced by an industry that is becoming consolidated on a global level at almost the same pace as the telecommunications industry. As the leading research-driven pharmaceutical company Merck & Co. develops their drug PRAISE as an antidote to Alzheimer's disease and Mild Cognitive Impairment ("a memory problem characterized by increasing forgetfulness and memory difficulties such as not remembering . . . items from a grocery list"), it has merged with the biotech company Sibia Neurosciences (a company that researches nervous system disorders), buying it intact for $87 million in cash ("Chicago Team Joins Alzheimer's Prevention Study").

The meaning of intelligence is conflated with the ability to buy and to consume, and just as in Giuliani's depictions of the homeless, the ability to buy, to deal economically—to think freely and rationally rather than irrationally—is guaranteed in the withdrawal of government from regulating business practices allowing for corporate consolidations. Intelligence is instituted through globalization and the gutting of public interventions. As Donna Haraway has argued, the consolidation of biotechnological companies has led to a few people getting rich off of speculation while the public itself gets locked out of decision-making about the direction of science and technology, even when the government is involved and tax money is invested: corporate power is replacing democratic processes and debilitating a public assessment of the common good. Writes Haraway, "In 1994, the new director of the National Institutes of Health (NIH), Nobel Prize winner Harold Varmus, as he looked for new ways to link NIH, academia, and industry, was quoted as saying, "We're not interested in giving grants to Merck. We're interested in giving grants to small business. . . . It is hard to find solace in such reassurance."[63]

PUBLIC ACTION

This is the same anti-government logic that informs *So Far from God*. The homeless and the mentally ill need to take care of themselves, the logic goes, and such a diminishment in the government's obligations to its citizens is for everybody's own good because it produces self-sufficiency and autonomy. This belief fails to assess six outcomes: (1) that everybody is not equally advantaged nor equally free nor equally able to provide for him/herself privately, and certainly the social playing field favors some

(2) that service and corporate labor are not adequate ways of ˥uman potential because they reduce freedom to a market ͜t, in the liberal tradition, "rights" discourse is based in property ownership, and that the current emphasis on "identity" supports a politics founded in private rights to ownership; (4) that government is not the only possibility for forming public contestations or public cultures; (5) that critiquing government does not necessarily require a vilification of all-things-public; and (6) that privatization means the consolidation of power at the global, corporate level at the expense of democratic culture and, indeed, the personal empowerment of citizens. Instead of stepping in to create the conditions of equality, the government in *So Far from God*— representing the only source of public action—is prohibits fairness and prosperity. Meanwhile, Giuliani supports an anti-federalist agenda where the individual can and, indeed, must determine his or her own well-being, thus making individuals accountable for their own quality of life while denying any kind of possible public action in defense of a wider public good. Citizens who are not homeless can safely believe that the homeless and the mentally ill are responsible for their own hardships, or at the very least, if they wanted to badly enough or if they worked a little harder, could change their situations, overcoming all those silly little obstacles like racism, sexism, the stigmatization of the poor and of immigrants, the criminalization of drug addicts, housing crises, educational inequalities, the growth of a police state, the deskilling of labor, the gutting of the inner city, welfare cuts, and other barriers to economic mobility, both institutional and ideological.

Despite the present austerity and hard-discipline face of the modern state, there are still spaces within state-supported institutions like public schooling where democratic dialogues, critical perspectives, and imagined futures can be developed. One might wonder here, too, if governmental institutions are the only viable tool for rekindling a beleaguered public sphere, or if the public can be reconceived through social movements (like the anti-WTO rallies in Seattle and Washington, D.C.) rather than being solely dependent on state support. After all, with the ascension of transnational corporations as the standard operative political power, nation-state-based interventions in support of the public have dissipated.[64] As a result, citizens, voters, public advocates, and activists are at a loss: given the way the current nation-state seems nested in the interests of big capital, rendering it virtually incapable of working for the promotion of democratic politics or providing institutions for public agency, the question remains, then, as to whether or not the creation of global institutions to implement checks on corporate power is feasible, in the current context, outside of the traditional framework of the nation, that is, whether globalization can and will allow for a divorce between the state and the public for the strengthening of broad-based public action and resistance movements, and also whether or not serious economic redistributions on a global scale can be carried out outside of the welfare state model.

Certainly, there are examples of literatures which have adamantly critiqued and resisted state power without thereby relegating all public power to the private, the sentimental, and the individual consumer. For instance, Brazilian novelist Clarice Lispector's *The Hour of the Star* tells of Macabéa, a poor orphaned migrant mixed-blood woman from the northeast who has come to the city to work as a typist. Addicted to cold-cream, advertising slogans, and Coke, Macabéa, riddled with malnutrition and tuberculosis, imagines herself to be Marilyn Monroe. When a fortune teller predicts that she will meet a foreigner who will fall in love with her and she will inherit his fortune, she at last feels alive, happily steps off the curb, and immediately gets run down by a golden imported Mercedes-Benz. She bleeds to death on the sidewalk as a crowd gathers around to watch. The novel's narrative is periodically interrupted by the play of military drums. As Brazil at the time was under the rule of a military dictatorship, the references to an ever-present military band evoke the state's indifference to, and even casual acceptance of, the plight of such citizens as Macabéa, and suggest that the public itself has been tragically atomized and impoverished by the government's support of economic liberalization, the selling of the poor and of labor to foreign trade. Instead of depicting the restrictions to individuals posed by public actions, Lispector indicates that individuals are forced into desperation because of the state's dismantling of public responsibility. Additionally, a book like *I, Rigoberta Menchú* clearly proposes organizational politics that defy state oppressions by empowering communities. Menchú shows how indigenous peoples in Guatemala established resistant coalitions that served to educate a marginalized population and then to defend themselves against the oppressions of the military. Here, opposing the unjust policies of states does not mean withdrawing into family privacy, affective attachments, or psychological idiosyncrasies but rather creating alliances for future insurrections.[65]

Culture work needs to consider how it operates politically and pedagogically to expand the possibilities for envisioning new types of governing which do not simply feed ideologies of corporatism and back the growth of capitalist affluence. This will entail creating the possibility of imagining different social relationships, including a politics of public responsibility and resistance to the crushing spread of ever more consolidated corporatist power and the governments which support it, with all the accompanying destructive and even deadly consequences, with all the resulting racist and sexist practices. As Peter McLaren observes, "The struggle for a revolutionary socialism is the preeminent struggle of our time. While not all social relations are subordinate to capital or overdetermined by economic relations, most social relations constitutive of racialed and gendered identities are considerably shaped by the social division of labor and the social relations of production. . . . I agree . . . that 'at the very heart of the new pluralism is a failure to confront (and often explicit denial of) the overarching totality of capitalism as a social system, which is constituted by class exploitation but which shapes all "identities" and social relations.'"[66] Neglecting the politics of capital and policies of distribution when considering literary production and analyses will certainly undermine any move towards recognizing and establishing an equitable pluralism, opportunities for organizing towards freedom and imagining alternatives.

NOTES

1. As cited in David M. Herszenhorn, "Mayor Accuses Critics of Scare Tactics," *New York Times*, 17 October 1999, B3.

2. See, for example, "Misguided Shelter Reform," *New York Times*, 28 October 1999, A30, late edition; and Kathi Wolfe, "Who Will Care for Their Children? Aging Parents Worry About Ill Sons and Daughters Whom They Will Leave Behind," *Washington Post*, 26 October 1999, Z09.

3. Citizens Housing & Planning Council, "Paying the Rent: An Evaluation of the Section 8 Housing Program in New York City," www.housingnyc.com/research/html_reports/chpc/chpc3.html, October 1997.

4. Herszenhorn, "Mayor Accuses Critics," B3. Giuliani's policies towards the homeless do have historical precedent. See Ron Scapp, "Lack and Violence: Towards a Speculative Sociology of the Homeless," *Practice* 6, no. 2 (Fall 1988) for an analysis of how the Koch administration rounded up and mistreated the homeless. Scapp argues that homelessness keys into very deep anxieties in American culture having to do with an ideology that determines personhood and rationality through property ownership as well as with the history of domestic settlement—the "homestead"—on the western frontier.

5. As cited in J. A. Lobbia, "Wake-Up Call For Rudy," *Village Voice*, 14 December 1999, 56.

6. Kamala Platt, "Ecocritical Chicana Literature: Ana Castillo's 'Virtual Realism,'" *Interdisciplinary Studies in Literature and Environment* 3, no. 1 (Summer 1996): 87.

7. Robert Kuttner, *Everything for Sale: The Virtues and Limits of Markets* (New York: Columbia University Press, 1998), 7.

8. Zygmunt Bauman, *In Search of Politics* (Stanford, Calif.: Stanford University Press, 1999), 98.

9. Edward S. Herman and Robert W. McChesney, *The Global Media: The New Missionaries of Corporate Capitalism* (London: Cassell, 1997), 3.

10. Henry A. Giroux, *The Mouse That Roared: Disney and the End of Innocence* (Lanham, Md.: Rowman & Littlefield, 1999), 20.

11. Bauman, *In Search of Politics*, 96. "One often hears alarms about the invasion or surreptitious colonization of daily life by public powers. As a rule the argument used to justify the alarm is an updated, rehashed version of once well-grounded fears of the state usurping undivided rule over the *agora*. Under present conditions, however, such an argument in any of its many renditions seems less to derive from the diagnosis of the current dangers as to be a recycled product of historical memories."

12. Randy Martin, "Globalization? The Dependencies of a Question," *Social Text 60*, 17, no. 3 (Fall 1999): 4.

13. See Robin D. G. Kelley, *Yo' Mama's Disfunktional!* (Boston: Beacon, 1997) for an insightful analysis of this phenomenon and the ideology of self-help, particularly as it refers to African-American political movements like the Nation of Islam.

14. Ana Castillo, *So Far from God* (New York: Plume, 1993), 139.

15. Bauman, *In Search of Politics*, 199.

16. Roland Walter, "The Cultural Politics of Dislocation and Relocation in the Novels of Ana Castillo," *MELUS* 23, no. 1 (Spring 1998): 82–83.

17. Theresa Delgadillo, "Forms of Chicana Feminist Resistance: Hybrid Spirituality in Ana Castillo's *So Far from God*," *Modern Fiction Studies* 44, no. 4 (Winter 1998): 889.

18. Delgadillo, "Forms of Chicana Feminist Resistance," 888.

19. Ana Castillo, *Sapogonia* (New York: Anchor Books, 1990), 312–13.

20. As cited in Jodie Morse, "Cracking Down on the Homeless," *Time*, 20 December 1999, 70.

21. Michel Foucault, *Madness and Civilization: A History of Insanity in the Age of Reason*, translated by Richard Howard (New York: Vintage Books, 1965), 46.

22. Foucault, *Madness and Civilization*, 51.

23. Christian Parenti, *Lockdown America: Police and Prisons in the Age of Crisis* (London: Verso, 1999), 83.

24. Herszenhorn, "Mayor Accuses Critics," B3.

25. Walter, "The Cultural Politics of Dislocation and Relocation," 89.

26. Walter, "The Cultural Politics of Dislocation and Relocation," 88.

27. Castillo, *So Far from God*, 217.

28. Castillo, *So Far from God*, 163.

29. Ana Castillo, *Massacre of the Dreamers: Essays on Xicanisma* (New York: Plume, 1994), 225.

30. Ellen Willis, *Don't Think, Smile! Notes on a Decade of Denial* (Boston: Beacon, 1999), 8.

31. Willis, *Don't Think, Smile!* 184.

32. "Returning Sanity to Mental Policy," *Daily News*, 15 November 1999, 32.

33. Thomas J. Lueck, "Police Predict Few Arrests of Homeless," *New York Times*, 21 December 1999, 45.

34. Castillo, *So Far from God*, 23.

35. Michael Specter, "Neglected Years, TB Is Back with Strains that Are Deadlier," *New York Times*, 11 October 1992, 1.

36. Thomas Hayden, "Tuberculosis Is Making a Comeback," *Newsweek*, 8 November 1999, 77.

37. Castillo, *So Far from God*, 25.

38. Hélène Cixous and Catherine Clément, *The Newly Born Woman*, translated by Betsy Wing (Minneapolis: University of Minnesota Press, 1986), 150.

39. Julia Kristeva, *Revolution in Poetic Language,* translated by Margaret Waller (New York: Columbia University Press, 1984), 15–16.

40. Jean Franco, *Plotting Women: Gender and Representation in Mexico* (New York: Columbia University Press, 1989), 4–5.

41. Gloria Anzaldúa, "Speaking in Tongues: A Letter to 3rd World Women Writers," in *This Bridge Called My Back: Writings By Radical Women of Color,* edited by Cherríe Moraga and Gloria Anzaldúa (New York: Kitchen Table: Women of Color Press, 1981), 167.

42. Daniel Paul Schreber, *Memoirs of My Nervous Illness,* edited and translated by Ida Macalpine and Richard A. Hunter (Cambridge, Mass.: Harvard University Press, 1988), 78.

43. bell hooks, "Homeplace: A Site of Resistance," *Yearning: Race, Gender and Cultural Politics* (Boston: South End, 1990), 48.

44. Carmela Delia Lanza, "Hearing the Voices: Women and Home in Ana Castillo's *So Far from God,*" *MELUS* 23, no. 1 (Spring 1998): 67.

45. Castillo, *So Far from God,* 215.

46. Castillo, *So Far from God,* 217.

47. Castillo, *So Far from God,* 142.

48. Castillo, *So Far from God,* 146.

49. Castillo, *So Far from God,* 64.

50. Castillo, *So Far from God,* 33.

51. Deborah Stone, "Why We Need a Care Movement," *The Nation,* 13 March 2000, 14.

52. Tina Kelley, "City Told to Give Homeless AIDS Patients Immediate Shelter," *New York Times,* 17 November 1999, B4.

53. Castillo, *Massacre of the Dreamers,* 12.

54. Castillo, *Massacre of the Dreamers,* 187.

55. Castillo, *So Far from God,* 222.

56. Castillo, *So Far from God,* 251.

57. As cited in Peter Applebome, "Interview with Marc Singer," *New York Times,* 27 August 2000.

58. Anthony Kaufman, "Marc Singer's Tunnel Vision," *The Village Voice,* 5 September 2000, 122.

59. Kaufman, "Marc Singer's Tunnel Vision," 122.

60. John Cloud, "Mental Health Reform: What Would It Really Take?" *Time,* 7 June 1999, 54–56. This idea conforms to the Clinton administration's policy of providing mental health care to federal workers and encouraging other employers to do the same: "President Clinton backs a bill in Congress to force employers to help too by providing equal insurance coverage for mental and physical health. (Currently, insurance plans can charge higher co-payments for psychiatric visits than for other medical care.) Clinton aims to set an example by announcing . . . that the Federal Government will begin providing its employees equal benefits for mental and nonmental ailments." Clinton's plan sees mental health as dependent on assimilation into the workforce, not even acknowledging the large problem of mental health among the uninsured, the unemployed, the semi-employed, and the homeless. For Clinton as well as for Giuliani, government intervention retards economic rationality demonstrated in the desire to work and get ahead; intelli-

gence is a product of the free market.

61. Tammerlin Drummond, "Elixirs for Your Memory," *Time,* 13 September 1999, 61.

62. Eugene Linden, "Can Animals Think?" *Time,* 6 September 1999, 58.

63. Donna J. Haraway, Modest_Witness@Second_Millenium.FemaleMan©_ Meets_OncoMouse: *Feminism and Technoscience* (New York: Routledge, 1997), 92. The consolidation of power in the pharmaceutical industry not only leads to an undermining of citizen support and public life, but also functions on the international level against the interests of public health and development in less powerful nations. Using international law on intellectual property and licensing rights, the pharmaceutical industry has succeeded in challenging South Africa's development of generic AIDS drugs or their attempts to diminish the AIDS epidemic by importing drugs from other markets worldwide that undersell U.S. competitors. "The Clinton/Gore Administration has been using political and economic blackmail to keep Third World countries from manufacturing or importing cheap, generic versions of patented AIDS-fighting drugs, many of which were developed with U.S. taxpayer-funded research": Doug Ireland, "AIDS Drugs in Africa," *The Nation,* 4 October 1999, 5. These recent initiatives to end small domestic manufacturing of AIDs-preventive drugs in South Africa threaten to spread a deadly epidemic which has the potential of killing a third of the continent as well as to force South Africa's economy into a global market, weakening government supports and the efforts of the black labor force to move beyond their history of colonization. South Africa is not the only country to find itself facing the choice between mass deaths or neoliberal punishment: Brazil has recently decided to defy Big Pharma by producing its own generic brands of AIDS drugs, while India legalized the mass-production of copycat pharmaceuticals in order to improve its own health-care system.

64. Bauman, *In Search of Politics,* 98. "This effect can be traced back to the seminal, previously mentioned departure in the history of the modern state: the separation and increasing gap between power and politics. Claus Offie gave a most precise expression to the various aspects of this most fateful of divorces. Among these aspects he names the implosion of the orthodox centres of economic, military, and cultural powers once condensed in the nation-state, but now sapped and eroded simultaneously from 'above' and 'below'; the postmodern transformations of social morphology, which led to the progressive decline of the established elites' support and of the overall trust in political institutions, both resulting in the new/volatility, fragmentation, and rapid fluctuation of the issues and foci of public attention; and—last but certainly not least—the fact that 'political agents have lost the certainty of their roles and domains because the political economy of postindustrial and global capitalism no longer provides the clear-cut categorization of "places within the system of production" in which forms of collective action (political parties, associations, trade unions) were once anchored.' The overall outcome of all these closely intertwined transformations is a situation in which 'sovereignties have become nominal, power anonymous, and its locus empty.'"

65. We are aware of the controversy surrounding Menchú's work because of David Stoll's allegation that she distorted her own history of involvement: David

Stoll, *Rigoberta Menchú and the Story of All Poor Guatemalans* (Boulder, Colo.: Westview, 1999). This allegation does not, however, contradict the point we are making here, that *I, Rigoberta Menchú* is able to recognize and build a public in opposition to the state. In other words, Menchú's critique of the state does not, at the same time, dismantle the possibilities of public organization and action.

66. Peter McLaren, *Revolutionary Multiculturalism: Pedagogies of Dissent for the New Millennium* (Boulder, Colo.: Westview, 1997), 260.

5

Enemy of the State

Pedagogical machines such as mass media and corporate curricula translate political choice into consumer choice. This manufactured common sense proclaims universal freedom as consumer choice, because if citizens do not like McDonald's there is other available fast food to eat, or, as *New York Times* foreign correspondent Thomas Friedman says, as he celebrates supposedly rising standards of living in the new global age, "Political choices get reduced to Pepsi or Coke."[1] Ironically, the 2000 U.S. national elections demonstrated that the vast degree of political choice has been reduced, not only in the reversal of the democratic vote in a Supreme Court decision, but also in the similarity of the two major candidates' stands on issues of economic parity, redistribution, and corporate power. At stake here are more than the foundations of the democratic process and the possibilities for allowing a public debate over legitimate political issues. As M. Jacqui Alexander and Chandra Mohanty point out, "The myth of 'private property as fundamental to human development,' wherein ownership of land is conflated with personal value, prestige, and evolution of the owner . . . all suggest a systematic world view whereby capitalist values infuse ideas about citizenship and liberal Democracy."[2] Moreover, ideas about what democracy could mean outside of casting a vote in an election, about what an engaged civil society might do to transform political possibilities, seem defeated from popular consciousness. Following the September 11 attack, U.S. citizens were told by their television sets, radios, and newspapers that they should "get back to normal," go to the mall and sporting events, and buy stock rather than engage with the political and historical context for the attack as the basis to reconsider

U.S. actions globally. U.S. economic and military imperialism was not open for review but rather affirmed.

New alternative pedagogies need to be developed to battle against mainstream machineries of power in order to expand possibilities for a democratic public. Hence, one of the tasks of an alternative pedagogy involves translating choice understood within the bounds of the market to choice as being about individuals' developing the capacities for political agency, engaged citizenship, and critical intervention in the conditions in which they and others live. Of course, such a pedagogy is not simply about individual political agency but needs to be conceived as the preconditions for collective political struggle for broader social transformation.

Choice, understood through the logic of consumption, is at present determining and defending the movement towards market integration on a global scale, and this movement has not been beneficial for everyone. Indeed, as an ideology, consumerism obscures the underlying politics and inequalities that largely give its forms of capitalist expansion their force and propulsion. As Robert McChesney points out,

> Large corporations have resources to influence media and overwhelm the political process, and do so accordingly. In U.S. electoral politics, for just one example, the richest one-quarter of one percent of Americans make 80 percent of all individual political contributions and corporations outspend labor by a margin of 10–1. Under neoliberalism this all makes sense, as elections then reflect market principles, with contributions being equated with investments. As a result, it reinforces the irrelevance of electoral politics to most people and assures the maintenance of unquestioned corporate rule.[3]

In explaining the new global system of capital, Thomas L. Friedman argues that it operates on the principle of consumer desire, of what people want. Even large global shifts like the end of the Cold War are fueled by a global clamoring, people themselves demanding and implementing changes through their holds on the pocket books of large corporate and financial institutions. "Because what globalization does," he writes,

> is to empower the common man. It empowers common men and women to have all these choices, and when that happens it is inevitable they will make choices that seem the most attractive, the most modern, the most appealing, the most convenient and the most commercial. And they may want strip malls along every street and Taco Bells on every corner—even though in the short run that will steamroll their local and national cultures.[4]

The logic of consumerism resolves a very old theological debate by coming down on the side of free will over determinism, coming down so defensively on the side of free will, in fact, that the very notion of power and politics is all but wiped out. Gone is any mention of how strip malls and Taco

Bells, along with the entire corporate and financial infrastructure, have a much more solid and determining role in deciding how these landscapes will look than the common man or woman out to buy a new lipstick or wanting to watch a half-hour's decent TV programming. Missing, too, is an acknowledgement of how Taco Bell can price out competitors, cutting costs by paying farm workers 40 cents for every 32-pound bucket of tomatoes they pick, the same wage Taco Bell has paid since 1978.[5] The problem here is not only Thomas Friedman's lack of attention to the ways ideology interacts and affects and even controls consumer desire, or to the ways that people's purchasing powers are limited by other forces than just the desire for aesthetic pride and appreciation, or to how consumer desire works to enforce inequalities in the class structure, or to how consumerism creates discontentment, or to the ways that capitalist power and institutions are able to dictate what people see as their choices. The problem is also, and more fundamentally, that many people actually *believe* that their freedom is defined as their ability to purchase things. "The consumer experiences his distinctive behaviours as freedom, as aspiration, as choice."[6]

Furthermore, many people also believe that this is the way it should be and that fairness will ensue, or rather, that this is the way it is and has to be, for, as Thomas Friedman admits, "You have to make capitalism work, because you don't have a choice. . . . Only the competitive will survive."[7] So which is it? Is there choice, or isn't there? "Globalization isn't a choice," he continues. "It's a reality."[8]

Consumerism voids political concerns. Mass media assumes the following myths:

1. Everybody consents to a free market system.
2. A free market system is the best and most rational choice because it benefits most people and institutes fairness.
3. Consumerism is also the best possible choice because there are no choices.
4. Markets are natural and so devoid of ideological content.
5. All political alternatives to free market capitalism and liberal democracy have failed.

"Politics," writes Thomas Friedman, "becomes just political engineering to implement decisions in the narrow space allowed you within the system."[9] Such pundits assume that the so-called triumph of free-market consumerism, deregulation and unlimited growth marks an ideological vacuum. Taco Bell and McDonalds "proliferate because they offer people something they want"[10] not because of advertising, product placement or the ways they have monopolized certain public spaces like highways. Such pundits of consumerism use the laws of nature as evidence that "those cultures that are not robust enough . . . will be wiped out like any species that cannot adapt to changes in its environment"[11] instead of indicating that consolidated capital makes competition obsolete by allowing the powerful to control commercial infrastructures. In reality, such ideas about the morality and justice of the market are being shoved down everybody's throats at twenty-four frames per second and supported by a powerful system of pedagogical production. This pedagogical production is able to take the most cruel repercussions of global capitalism and make them into statements of love.

FORECAST

This chapter uses Tony Scott's 1998 film *Enemy of the State* to examine how global capitalism appears as love in part as it represents global consumerism as familial devotion. We examine Thomas Friedman's *The Lexus and the Olive Tree* in relation to *Enemy of the State* in order to show how representations of family freedom and privacy are used to bolster ideals about market freedom and consumerism.

Representations of the family's freedom from the state show globalization as a new guarantee of freedom. In such representations, only within the free field of the economy is the individual safe from state terror, and the ability to participate within this economy is only possible when the state withdraws, leaving the individual comfortable and secure as a consuming unit in his home. Our reading of *Enemy of the State* and *The Lexus and the Olive Tree* intends to link representational analysis to opening up possibilities for imagining political choice beyond its reduction to the market. Such an analysis presupposes that cultural work involves politically and pedagogically intervening in the ways that representations take the material force of ideology. In other words, we are less concerned with what such cultural products mean than with what they do, how they shape reality and are wielded as weapons of power.

Enemy of the State tells the story of a black labor lawyer who is surveilled by the state to the point where the state is able to change his identity, get him fired from his high-level executive lawyer job, ruin his family and his marriage and, most tragically, cancel his credit cards. Will Smith plays the part of the main character (Robert Clayton Dean) who, by a fluke of circumstance, ends up as the target of the state's vast surveillance. Dean is in a store buying Christmas presents for his family when an old college friend runs through pursued by the thugs of the state for carrying a video recording. This video witnesses the murder of a Republican senator who was blocking the passage of a telecommunications bill which would have severely curtailed civil liberties by allowing the government's increased usage of surveillance technologies, satellite tracking equipment, sophisticated bugging and taps, video rovers, and the like, all in the name of democracy and national security. The film exposes some of the cruel consequences of global consumerism—oppression, terrorism, racism, sexism, and classism—but insists that they are aberrations within a system whose real outcomes and intentions are integrity, suburban bonding, and human tenderness all expressed through consumerism.

THE GOLDEN STRAIGHTJACKET

Enemy of the State stages a conflict between the individual and the state where the state's technological intervention limits the individual's freedom of movement and choice defined as his ability to buy. As one reviewer puts it, "The movie briefly touches on the privacy issues that are an outgrowth of such technology." " 'Privacy has been dead for 30 years because we can't risk it,' [Jon] Voight's character [the leader of the bad guys] announces."[12] Even if the film takes privacy to the morgue, it also resurrects it as the salvation of a dangerously technologized world. The film shows how the individual can only achieve freedom once the state has disappeared and things have returned to normal, leaving the individual free to enjoy the products of late capitalism with his wife and kids in the privacy of his own home. Missing is any consideration of how the state in its present form actually redistributes wealth to the most wealthy predominantly by investing in such military surveillance equipment as the film foregrounds.

For Scott as for Thomas Friedman, individual freedom is presaged on the freedom of the market, and the freedom of the market demands the shrinking of the state. The rules that allow for the freedom of the consumer to choose whatever she or he wants are what Friedman calls, paradoxically, "The Golden Straightjacket," a label that Thomas Frank has defined as "the absence of political options," where the possibility of imagining "ways to order human affairs other than through the free market"[13] was nullified. Margaret Thatcher and Ronald Reagan initially developed these rules because government intervention in the market, Friedman says, made levels of economic growth insufficient (Friedman never specifies for whom they were insufficient). Such rules include "making the private sector the primary engine of its economic growth, . . . shrinking the size of state bureaucracy, . . . eliminating and lowering tariffs on imported goods, removing restrictions on foreign investment, . . . privatizing state-owned industries and utilities, deregulating capital markets," and the like, all of which amounts to this: "your economy grows and your politics shrinks."[14] In other words, any state function that would limit the unlimited growth of capitalism is a virtual horror show with the state itself starring as the blood-sucking vampire. There is no sense here that the state could be protectionist, compassionate, the enforcer of nonmilitary justice, or redistributive, but it is always, as in *Enemy of the State*, the evil enemy, the agent unjustly pursuing to the death the innocent, unwary consumer.

This vision of deregulation, privatization, and unlimited growth that Friedman espouses requires that multinationals take over the role of the state. The problem that Friedman spots, however, is that people themselves will start to feel alienated, for corporate control and the consequent technologization of the workplace could counter "what give us the warmth of family, the joy of individuality, the intimacy of personal rituals, the depth of private relationships, as well as the confidence and security to reach out and encounter others."[15] What needs to be developed is "a sense of home and belonging" lest "life becomes barren and rootless"[16] in the instabilities created by the new global order of work and production. In other words, it is consumer capitalism's job to produce feelings of intimacy because it has been so successful in destroying human relationships.

FREEDOM IN MOBILITY

The film actually depicts the effects of globalization in a very real way. Here, power is compelling people to move by controlling their access to jobs, as Robert Dean is fired and expelled from his home, forced onto the street. Zygmunt Bauman has identified this type of power as "'anonymous forces,' operating in the vast—foggy and slushy, impassable and untamable—'no man's land,' stretching beyond the reach of the design and action capacity of anybody's in particular."[17] For Bauman, global power has the capacity to create the conditions of freedom in mobility for the touristic elites, while enforcing other people—the vagabonds—into immobility or, as in the case of Dean, mobility without choice where all his human relationships and responsibilities, all his connections to material existence, have been confiscated through the operations of power. Command over movement is what separates the powerful in the era of globalization from the not-so-powerful, and is consequently what Dean spends the entire movie claiming back, but the kind of mobility which he pursues as rightfully his is the freedom to have and to hold commodities, and not to have the arbitrary arm of government take away his earnings, his collections, his wife, and his blender. Dean's home filled with the commodities of intimate life guarantees, as Bauman says of consumer society, "the disguise of a free exercise of will":

> on every successive visit to a market-place consumers have every reason to feel that it is they—perhaps even they alone—who are in command. They are

the judges, the critics and the choosers. They can, after all, refuse allegiance to any one of the infinite choices on display. Except the choice of choosing between them, that is—but that choice does not appear to be a choice.[18]

Dean's drive to reinhabit his lost home means that he wants a mobility of will, the choice of what to invest his allegiance in, and the freedom from state impositions which only the commodity can promise.

Enemy of the State shows capital as protecting the consumer against the state, but capital in the guise of the family. A sense of home and belonging is, indeed, being forged as an alliance with capital against the state. The film misplaces blame by making it seem as though the state is destroying human relationships. What this view obscures is that the shrinking of the compassionate function of the state has actually been a major weapon wielded by the corporate sector in razing the family and weakening human bonds. This takes the form, on the domestic front, of the dismantling of welfare, states' rights, the failure of the U.S. government to institute a national health care program, the assault on affirmative action, the predicted end to social security, and, on the international front, the impoverishment of regions, forcing the migration of labor, the expansion of for-profit militarization, and the transformation of poorer nations into high-tech war zones. Corporations, media corporations in particular, have successfully created a culture of fear through cop shows, horror flicks, and blood-drenched headlines, and even in endless repetition of terrorist events.

Corporate media now seek to sell security, intimacy, and community back to people. This is evident in "My McDonalds" advertisements and "My Computer" icons which suggest that the most generic and depersonalized mass produced and mass marketed commodities can be possessed in the most personal and intimate fashion. At the same time, these highly personalized logos suggest community—yet this is a community defined by consuming identical products. So the identical and undifferentiated commodity becomes that which links different citizens. It becomes the glue of the social bond, the liberal democratic consensus that joins different identities and interests.

Thomas Friedman's best-selling book *The Lexus and the Olive Tree* describes consumerism in terms that correspond to the worldview Dean seems to be fighting to protect in the movie. For Friedman as (we will see later) in *Enemy of the State*, consumerism is an ideology that assumes freedom in places where freedom is, in actuality, most limited. Even citizenship is just another item for sale, as "To be an American you just have to want to be an American,"[19] and, of course, everybody does want to be an American because, according to Friedman, due to this marvelous revolution in communications and information technology, everybody can see what Americans have (e.g., cars, sexy girls, and Michelob week-ends) and so everybody wants what Americans have. This assertion com-pletely denies that Latin American immigrants caught along the U.S.–Mexican border will get imprisoned and/or sent back to Mexico, and that U.S. products are not just lying out ready for the taking.

The idea that the United States has and will give the opportunity to ac-quire everything that one might want is actually a carefully constructed discourse of the American Dream, expressed through an elation every-where in the media about the possibility of buying one's way into the rul-ing classes by acquiring their signs of status, or of working really hard to get ahead to the point where one can buy better cell phones, vacations, and luxury cars: guarantees of happiness and the good life. Corporate me-dia sell identifications with power predicated on merit and diligence. Supporting the belief that America has everything to offer, these messages belie the contemporary situation of labor, where even when it is true that people have work, they have work without benefits, contracts, longevity, security, or satisfaction. As Friedman himself applauds, labor flexibility "enables workers to move easily from one economic zone to another, and . . . enables employers to hire and fire workers with relative ease."[20] This promise of freedom is false in a double sense:

1. National laws and enforcement carefully limit the movement of workers from one economic zone to another, or restrict what kinds of movements are available.
2. Employees do not necessarily want to be fired just so that they can acquire all this freedom of movement, which being American sup-posedly promises.

Yet, Friedman insists that the loss of jobs is a positive sign of an ascen-dant economy since "the easier it is to fire workers, the more incentive employers have to hire them."[21] This is especially untrue as automation yields higher production with fewer workers. Furthermore, women who work in situations of flexible labor have been actively recruited by West-ern manufacturers, and have often left their homes and families behind in rural villages. Such migrations are caused by a series of factors, most no-tably the way that commercial agriculture often makes traditional modes of life unviable. Sassen states that "young women in patriarchal societies are seen by foreign employers as obedient and disciplined workers, will-ing to do tedious, high-precision work and to submit themselves to work conditions that would not be tolerated in the highly developed coun-tries."[22] One might wonder, indeed, why, if their exposure to Western life is through unhealthy work conditions, women would desire still to give themselves over to it. What makes Western life necessarily so appealing for everybody? How has this logic of consumption become so unmarked, so unnoticeable that even the most cruel corporate practices are justified on the grounds that to continue them is what most people want?

The fact is that there are countless people who do not want to be American, because they feel they live better than Americans, not boxed off into regulated time slots and subjected to the nuisances of urbanism, industrial pollutants and the claims of ever faster rates of production. Exposure to American systems of production does not necessarily create happiness. Additionally, exposure to American lifestyles does not automatically produce the desire to have one like it, but is accompanied by a vast campaign of advertising, commercial films, news reporting, satellite TV, product flooding, and books like Thomas Friedman's, all of which unabashedly offer America and American products as salvation. The United States blasphemously sells itself to the world as God, a new and improved God with 30 percent more free. How has this image of America the Beautiful been sold and made so pervasively acceptable across the political spectrum?

The bleak realities of the labor situation in the United States do not stop Friedman from assuming that all those people out there would and could be American, since American products are so appealing. In this logic, remember, being American simply entails consuming American products. What is more, these products are naturally appealing and possess a natural, almost magical magnetism, as Friedman never thinks it necessary to explain exactly *why* so many people are so thrilled and seduced by the images which the U.S. projects of itself around the world. For example, he never considers that U.S. companies are pasting their ads ever more pervasively, so that in Manhattan's Soho there scarcely remains a building that does not have happy faces of consumers plastered colorfully all over its surfaces. Nor does Friedman think it relevant that the United States exports its commercial cinema, filling the world outside with messages of the good, happy life. "With all due respect to revolutionary theorists," Friedman writes, "the 'wretched of the earth' want to go to Disney World—not to the barricades."[23] Even overlooking Frantz Fanon's in-depth historical analysis in *Wretched of the Earth* of why people give up material comforts to fight for liberation, one would wonder, indeed, why Friedman supposes that the choice is between Disney and war if everybody so much wants Disney. Indeed, Fanon himself shows that the worldwide system of capitalist exploitation—and the hierarchies of power that support it—is kept in place only through recourse to force: "In the colonial countries," he writes, ". . . the policeman and the soldier, by their immediate presence and their frequent and direct action maintain contact with the native and advise him by means of rifle butts and napalm not to budge" (38).[24] Basically, Fanon acknowledges that anti-colonialist violence begins with colonialist violence, systems of oppression kept in place by private companies, debt structures, and unjust distributions of wealth. "[Colonialism]," he writes, "is violence in its natural state, and it will only yield when confronted with greater violence." While Fanon, perhaps, overstates the inevitable necessity of violence to successfully counter hegemonic violence, he understands that capitalism originates in violence, requires violence to perpetuate itself and, in turn, gives rise to an oppositional violence that seeks to abolish it. Consistent in this regard with the founders of the United States, Fanon thought that revolutionary violence is part of a political movement, not merely wanton destruction. Indeed, if everybody wants to be American and to have the things (like Disney) that Americans have, and if everybody *can* have these things just by wanting them, and if everybody is so happy about all of this, then why is it that America needs to have, as Friedman boasts proudly, "a large standing army, equipped with more aircraft carriers, advanced fighter jets, transport aircraft, and nuclear weapons than ever, so that it can project more power farther than any country in the world"?[25]

Enemy of the State likewise positions America as a desire that needs to be protected through technologies of violence. Indeed, the protection of American citizens from the possibilities of external aggression and competition gets completely absorbed into a narrative about the protection of American citizens from the excesses of an overly demanding government. As the film opens, the politician who is about to murder the hold-out senator explains the needs for the deregulation of powers of surveillance: "This is the richest most powerful nation on Earth," he reasons, "and therefore the most hated. You and I know what the average citizen does not: that we are at war 24 hours of every day. Do I have to itemize the number of American lives we've saved in the past 12 months alone with judicious use of surveillance intelligence?" In other words, as in Friedman, military equipment will defend America, upholding America's ability to have riches and power by denying it to others. Asserting its mastery, flexing its financial weight with the backing of its mighty armaments, the United States enforces austerity, opening foreign economies to U.S. investments and domination while shrinking the means of domestic development and even of subsistence production, especially in smaller and less capital intensive countries (and still often failing to achieve its goals). "While [the First World's Structural Adjustment Programs] are ostensibly intended to promote efficiency and sustained economic growth in the 'adjusting' country," reports Grace Chang in a study on the causes of global immigration, "in reality they function to open up developing nations' economies and peoples to imperialist exploitation. . . . The phenomenon consistently reported is that overall standards of living, and conditions for women and girls in particular, have deteriorated dramatically since the onset of SAPs. Often this has occurred after periods of marked improvement in women's employment health, education, and nutrition."[26]

In the movie, however, Friedman's prized equipment gets turned on the very citizens of America as the real enemies of the state. Indeed, the movie ends with the extrapolation that these technologies should be used as "protection of civil liberties, particularly the sanctity of my home" instead of for such crimes of intimidation and harassment against Americans themselves. The military should be used, the movie demands, to protect Americans against enemies from without. The logic of the movie insists that the use of the military is justified but only on exterior targets to ensure internal security in the guise of bankrolls and suburban peace.

The question of what creates America's enemies is never taken up, as Robert Dean eventually settles back in his comfortable life knowing that the equipment used to thwart him is certainly a formidable force of national defense, ready to pulverize those who would pose challenges from anywhere—an unacknowledged but still very real prize for his efforts as he wins the American military over to his side. "Do you think we're the enemy of democracy you and I?" says the Republican senator's murderer to Brill right before the shoot-out with labor. "I think we're democracy's last hope. There's always going to be power." What has disappeared is the idea, introduced in this beginning conversation about the telecommunications legislation, that militarization is not only a danger to American nationals, but especially to those outside the nation who oppose the imposition of American ideology and equipment in their homes.

Even with the inkling of an admission on Friedman's part that capitalism does restrict choice and that everybody is not so happy after all (but must be forced to be happy), he goes on to insist that these new capitalist formations are actually raising standards of living, and this is what everybody wants. To prove this, Friedman uses no statistics or other standard forms of evidence, but instead comes up with a utopian view in which capitalism has wedged its way into every corner and crevice of modern life, becoming synonymous with life itself. Consumerism is consciousness. "We can now," he says, "have a bank in our homes, a bookstore in our homes, a brokerage firm in our homes, a factory in our homes, an investment firm in our homes, a school in our homes. . . ."[27] Hooray! In this view, privacy and family are both in the lap of capital, and this does not produce any friction because this is the way it should be. So, has the factory become just another trendy mode of interior design, completely interchangeable with other institutions as a question of style, and should we all therefore feel as comfortable reclining on a conveyer belt as on a sofa?

Though Friedman admits that U.S. manufacturing is moving abroad "to take advantage of lower labor costs,"[28] missing here is any consideration that labor is not just a matter of changing scenery and that the factory is not just a new type of wallpaper and a few extra pieces of furniture, but rather an economic and political method for coordinating productive labor. For example, Friedman neglects to mention, as Chandra Mohanty has pointed out, that NAFTA has facilitated the use of the home as an extension of the factory. Mohanty has shown, through her analysis of Mexican women's labor, how craft production has been complicit in relegating women, in particular, to less lucrative and more exploitable positions. Working in "leisure time" in their homes, female workers have been easily underpaid, and denied contracts and benefits, because of the way they are considered non-economic, non-measurable, outside of general accounting, outside the jurisdiction of labor law, and outside of the main, integral sites of industrial manufacturing, profits, and incomes. Mohanty writes, "Ideas of *flexibility, temporality, invisibility,* and *domesticity* in the naturalization of categories of work are crucial in the construction of Third-World women as an appropriate and cheap labor force."[29]

The definition of Third-World women's work as domestic has eased a capitalist strategy for colonizing the poor. U.S. companies are indeed taking advantage of the lower costs of home labor, a no-contract, no-benefits type of labor ("flexibility") with no possibility of organizing, where people are paid by the piece, not supplied with equipment, easily dismissed, and having to pay for their own operating costs.

By ignoring this type of labor exploitation, Friedman is able seriously to extol the benefits of a rapidly integrating and growing world market. As Baudrillard has said, "We are speaking of the absurd gymnastics of *accounting illusions,* of national accounts. Nothing enters into these except factors which are visible and measurable by the criteria of economic rationality. . . . Research, culture and women's domestic labour are all excluded from these accounts, though certain things which have no business there do figure in them, *merely because they are measurable.*"[30] Certainly, it is not merely an aesthetic "choice" for things American that determines how outsourcing work at the *maquiladoras* has transformed the lives of women workers and their families by forcing a factory into their homes.

Popularly acclaimed, Friedman's descriptions of a global consumer society only barely glimpse and even sometimes celebrate the negative outcomes which globalization incurs, outcomes such as environmental destruction, the growing number of various disabling addictions and diseases, economic insecurity, expanding poverty, human rights abuses, cultural devastation, increasing militarization, and incarceration on a world scale, the decreasing abilities of governments to enforce just redistributive measures, deskilling and, indeed, lowering wages. "Those who don't [perform]," writes Friedman, "are left as road kill on the global investment highway."[31] The logic of consumption that Friedman outlines goes like this:

1. What is in the interests of global capitalist profit?
2. How is this bad for anyone?
3. In fact, it is good for whoever it is bad for.
4. So everybody is benefiting when only a few are benefiting. For instance, Friedman briefly acknowledges that large corporate expansions have caused severe environmental damage, but, he argues, this is not really bad because corporate destruction of the environment is also protecting it. Corporations are protecting the environment because consumers demand ethical behaviors, and consumers have complete control, through their purchasing power, of what corporations do.

"To be sure," Friedman specifies, "Ford is not saving the Pantanal because it's fallen in love with its endangered species, but rather because it believes that it can sell a lot more Jaguar cars if it is seen as saving the jaguars of the Pantanal. And if that's what it takes to save this incredibly beautiful ecosystem and way of life, then God bless Henry Ford and the Internet."[32] So, corporate investment and growth fuel environmental initiatives which in turn fuel more growth and pollution. The negative or nuisance from prior growth becomes the engine for more growth and exploitation. "If you want to save the Amazon," Friedman asserts, "go to business school and learn how to do a deal."[33] Friedman's reasoning takes the negative side of production and counts it on the positive side, making all production an advantage over non-production so that the accounting of globalism is heavily weighted on the side of assets and bloated optimism. "America has more assets," Friedman asserts, "and fewer liabilities, in relation to this system than any other major country."[34] What would be the response to this in an urban community such as those in Detroit, Oakland, Chicago, Philadelphia, or a rural community in Appalachia? Who determines what counts as an asset and what counts as a liability?

Friedman's idea is that unlimited growth is the principle driving everything, for better or for worse. Friedman's faith that capitalism in the end will produce worldwide happiness is similar to the smile that Coca-Cola promises even while it continues to exploit child labor in Brazil and to undermine local start-up industries everywhere. For Friedman, what is good for Taco Bell is good for America, and what is good for America is good for the world and is even good for other galaxies. "The Malaysians go to Kentucky Fried and the Qataris go to Taco Bell for the same reason Americans go to Universal Studios—to see the source of their fantasies. Today, for better or for worse, globalization is a means for spreading the fantasy of America around the world."[35] As the Kentucky Fried Chicken/Taco Bell/Pizza Hut advertisements for *Star Wars Episode I: The*

Phantom Menace profess, even outer space aliens want in on all this blissful satisfaction that fast food offers, and who wouldn't? Maybe aliens and intergalactic warriors do not get cancer, heart disease, or have strokes quite as easily as earthlings do, and maybe for them, indigestion is a source of quiet pride. A commercial poster for the movie depicts Colonel Sanders, the Taco Bell Chihuahua, and a Pizza Hut waitress posing as Luke Skywalker, Han Solo, and Princess Leia, outfitted with the weapons of the Rebel Alliance. This "rebel alliance" is poised to save the universe from the Evil Empire. Here, these icons of consumption and massive corporations offer redemption against a totalitarian state. The promise of freedom becomes the freedom of consumption.

This logic of consumption is presently so pervasive that it has become invisible, or common sense, and infrequently either noticed or challenged. *Time* published an article where it extolled the virtues of global capitalism and unlimited growth by commemorating the careers of the three men who called the plays under Clinton: Alan Greenspan (chairman of the Federal Reserve Board), Robert Rubin (Secretary of the Treasury), and Lawrence Summers (Deputy Secretary of the Treasury). *Time* begins its report by talking about the fragility of the world economy in the wake of the Asian crisis, and then argues that the only way to ensure future well-being is through neoliberal reform, faster and more open markets. The current "meltdown" in many countries' economies gave Greenspan, Rubin, and Summers the justification they needed to "sell a market-driven policy that could be labeled Realeconomik."[36] According to *Time,* the market-based growth policy means that there is no ideology involved, and no partisan bickering, but full consent, since the market, rather than the ideas of particular people, is governing the economy, and markets are non-ideological balancing forces, "the deepest truths about human nature" and ultimately, in most instances, "correct." The domination of world markets by U.S. interests seems both natural and necessary and proving, says *Time,* these men's ability and commitment to "Save the World." This "pragmatism," reports *Time,* is partially developed through Greenspan's readings of Ayn Rand's objectivist novels, where unlimited capitalist growth and supremacy result literally from the destruction of others, and particularly of the weak, as right-wing Nietzschean Supermen ascend through economic ruthlessness. While the "robust U.S. economy," says *Time,* has "turned nations like Malaysia and Russia into leper colonies by isolating them from global capital and making life hellish in order to protect U.S. growth," these men still "believe that a strong U.S. economy is the last, best hope for the world."[37] For *Time,* the fact that economies around the world are being squeezed to feed the growth of U.S. multinationals (and that this causes real human suffering) does not seem to contradict their assertion that, indeed, the expansion of U.S. multinationals is the last hope for a world tottering on the edge of economic turmoil. The example that *Time* gives of how these men's economic policies are saving the world is the 1995 Mexican bail-out, while no mention is made that the bail-out caused increasing pockets of poverty and labor exploitation among poor Mexicans while profiting the Mexican elite, U.S. currency speculators, and multinational manufacturing sectors.

In his early work, Jean Baudrillard provides a framework for exploring this aspect of the consumer society where a belief in affluence generates a vicious circle of growth and acquisition as a transcendent aim, and he shows clearly the cancerous underside and glaring cruelty of this global happiness. Baudrillard is most known for his postmodern theories of simulation, where all objects become immediately and automatically interchangeable as images devoid of content or reference, and the reality signified in these images has disappeared under a totalizing code. As in structural linguistics, the sign just refers to other signs in a chain, not to physical objects in the world. These theories have been criticized because they leave no room for oppositional action or agency, and relegate all revolution and dissent to the position of trendy commodities and fashion. As Baudrillard himself says, "No revolution is possible at the level of a code—or, alternatively, revolutions take place every day at that level, but they are 'fashion revolutions,' which are harmless and foil the other kind."[38] Such an approach dismantles the possibilities for change while circumventing a critique of the institutions who assign value to these signs and control both their production and their circulation. However, in *The Consumer Society* (written in 1970 and published in English in 1998), Baudrillard vividly describes the hazards in the type of society that Friedman so cheerfully lauds. In this text, Baudrillard talks about how consumer action differentiates people into hierarchies and that this is at odds with the principles of democracy and egalitarianism, yet, at the same time, consumption carries with it the suggestion of an "equality before the Object,"[39] i.e., in Friedman's case, all people are equal in desiring America.

The logic Baudrillard is recognizing is that consumer capitalism does just the opposite of what it says it is doing: it differentiates while appearing to homogenize and homogenizes while appearing to differentiate. For example, Friedman's assumption that all people want to be American and can be American just by wanting it homogenizes the global playing field while, at the same time, reproducing and even exacerbating class inequalities because not all people can be American in the same way. When a consumer makes a purchase, she or he is actually inserting her- or himself into a type of lifestyle, dream, and a set of social relations which are class specific and exemplified by the lifestyles depicted in advertising. At the same time, consumption homogenizes people by forcing them to desire and to compete for social recognition and valuation on a hierarchy tied to their consumption abilities.

It appears here that Baudrillard could have gone in another direction than collapsing all contemporary world problems into a problem of the image. His early theory suggests that he is on the edge of developing a critique of ideology and power, one that would take into account the cruelty done to real people under the very real material relations of capital.

> Modern (capitalist, productivist, post-industrial) social systems do not, to any great extent, base their social control, the ideological regulation of the economic and political contradictions by which they are riven, on the great egalitarian and democratic principles, on that whole system of ideological and cultural values that is broadcast to all corners of the earth and is operative everywhere. Even when seriously internalized through schooling and socialization, these conscious egalitarian values—of law and justice, etc., remain relatively fragile, and would never be up to the task of integrating a society whose objective reality they too visibly contradict.[40]

Like in the theories of ideology developed at the same time by Louis Althusser, Baudrillard here indicates that schools, the film industry, and other "State Apparati" are instrumental in calling citizens to believe that commodities and commodity systems allow for political positions which they in fact deny. Through these institutional apparati, the negative effects of capitalist development are re-envisioned as the positive power of relentless production:

> First, we have seen the degradation of our shared living space by economic activities: noise, air and water pollution, environmental destruction, the disruption of residential zones by the development of new amenities (airports, motorways, etc.). Traffic congestion produces a colossal deficit in technical, psychological and human terms. Yet what does this matter, since the necessary excess of infrastructural building, the extra expenditure on petrol, the costs of treatment for accident victims, etc., will all be totted up as consumption, i.e., will become, under cover of the gross national product and statistics, an indication of growth and wealth! . . . *Every article produced is sacralized by the very fact of its being produced.*[41]

What Baudrillard is invoking here is a type of double-speak, a religion of commodities where devils cross-dress as angels with wings and halos, whispering loving, enchanting poetry while poisoning us with vicious toxins. In talking about human subjection as inevitable and total under capitalism, however, Baudrillard is here starting to deny the possibilities of resistance or radical intervention either through critical pedagogical practices or through media opposition, guerrilla advertising, hacking, jamming, or graffiti, all of which do, in some degree, tear through the ideological curtain.

The market not only sells itself and its agenda by appearing sexy through visceral associations, as Jameson says, but also, in a different mode, sells itself as wholesome.[42] One of the main ways that the domination of capital is sweetened as the positivity of production is by reinventing the commodity as the assurance of familial love. Baudrillard, indeed, talks about advertising as a type of enticing solicitude where citizens are taught complicity. For Baudrillard, advertising gives the sense that someone is caring for you—"a continual consumption," he writes,

> of solicitude, sincerity and warmth, but consumption in fact only of the *signs* of that solicitude, which is even more vital for the individual than 'biological' nourishment in a system where social distance and the atrociousness of social relations are the objective rule. The loss of (spontaneous, reciprocal, symbolic) human relations is the fundamental fact of our societies. It is on this basis that we are seeing the systematic reinjection of human relations—in the form of *signs*—into the social circuit. . . . [43]

Advertising is the packaging of social control under the appearance of generosity. This appearance of generosity in advertising, "gradually rationalizing redistributive economy" (160) for the purposes of profit and greed, uses the family to project a feeling of tenderness and comfort. A feeling of complacency succeeds in putting a positive value on the desolation and hardships that commodity capitalism orchestrates. Syrupy, sweet, and sentimental extracts of family intimacy are, for Baudrillard, ideological operations of redistribution.

Enemy of the State captures vividly the cultural links between family and consumerism that are currently greasing the philosophy of capitalism, showing the state as in vital opposition to individual freedom. It shows how capitalism shreds human relations and then projects a sense of home and belonging so that the cruelty of capital comes to seem sweet and caring. The conflict between Dean and the government begins when an old college friend (Jason Lee) slides a videorecording in his shopping bag. The videorecording is evidence of the murder of a "good senator" orchestrated by a corrupt one, this latter one having been bought off by multinational profit-mongers and telecommunications' special interests. It is crucial that when Dean starts to be targeted by the government, he is engaged in an act of purchasing. In other words, as he steps over the line between his former freedom and his seizure by state surveillance, buying things becomes impossible for him. The very scene of buying becomes inaccessible and dissolves to demonstrate that his freedom is trickling away. When the videorecording lands in his pocket, Dean is shopping for sexy lingerie. It is exactly at the moment when illicit sexuality is introduced in Dean's busy business schedule that the state starts to police him, tracking him down to retrieve the videorecording that eventually gets destroyed even while the state continues to search him out.

While it is clear that Dean has never before taken an interest in such eroticism, it is ambiguous for whom the lingerie is intended. The saleswoman asks him if it is really for his wife (Regina King), and Dean insists that it is to such a degree that he introduces doubt, especially when the viewer knows that he from time to time has lunch with a college girlfriend whom he still loves and with whom he sometimes does business, transferring funds to her bank account in exchange for information and materials for blackmailing the mob. His consumerism is thereby linked to his masculinity, and throughout the film it becomes clearer and clearer that as "object of the gaze," Dean's sexuality, and his ability to purchase, come simultaneously under question, as his wife complains that he falls asleep whenever she attempts seduction.

The interventions of the government into Dean's private life end up fragmenting his identity by weakening his marriage bonds. One of the government's methods of torment was to send Dean's wife photographs of him with his college sweetheart Rachel (Lisa Bonet). The state actually produces an affair between the two, coming up not only with photographs but also with other types of circumstantial evidence like bank statements showing that funds had been transferred between their accounts and, at last, leaving his clothes in her apartment when she is brutally murdered.

ACCOMMODATION OF THE MACHINE

The film is a celebration of technology. The technology functions seamlessly, strengthening the state's authoritarian power by displaying the excessive power of a state that intervenes in the private lives of citizens. Every phone is tapped, TV screens are rigged, and the government even has satellites through which it can monitor Dean's movements in the chase. There are no mistakes, no snafus, no gaps, or, as one reviewer remarks, "the real world's hourglass icon, the one that indicates a computer is taking its sweet time about something, is nowhere to be seen."[44] Another reviewer also describes the way that technology in the film gives to people in power complete control over social configurations:

> [The Powers that Be] are, as everyone knows, evil, all-powerful, and hooked directly into every single phone line, computer screen, and convenience-store security camera in those United States. . . . As Dean's world comes crumbling down around his ears, these federally employed nudniks watch his every

move, and the action switches back and forth between Smith in close up, aerial long shots of his movements, quickie cuts to the NSA control room ("he's turning left, he's bending down, . . ." the breathless young guys report to their boss, who keeps barking things like "prioritize his phone bill!") and even to 2001-styled shots of a satellite spinning round the globe.[45] (Hoffman)

The "enemy" of the state is not the one who attacks the state but the one who is attacked by it. Though Dean occasionally does manage to escape the government's omniscient, roving, Big-Brother eye—by, for instance, hiding out in an old Dr. Pepper factory in an abandoned old-industrial sector of the city with co-actor Gene Hackman playing Brill—the government's tracking always catches up with him, sending in its fire-and-air power and summoning war-time helicopters and equipment. Not only do the techniques of surveillance become techniques for a military corralling of the enemy, but also the cinematic apparatus itself becomes a weapon of search, seizure, and assault. As one reviewer notes, "The film's juxtapositions, sharp angles, jump cuts and aerial surveillance shots (à la the Gulf war) have a rhythm that suits the material."[46] The film, in fact, makes technologies of destruction into aesthetic products and even targets of desire. *Enemy of the State,* a reviewer comments, "treats technology as its biggest turn-on."[47]

THE PARENT ORGANISM

Dean's identity as a consumer derives from his status as a "family man." State surveillance undermines Dean's family privacy, thereby threatening the foundations of his consumer identity. The film's main agenda is to restore this privacy, making privacy and private property together into the aspiration of the plot and the divine ideal of liberty and transcendence. One reviewer remarked on the ways in which this film resonated in national politics, pitting the government against the family, as it was released in the very same week that Linda Tripp publicized her recorded phone conversations with Monica Lewinsky.

> Though *Enemy of the State* finds a flimsy excuse for setting one scene amid lingerie models, babes have nothing to do with its notion of sex appeal. Instead, it's the gigahertz that are hot in a thriller that treats technology as its biggest turn-on. High-tech surveillance ("Enhance, then forward frame by frame!") is at the heart of this latest splashy collaboration between Tony Scott and Jerry Bruckheimer with its premise that privacy is imperiled by runaway electronics. In a week that finds the nation listening to surreptitiously taped Washington telephone calls, who's to say that *Enemy of the State* doesn't have a point?[48] (Maslin)

Indeed, it is tempting to think of the whole Monica Lewinsky affair as evincing a high-tech political wash-out where the real crimes of the administration—breaking international law, contributing to the deterioration of U.S. inner cities, performing acts of murderous aggression (amounting to genocide) on defenseless populations, and so on—become subordinated to a national focus-debate on the dramatics of a family crisis.

In *Enemy of the State,* indications that the patriarchal family is threatening to unravel appear in the suggestion of illicit temptation posed by Rachel. Rachel presents a danger to Dean's family privacy because she dissipates his bank account and therefore his ability to consume. Dean pays her to retrieve vital information for his law practice, transferring cash from his account into hers. The transfer of money later becomes evidence for an allegation of their sexual relations. Rachel temporarily challenges privacy, making illegible the separation between desire and a cash economy.

The history of prostitution surfaces in Rachel's contingency to capital. Part of what makes Rachel's sexuality dangerous is her skin-color, as she is much lighter than Dean's wife. Sander Gilman has traced historically the discourse of female sexuality and has shown how what brings out sexuality in women and characterizes images of prostitution is, exactly, the surfacing of racialized traits as signs of sexuality. "The black," Gilman finds, "both male and female, becomes by the eighteenth century an icon for deviant sexuality in general."[49] According to bell hooks, "[popular] films portray the almost-white black woman as tragically sexual."[50] This is certainly true in *Enemy of the State,* where the racial distinctions between the two opposing black women make Rachel, indeed, tragic, first in her aloneness, her emphatic search for independence, which leads ultimately to her brutal murder. It is not only, however, the history of prostitution with its contingency to capital that frames Rachel's character. It is also the history of slavery with its practices of turning black bodies into barterable commodities. Rachel's whiteness threatens the stability of identity and racial purity. As Anne McClintock observes,

> [In Enlightenment discourse,] the relationship between the "normal" male control of reproduction and sexual pleasure in marriage, and the "normal" bourgeois control of capital was legitimized and made natural by reference to a third term: the "abnormal" zone of racial "degeneration." Illicit money and illicit sexuality were seen to relate to each other by negative analogy to race. . . . Prostitutes became associated with black and colonized peoples within a discourse on racial degeneration that figured them as transgressing the natural distributions of money, sexual power, and property, and as thereby fatally threatening the fiscal and libidinal economy.[51]

Rachel's sexuality is dangerous because it cannot be kept in place through rules of property, location, and belonging, but instead moves around, deracinated, unattached along with the migrations of capital. She represents the possibility of the effacement of differences. The film's resolution does depend upon such an effacement as suburban, consumerist conformity replaces and destroys racial differences.

Dean's character must assume the disguise of a black street person and terrorist until he can prove his own innocence, regain his identity, and claim back his Rolex watch, his cell phone, and Mont Blanc fountain pen along with the love of his wife, respect of his kid, and the obedience of his dog, as his wife finally accepts his sexual advances, restoring him to manhood by acknowledging his property. When the state turns against the citizen, it is then that the real takes over: it is, for instance, when the state cancels his credit cards and steals his blender that Dean chooses to assume the "black man" stereotype with a wool-knit watchcap and raggedy gangsta rap clothing, becoming interchangeable with the city sanitary worker with whom he trades places. In *Enemy of the State,* race only becomes noticeable as difference when Dean "plays" or "performs" blackness—a blackness that he can, indeed, in the logic of the film, choose to renounce when he puts back on his Rolex and fancy suits.

The return to the safety of suburbia results in the effacement of difference. Race is actually shown as in opposition to the family and its propensity to consume, only becoming apparent when the state is too large, too insidious, too encumbering and overbearing. The insinuation here is that the state produces race as difference, while without the state, race really is unnoticeable and racism is not an issue. This idea keys into contemporary criticisms of welfare and affirmative action, where opponents are claiming that these state actions cause racism rather than putting a lid on its more outrageous institutional manifestations. In *Enemy of the State,* however, steamrolling black local and national cultures seems to be the first step in allowing and protecting the family bond. This disappearance of blackness seems to be a desirable end and is conducted only through Dean's requisition of his purchases, when he proves himself equal before the objects and therefore adequate before his wife.

Cultures of poverty in *Enemy of the State* are, indeed, shown to be a matter of personal choice and even a personal strategy for achieving personalized goals. For example, Gene Hackman (Brill, a former intelligence agent who later becomes Dean's ally) has chosen to live in a burned-out factory with minimal technological support because he himself has chosen to distance himself from state power, leaving out any mention that mostly housing shortages force people to squat. Most notably, during Dean's walk in the park with his college girlfriend, the government surveillance crew is all undercover as homeless people. The message is: poor people are really like "us," but wearing different clothes, and might even be faking it or disguised. Homelessness is a fashion choice and a good strategy for getting what you want, just like making your home out of a factory. This keys into certain cruel commentaries that profess that poor people are cheating the welfare system or disguising themselves as needy, having babies, for instance, just to collect more. Such images deny the realities of economic depravity, showing poverty as simply a matter of wardrobe choice. They also use the fact that the helpless are unnoticed to talk about the cleverness of the powerful.

BAD SEEDS

In *Enemy of the State,* the sanctity of the state is protected because it is not the state itself, but a marginal criminal element which is the source of the danger. The state is not seen as a predominant enemy of the family, but both the state and the family are simultaneously produced, in the end, as signs of a healthy society and a just resolution. The protection of privacy that the family represents also means that private business practices will become part of the natural order of human relationships. The Republican senator refuses the telecommunications deal by adamantly insisting that he will not let his privacy be invaded, an ethical position (in the film's own logic) that leads to his murder. Yet, the privacy that the senator dies defending is the privacy of corporate agenda-setting: "I've got three major employers in the Syracuse area alone that are going to get killed by this bill," he rejoins. "I'm talking about my constituents being out of work." Gone here is the implication that global corporations are no longer protecting workers' jobs but rather making them insecure, assuring compliance by threatening to move abroad to lower pay-roll costs or to avoid costly labor confrontations, environmental regulations, or inhibiting legal processes. In the film, however, corporations are seen as protecting the privacy of workers *against* labor organizing and government interventions. In fact, in the first scene after the credits, labor lawyer Robert Dean is called on a case to defend a laborer's choice of voting against the choice of the union. Clever pitting of the government against the mafia/labor union results, in the ending scenes, in a deadly shootout which kills those malignant predators in the state and in the unions. This culmination shows labor organization as infused with criminal elements, rotten and ineffectual at the core, just like the government. The evil in the state and the evil in the unions face off and shoot each other, each punished for the same reason: limiting the individual's abilities to choose. In the shoot-out scene, the corruption of labor—which was limiting the individual's right to vote—and the corruption of federal government—which is jeopardizing his right to buy—wipe each other out, leaving Will Smith and Gene Hackman alone and finally unguarded, walking freely away from the cordoned off crime scene being put back to order by the suddenly actively concerned agents of the FBI.

These few "bad seeds" in the state can be easily eliminated, and the state can function again as a sign of justice and order. All the recording equipment gets removed from Dean's house, his credit cards are reinstated, and the film's dénouement progresses into a quaint family scene with Dean, his wife, and his son snuggled up in front of the television set, and then Dean coquettishly inviting his wife to frolic (*"You* have a lot of monitoring to do," she responds, handing over to Dean the right to be subject of the gaze). Dean returns to his suburban fantasy life of his blender and remote control.

In the end, objects are what create equality. Dean's identity as upper class lawyer and a suburban family man is cemented in place through his self-recognition on his TV screen. Then, Gene Hackman dressed as a cop slips off only to resurface on Dean's TV as a pair of white hairy feet on a fantasy island displayed on the screen. Hackman's toes write in the sand, "Wish You Were Here." Smith waves to himself with a bewildered half-smile through the camera that had been hidden by Hackman in the smoke-detector on the ceiling. Intimacy between the buddies is forged through the surveillance technology that the buddies spent the film combating as a threat to their respective families. It turns out that the surveillance technology is not the problem when it can be bought as home furnishings, but only when it supports the public function of the state. Here the alliance of the life-saving technology of the fire alarm and the life-saving (identity restoring) technology of surveillance come together, and both serve to re-affirm the sanctity and comfort of the home. The technology has the power to take life, dismember identity, but also to restore it. The technology takes on an omnipotence which seems to be outside of the scope of human struggles over politics, class and racial interests, or questions of who controls the technology and hence has the power of manufacturing and deploying the fantasy.

In contrast to the cruel vision of *Enemy of the State*, a compassionate democratic politics recognizes that the real enemy of the people is the unfettered global corporate sector—precisely, the private—with its unfettered greed, singular ideal of market domination, perpetuation of unequal distributions of wealth and power, white supremacist, colonial, and patriarchal institutions, and that a strengthening of the public—of community, collaboration, alliance, dialogue, association, and compassion—is the groundwork for countering the logic of consumption and corporatism with practices of democracy and justice. A compassionate democratic politics works to dismantle corporate rule, works to make the corporation subject to the public interest, and recognizes the following: a social fabric defined by consumption renders highly unequal relations; technology needs to be thought of as a tool for countering unequal distributions of wealth, power, and cultural value; economic inequality cannot be over-come through increasing macroeconomic growth but rather through expanding the political power of the least enfranchised members of society. This includes democratizing control over cultural production so that culture, language, and ideologies can represent the interests of most people rather than an economic elite; strong, secure, and healthy families require public initiatives for high quality universal housing, education, health care, and political participation; economic inclusion requires not merely opportunities for consumption but opportunities for citizens to be involved in decisions about what is available to consume and what kinds of production should be done to achieve this. Developing this requires the formation of a critical, educated, and informed citizenry that understands the political, ideological, dimensions and implications of policy and cultural representation. But alongside educative initiatives for changing levels of awareness, new and progressive institutions need to be built, institutions that bring about democratic participation in decision-making about production while recognizing that issues of racial, ethnic, class, gender, and sexual equality involve economic redistribution. A politicized and critical democracy means the necessity of creating the conditions for different groups to be empowered to struggle and compete for diverse human values and interests rather than being subjected to the monological dictates of the dehumanizing values of the market.

NOTES

1. Thomas L. Friedman, *The Lexus and the Olive Tree: Understanding Globalization* (New York: Farrar, Straus & Giroux, 1999), 87.

2. M. Jacqui Alexander and Chandra Talpade Mohanty, "Introduction: Genealogies, Legacies, Movements," in *Feminist Genealogies, Colonial Legacies, Democratic Futures,* edited by M. Jacqui Alexander and Chandra Talpade Mohanty (New York: Routledge, 1997), xxxiii.

3. Robert W. McChesney, introduction to *Profit over People: Neoliberalism and Global Order,* by Noam Chomsky (New York: Seven Stories Press, 1999), 11.

4. Friedman, *The Lexus and the Olive Tree,* 241.

5. "Let Freedom Ring . . . Boycott the Bell!!!" Coalition, www.ciw-online.org.

6. Jean Baudrillard, *The Consumer Society: Myths & Structures* (London: Sage, 1998), 61.

7. Friedman, *The Lexus and the Olive Tree,* 84.

8. Friedman, *The Lexus and the Olive Tree,* 93.

9. Friedman, *The Lexus and the Olive Tree,* 89.

10. Friedman, *The Lexus and the Olive Tree,* 236.

11. Friedman, *The Lexus and the Olive Tree,* 236.

12. Jeff Strickler, "'Enemy of the State' at the top of the year's action-thriller list." *Star Tribune* (Minneapolis, Minn.), 20 November 1998, 1E.

13. Friedman, *The Lexus and the Olive Tree*, 13.

14. Friedman, *The Lexus and the Olive Tree*, 87.

15. Friedman, *The Lexus and the Olive Tree*, 27.

16. Friedman, *The Lexus and the Olive Tree*, 27.

17. Zygmunt Bauman, *Globalization: The Human Consequences* (New York: Columbia University Press, 1998), 60.

18. Bauman, *Globalization*, 84.

19. Friedman, *The Lexus and the Olive Tree*, 301.

20. Friedman, *The Lexus and the Olive Tree*, 302.

21. Friedman, *The Lexus and the Olive Tree*, 302.

22. Saskia Sassen, *Globalization and Its Discontents: Essays on the New Mobility of People and Money* (New York: The New Press, 1998), 42.

23. Friedman, *The Lexus and the Olive Tree*, 194.

24. Frantz Fanon, *The Wretched of the Earth: The Handbook for the Black Revolution that Is Changing the Shape of the World*, translated by Constance Farrington (New York: Grove Press, 1968), 61.

25. Friedman, *The Lexus and the Olive Tree*, 304.

26. Grace Chang, *Disposable Domestics: Immigrant Women Workers in the Global Economy* (Cambridge, Mass.: South End Press, 2000), 124–26.

27. Friedman, *The Lexus and the Olive Tree*, 42.

28. Friedman, *The Lexus and the Olive Tree*, 46.

29. Chandra Talpade Mohanty, "Women Workers and Capitalist Scripts: Ideologies of Domination, Common Interests and the Politics of Solidarity," in *Feminist Genealogies, Colonial Legacies, Democratic Futures*, edited by M. Jacqui Alexander and Chandra Talpade Mohanty (New York: Routledge, 1997), 20.

30. Baudrillard, *The Consumer Society*, 41.

31. Friedman, *The Lexus and the Olive Tree*, 214.

32. Friedman, *The Lexus and the Olive Tree*, 232.

33. Friedman, *The Lexus and the Olive Tree*, 225.

34. Friedman, *The Lexus and the Olive Tree*, 298.

35. Friedman, *The Lexus and the Olive Tree*, 235.

36. Joshua Cooper Ramo, "The Three Marketeers," *Time*, 15 February 1999, 39.

37. Ramo, "The Three Marketeers," 36.

38. Baudrillard, *The Consumer Society*, 94.

39. Baudrillard, *The Consumer Society*, 50.

40. Baudrillard, *The Consumer Society*, 94.

41. Baudrillard, *The Consumer Society*, 39–41.

42. Fredric Jameson, "Notes on Globalization as a Philosophical Issue," in *The Cultures of Globalization*, edited by Fredric Jameson and Masao Miyoshi (Durham, N.C.: Duke University Press, 1998), 69.

43. Baudrillard, *The Consumer Society*, 161.

44. Janet Maslin, "The Walls Have Ears, and Eyes and Cameras," *New York Times*, 20 November 1998, E1.

45. Adina Hoffman, "Bogged Down by Heavies," *The Jerusalem Post*, 22 January 1999, 5.

46. Maslin, "The Walls Have Ears," E1.

47. Maslin, "The Walls Have Ears," E1.

48. Maslin, "The Walls Have Ears," E1.

49. Sander L. Gilman, *Difference and Pathology: Stereotypes of Sexuality, Race, and Madness* (Ithaca, N.Y.: Cornell University Press, 1985), 81.

50. bell hooks, *Black Looks: Race and Representation* (Boston: South End Press, 1992), 74.

51. Anne McClintock, "Screwing the System: Sexwork, Race, and the Law," in *Feminism and Postmodernism,* edited by Margaret Ferguson and Jennifer Wicke (Durham, N.C.: Duke University Press, 1994), 113–14.

6

A Hilarious Romp
through the Holocaust

No longer is fear deployed to stifle and silence laughter. It is as if power has picked laughter as its most secure shelter; as if fear wants more laughter so that it will have more room to hide in and so that resistance to fear-wielding power could be paralysed before it started, and if it did explode, it would leave the fearsome intact. Like the phoenix from the ashes, or the ageing witch from the bathtub full of virgin blood, power arises from laughter reborn and rejuvenated.[1]

In the late nineties, a sudden blitzkrieg of films about the fascist threat came goose-stepping out of Hollywood. Some, such as *American History X* and *American Beauty,* located fascism at home, while others, such as *Saving Private Ryan* and *The Thin Red Line,* brought back the axis enemy from abroad. In both cases these films usually represent collective political action as either impossible, non-existent, or as inevitably authoritarian. As private concerns with family, sex, romance, and childhood innocence appear as the only reprieve from a total repressive authority, the possibility of public solidarity is rendered obsolete (*Milena, Before Night Falls, Life Is Beautiful, American Beauty, Quills, Fight Club, Elizabeth, Enemy at the Gates*). Such films eradicate the possibility of political action and represent personal liberty as an escape from the evil of politics by reducing agency to a strictly individual matter. What results from the removal of collective action from the popular imagination is an annihilation of the very thought of public culture and avenues of dissent. Endless films, books, and TV documentaries (like almost every program on the History Channel) define evil as embodied in the Nazis, thereby diverting attention from the United States's historical record and current practice of human rights abuses, including military actions like the Kosovo invasion, corporate actions like Amoco's use of paramilitaries in Colombia, and domestic actions like cuts in housing. What is at stake in such representations of politics itself as fascism is the imaginable role that the public sphere can have to institute fairness and equity, to create institutions which support the basic needs, health and well-being of citizens, to increase equality through public services and expenditures, and to promote democracy.

What is more, the material and representational assault on the public sphere produces anxiety, insecurity, and uncertainty about a future filled with flexible labor, capital flight, and political cynicism. The dismantling of social safety nets and other public infrastructure (such as social security, public schools and universities, welfare, public transportation, social services, health care, public legal defense, public parks, and public support for the arts) intensifies and accelerates this insecurity. Mass-mediated representations translate economic insecurity into privatized concerns ranked with public safety such as street crime, school dangers, viruses, and even terrorism. As well, mass media channels this anxiety into private preoccupations with controlling and ordering the body, its fitness, its appearance, its fluids, pressure, caloric intake. The widespread insecurity resulting from the dismantling of the public sector undermines the kind of collective action that could address the very causes of insecurity.[2] As Zygmunt Bauman insightfully writes,

> The need for global action tends to disappear from public view, and the persisting anxiety, which the free-floating global powers give rise to in every growing quantity and in more vicious varieties, does not spell its re-entry into the public agenda. Once that anxiety has been diverted into the demand to lock the doors and shut the windows, to install a computer checking system at the border posts, electronic surveillance in prisons, vigilante patrols in the streets and burglar alarms in the homes, the chances of getting to the roots of insecurity and control the forces that feed it are all but evaporating. Attention focused on the 'defence of community' makes the global flow of power freer than ever before. The less constrained that flow is, the deeper becomes the feeling of insecurity. The more overwhelming is the sense of insecurity, the more intense grows the 'parochial spirit'. The more obsessive becomes the defence of community prompted by that spirit, the freer is the flow of global powers. . . . And so on.[3]

A clear example of this type of insecurity can be found in calls for a missile defense system. The need for a missile defense system is grounded, its advocates proclaim, in threats posed by rogue nations and possible mistakes rendered by other, perhaps less cautious, nations. What is left out of these arguments is why so many nations would be U.S. adversaries. While talk of the missile defense system creates a sense of radical insecurity, the insecurity, is created as a tool to extend the public-to-private transfer of resources: defense contractors and high tech sector win out while the public loses. Resembling an organized crime protection racket, this example highlights the extent to which security is sold back to the public as the same powers that sell security rob the public of security by destabilizing the labor system, eradicating social safety nets, and fostering a militaristic posture domestically and globally, angering both allies and non-allies.

What could be more of a site of radical insecurity than the concentration camp or the battlefield? One can look to *Fight Club* and *American History X*, in which collective action inevitably becomes fascism, or one can look to *Saving Private Ryan* and *The Thin Red Line*, in which public service is for the restoration of the family or the redemption of the individual rather than the public. In these films, characters faced with social insecurity can pursue freedom from this insecurity only individually. These representations function pedagogically by producing identifications and understandings that are distinctly at odds with democratic social relations.

In this chapter, we discuss how representations of fascism, exemplified in the popular film *Life Is Beautiful*, are currently stoking cynicism about the possibility of collective political action. In what follows, we elaborate on the way that freedom is defined in opposition to politics. What makes *Life Is Beautiful* particularly egregious is the way that it accomplishes this vilification of public power by opposing politics and knowledge of political realities to childhood innocence, the safety of the family, and love. No doubt, the widespread popularity of such films about fascism owes in no small part to growing anxieties about the insecurity that individuals and families face amidst rapidly changing and volatile prospects about the future of livelihood. Rather than providing the public with collective solutions to the causes of insecurity, these films offer only sentimental and private responses that translate public concerns into private anxieties. Finally, we suggest that the translation of public concerns into private anxieties can be countered with a pedagogy that translates private anxieties into matters of public action.

REPRESENTING POLITICS

Why were so many blockbuster films about World War II produced at millennium's end (e.g., *Saving Private Ryan*, *The Thin Red Line*, *Schindler's List*, *The Last Days*, and even the documentary testimonials of survivors being collected by Steven Spielberg and screened at the Jewish Museum in downtown New York)? Contingently, why has there been such an interest in making films about fascist segments of U.S. culture (e.g., *American Beauty*, *American History X*)? And why do these films about fascism—in particular *Saving Private Ryan*—seem to show how fascism is out to destroy the family which is the root of American salvation? As in *Life Is Beautiful*, the entire U.S. war effort in *Saving Private Ryan* is mobilized to return the son to his tragically abandoned mother.

Current filmmaking about fascism, however, tends to restrict fascist practices to either a historical distance (*Life Is Beautiful*) or a marginal position adopted by extremists (*American History X, American Beauty*) while envisioning a safe place outside of fascism in which to situate the present. The present and the mainstream are, we are assured, free of fascism: the forces of freedom have overcome, and the forces of evil fascism get punished deservedly by their own excesses and pathologies and then are diminished to point zero, wiped out, literally shredded and turned to ashes. However, as Bill Martin argues, "We want to talk about the U.S. response to European fascism, the U.S. recruitment of Nazis and fascists at the end of the war into intelligence, defense and aerospace work, the sheltering of many Eastern European fascists in the Republican Party, and, most importantly, the fascism of leading figures in the U.S. government and political scene, from Pat Robertson and Jesse Helms, on up to Ronald Reagan."[4] Certainly such an allegation continues to be applicable, even as U.S. warplanes attacked Kosovo with little input from the citizenry, UN Security Council or Congressional approval, or when the Supreme Court decides who should be president based on make-believe legal principles. Furthermore, these representations of fascism preclude consideration of the ways democracy is prevented from developing in such obvious facts as the corporate control of congressional decision making and election outcomes through lobbying, soft-money contributions, and the consolidated control of information-production that keeps political issues framed in the interests of ruling elites.[5]

Yet, what is at stake here is not only the denial of fascist elements of the contemporary political scene. As well, representations of fascism are serving the neoliberal attack on the public sphere. A substantial ideological campaign enforces the erosion of public power in favor of deregulation and corporate control. As Herman and McChesney put it, "To no small extent the stability of the system rests upon the widespread acceptance of global corporate ideology.... [One]... element of global corporate ideology is that government intervention and regulation tend to impose unreasonable burdens on business that impede economic growth. . . . [Governments] should ideally confine themselves to the maintenance of law and order and the protection of private property."[6] Hence, *Life Is Beautiful* (along with the myriad other popular cultural programming of fascism) projects a neoliberal dystopian ideal of the state and the public rather than a fascist one. This dystopian ideal, in turn, feeds a more widespread ideological projection of the no-good state.

Events such as the Branch Davidian hold-off of federal police in Waco as well as the growing organization of militias culminating in Timothy McVeigh's bombing of the federal building in Oklahoma City give voice to a popular distrust of the state, particularly among right-wing extremists. Of course, this anti-state sentiment is hardly restricted to political extremists. Rather, as a central component of neoliberal ideology, anti-state sentiment symptomizes the general elevation of the market as preferable to the public sphere on the grounds of its inherent efficiency, accountability, competitiveness, freedom, and fairness. This appears, for example, in popular accusation that the federal government taxes excessively, taking away the citizens' rights to choose what to do with their well-earned money, as well as in debates over school vouchers, where public interventions are seen to have ruined education.

The weakening of government's power to protect the public's interests is one of the crucial factors supporting neoliberal consolidations, the transnationalization of capital and global market deregulations, and the insecurity that ensues. As Edward Herman and Robert McChesney have shown,

> [That the state is limited in serving a popular constituency] has a powerful channeling effect on policy choices: redistributing policies to rectify inequality and increase domestic demand will be treated harshly by the market, which will insist on policies that improve "competitiveness." Competitiveness in the world market depends on keeping costs down—including wages, benefits, and taxes on business and the wealthy—and avoiding inflation. Virtually all policy choices that directly serve ordinary citizens threaten "competitiveness" or inflation. By 1996 *Forbes* magazine exulted in the fact that the world's governments, be they ostensibly left or right, could no longer "interfere" with the prerogatives of business without suffering an economic punishment that would bring them down. Governments have effectively lost their power to govern.[7]

Of course, the anti-federalist perception that government power needs to recede is not accompanied by a diminishment of the powers of government but rather by an ideological belief that globalization requires and entails governmental limits. Military spending is on the increase as are subsidies for corporations and policing. The expansion of government power seems to be acceptable only when it is in the interests of the big money elites and the corporate sector while it is demonized when it comes to supports for civil liberties, basic needs, and public benefits. What is more, the growth of government to bolster the aims of capital is neglected in mainstream news coverage while "waste" and "inefficiency" pervade stories about public spending on education and welfare. *Life Is Beautiful* plays the game of hiding the ill effects of anti-federalism behind the absolute and heart-rending moralism that depictions of fascism tend to elicit.

THE POLITICS OF CHILDHOOD INNOCENCE

Life Is Beautiful was a raving first-run success, charming millions and winning an Academy Award and nominations for three others. It won runner-up grand jury prize at the renowned Cannes film festival and eight David di Donatello Awards (the Italian equivalent of the Oscar). The critics were mostly enthusiastic, lavishing abundant praise, saying, for instance, that "its sentiment is inescapable, but genuine poignancy and pathos are also present, and an overarching sincerity is visible too,"[8] with only an occasional half-hearted reproof that Benigni could regard "fascism as a laughing matter,"[9] or that he could turn "even a small corner of this century's central horror into feel-good popular entertainment,"[10] or that he could disregard the historical truth: "even a hint of the truth about the Holocaust," one critic proclaims, "would crush his comedy and reduce to absurdity his "fable" about a man named Guido making a sort of hide-and-seek game out of camp life."[11] As Benigni says in London's *Sunday Telegraph*, "People said, 'How dare he make a movie about this? We have to stop him.' I respect that opinion but I felt an urge to play a comic character in an extreme situation, and what could be more extreme than this?"[12]

Roberto Benigni's Chaplinesque two-part story joins a romantic comedy with a story of fatherly sacrifice and family survival during the Holocaust. In the first half of the film, Guido (Benigni), a Jewish newcomer to the city of Arezzo, comically attempts to seduce his future wife while she is being courted by an up-and-coming fascist magistrate. As he attempts to seduce this woman, Guido is also trying to negotiate with the state bureaucracy via the same magistrate to secure permits to open a store. Increasingly subjected to anti-Semitic attacks, Guido manages to steal the heart of his intended by literally rescuing her on a white steed from her marriage to the fascist. Guido marries his beloved, they have a son, Giosue, and eight years later the Nazis send the family off to a concentration camp. Part two takes place in the concentration camp. Guido lies to Giosue, saying that the concentration camp is really an elaborate game. Guido uses the game to save his child from the gas chamber by tricking him into staying quiet, hiding, remaining in good spirits, and not asking for food. Giosue endures the competition in hopes of winning the grand prize—a tank. Guido manages to communicate briefly with his wife who remains locked on the other side of the camp before he is finally shot attempting to save his wife and child as the war ends. The film finishes with the American military (via the prized tank) restoring Giosue to his mother.

The main problem of the film is not in its falsifications of a serious historical actuality where, as some viewers have claimed, the kid would have been turned to soap as soon as the Nazis had set eyes upon him. Realism does not seem his concern. "According to what I read, saw and felt in the victims' accounts," he explains, "I realized that nothing in a film could even come close to the reality of what happened. You can't show unimaginable horror—you can only ever show less than what it was. So I did not want audiences to look for realism in my movie."[13] The director's comments echo those of Claude Lanzmann, the director of *Shoah*, whose nine-hour-long documentary about Auschwitz uniquely refuses to represent visually the camp or the past. Lanzmann pieces together a history through survivor testimony as well as the testimony of those who lived near the camp and those who worked in it. Lanzmann's refusal to represent the Shoah comes on the ethical grounds that to do so would inevitably misrepresent an event that defies representation. Such misrepresentation would produce a false testament to the event. Whether or not one agrees with Lanzmann's deconstructionist approach to representation, unlike Lanzmann, Benigni's concern with representational politics had little to do with the ethical concern of doing injustice to the memory of the holocaust. Rather, as Roberto Benigni himself said, "I didn't want to make a movie about the Holocaust—I wanted to make a beautiful film."[14]

The principal problem of the film, however, is neither its failure to live up to an impossible aesthetic realism nor even principally the very big problem of aestheticizing politics. Rather, the main problem of the film, then, is that it functions pedagogically and politically by representing politics itself, not merely fascism, as a threat to family and youth. This is shown in four ways: (1) keeping children ignorant about political realities to protect them;[15] (2) depicting the only possibility of government as all authoritarian without any political opposition, dissent, or resistance; (3) posing the family and youth innocence as the only defense against totalitarian government;[16] and (4) resolving the film with the redemption of youth and family by the benevolent forces of the U.S. military. As Henry Jenkins writes,

This dominant conception of childhood innocence presumes that children exist in a space beyond, above, outside the political; we imagine them to be noncombatants whom we protect from the harsh realities of the adult world, including the mud splattering of partisan politics. Yet, in reality, almost every major political battle of the twentieth century has been fought on the backs of our children, from the economic reforms of the Progressive Era (which sought to protect immigrant children from the sweatshop owners) and the social readjustments of the civil rights era (which often circulated around the images of black and white children playing together) to contemporary anxieties about the digital revolution (which often depict the wide-eyed child as subject to the corruptions of cyberspace and porno websites). The innocent child carries the rhetorical force of such arguments; we are constantly urged to take action to protect our children. Children also have suffered the material consequences of our decisions; children are the ones on the front lines of school integration, the ones who pay the price of welfare reform. We opportunistically evoke the figure of the innocent child as a "human shield" against criticism.[17]

The myth of childhood innocence is employed not only in the service of class warfare and culture war nationally.[18] Additionally, it defends a politics of international globalization as can be witnessed, for example, in the ways representations of the starving child in Africa de-link the effects of systemic impoverishment of the Third World by the First World from its causes in the legacy of present day colonialism and economic imperialism.

As a cultural producer, Benigni wields pedagogical authority to frame issues of public import, to produce identifications and to suggest ideal social relations. With his pedagogical authority, however, Benigni does not contest the discourse on childhood innocence as it is used to legitimate material and symbolic violence, including the equating of childhood innocence with political ignorance.[19] For example, Guido attempts to protect Giosue from political oppression in the camp as well as from historical knowledge of anti-Semitism by keeping him ignorant, as if knowing the history of the oppression of the Jews makes Giosue more vulnerable to anti-Semitism and will lead to Giosue's slaughter at the hands of the Nazis. Prior to the camp incarceration, Guido lies to Giosue about anti-Semitic slogans written on his store, transforming these instances of pedagogical possibility into the erasure of politics and conflict. Giosue asks his father why the sign in the window says, "No Jews or Dogs Allowed." Guido responds by saying that sometimes people do not like other people for no reason, like the pharmacy down the street where they have a sign saying, No Chinese or Kangaroo. "Determined to protect his boy from the knowledge of what's going on" (as one critic admiringly puts it),[20] Guido turns hatred, racism, xenophobia, and intolerance into cute little quirks of personality or taste rather than explaining the very insidious ways they structure institutions and cause mass deaths.

Not the Nazis and the Fascists, but *knowing* about the Nazis and the Fascists is what Giosue needs to be guarded from in the film. Guido continues to conceal anti-Semitism from his son into the second half of the film, where Guido performs the ultimate lie in denying the existence of the Holocaust itself, supposedly for his son's benefit. Giosue learns through hearsay that the Nazis are turning the Jews into buttons and soap and burning their bodies in ovens. Guido's response is to laugh at the absurdity of this report, pointing out how unbelievable and fantastical and comedic is the very truth of their history. On the one hand, this may seem to erase the memory of the Holocaust, while, on the other, it serves to show (to the viewer, if not to Giosue) how political reality itself seems to be the product of absurd imagination, like a game rather than a result of historical material and discursive struggles.

Such a relationship between politics and innocence carries a number of unsavory implications for contemporary youth: (1) It suggests that kids are outside of politics, and that youth are incapable of acting as political agents. Yet, as Henry Giroux says,

> A democratic culture fulfills one of its most important functions when it views children as a social investment, whose worth and value cannot be measured exclusively in commercial and private terms. That is, a democratic culture provides the institutional and symbolic resources necessary for young people to develop their capacities to engage in critical thought, participate in power relations and policy decisions that affect their lives, and transform those racial, social, and economic inequities that close down democratic relations.[21]

(2) Furthermore, this strategy of using youth innocence as a defense from the political serves to define education as having the possibility of not being political; and (3) defensively challenges the idea, developed in the sixties, that youth is the hotbed of the political rather than its limits. As Maurizio Viano insinuates, Giosue represents a withdrawal from politics into the purely personal which needs to be taken seriously: "The game, then has a name: spirituality. . . . Our take on the game depends on our willingness to take seriously the sudden erupting of spiritual needs that characterizes this end of the millennium. . . . Differently put, the film/fairy tale/game suggests that we regard even the worst of nightmares as parts of a dream."[22] In other words, the only good politics is the absence of politics and the withdrawal into subjectivity, and the child is the embodiment of the absence of politics, the promise of the private. Additionally, the suggestion that there need to be spaces of refuge from the political implies that (4) community can only exist through affective bonds and therefore without politics; (5) the erasure of the social and the deification of the individual mean the embrace of consumerism; and (6) the private is the only good, denying the possibility of a social ethics. Tied to the autonomy of personhood and individual independence, freedom here is not a political arena to be struggled over but instead the outside of politics—transcendence and spiritual redemption.[23]

A central point of *Life Is Beautiful* is that protecting youth involves keeping youth ignorant of political realities. As one reviewer says, "Rated PG-13, *Life Is Beautiful* contains no profanity, nudity, sex, or violence. It is adult because of its theme of genocide."[24] Like Benigni, the critic assumes that knowledge of political violence in the form of genocide threatens youth innocence. Protecting kids from knowledge of politics is not only a subject of this particular film, but part of a broader conservative cultural discourse where youth seems endangered by such knowledge in, as the critic suggests, such mass-mediated items as pornography, cinematic violence, the Internet, and video games. How is knowledge being redefined as a threat to youth? What kind of knowledge is it, and how is the idea of youth being re-envisioned as vulnerable, or somehow contrary, to this sort of knowing? What is particularly egregious is that such rhetoric says youth is threatened by knowledge of political realities rather than by the political realities *themselves*, as though the mere knowledge of who the Nazis were would kill Giosue, rather than the Nazis themselves. This understanding denies the damage done to kids not by knowledge[25] but rather by oppressive political action performed by governments and corporations, for example, like cuts to welfare, cuts to social services in poor neighborhoods, reducing education to quantifiable competition, defending police who shoot unarmed civilians, etc. Let's see, rather, a comedy about how the United States financed and armed Indonesian genocide in East Timor. Maybe a musical about the lack of textbooks in Camden, New Jersey? A slapstick revue of the New York City police department's torture and murder of unarmed black civilians? Stuart Liebman writes in *Cineaste,* "Benigni could have rooted his story in facts that would anchor our understanding of the continuity of parental devotion in an awareness of its fragility and limits. Instead, he substitutes accessible, crowd-pleasing formulas that trivialize experience and displace despair to contrive a 'triumph of the human spirit.'"[26] Rather, *Life Is Beautiful* insists that knowledge of political realities should be replaced with entertainment. In the current context with knowledge and information so extensively controlled by the corporate sector, such a position powerfully affirms the extent to which corporate media fails to provide the kind of informative content necessary for citizens to participate in a democracy.

How does ignorance come to hold such a place of value, and how does it become so acceptable, indeed so entertaining, to talk about ignorance as the supreme pathway to deification and salvation? One could argue that there is "bad knowledge" that harms youth. We contend, however, that knowledge is made meaningful by being contextualized as part of the operations of power. A democratic approach towards knowledge production involves the pedagogical task of helping youth understand the power relations that inform the way representations and knowledge are made meaningful. This suggests that critical engagement with multiple forms of knowledge offers youth the possibility of political agency. As communications scholar Robert W. McChesney[27] has suggested, the current media monopoly functions as de facto censorship preventing diverse viewpoints and ideological positions from being widely distributed. Rather than turning to censoring "dangerous knowledge," dismantling the corporate monopoly on knowledge production would promote the likelihood of vigorous public participation and debate vital to the possibility of a genuine democracy. (It would also be the first step in turning over media production to citizens.)

The innocence of the child is further reproduced as the infantilization of the viewer. The film protects viewers from the realities of genocide just as Guido protects Giosue. As one movie review puts it, "The genocide and cruel conditions are there, but Benigni protects us a bit from harsh reality as Guido completely veils the horrors from his son."[28] Though Guido's physical deterioration due to conditions in the camp is visible on screen, Giosue's is not. The movie preserves the healthiness and strength of the white child to foreground how the protection of innocence is at stake. What would happen, for example, if Giosue caught lice, came down with dysentery, had a cut that got infected as he was hiding away in the barracks? What would happen if somehow his physical integrity were compromised, a body part made disgusting or hideous, his chubby cuteness turned to emaciation? In the face of the unavoidable visual evidence of physical deterioration of Giosue's beauty, would the viewer lose sympathy? If Giosue were ugly or nasty, *if Giosue were made to look like the children in the camps,* could the viewer invest enough in the desire for his survival to accept the fantasy of the U.S. military as loving, or that a father's lie to his child constitutes the ultimate sacrifice and martyrdom?

In contrast, *Born on the Fourth of July* provides an example of a film in which the political ignorance of youth has tragic consequences, but this tragedy becomes the basis for political engagement. The more recent *Light It Up* depicts the reality that politics is inescapable for many youth. In this case, working class and non-white inner-city students who are subject to racism and class oppression choose to fight back. As well, John Waters's *Cecil B. Demented* offers a picture of kids who, understanding the ways that corporate power oppresses them, go on an anti-corporate rampage in the name of free expression. *A Dry, White Season* shows both the necessity and the inevitability of the child as a witness to the cruelties of the South African Apartheid regime. In that film the white child not only helps his father realize the need to take action against political tortures of blacks and other resistance movers, but also is a pedagogical link who brings knowledge of the atrocities into wider public circulation by transporting important photographs for the Resistance. The first feature-length

Kurdish film, *A Time for Drunken Horses*, demonstrates how kids younger than Giosue by necessity acquire economic ingenuity to survive through the hardships, deprivation, and the unequal distribution of shortages implemented through the internationalization of commerce. Unlike in these other films, in *Life Is Beautiful* youth knowledge of political realities is deadly. Salvation is ignorance. What does this approach to the relationship between youth and knowledge suggest about the role of education? Even as the news insists on the impossibility of keeping the knowledge of cruelty from children—violence on TV; sex on the Internet; guns in the projects—why is such an extreme value—the value of life itself—placed on preserving this fictitious world of childhood uncorrupted by the sins of twentieth-century politics?

The important point is not whether or not kids are innocent, but how the myth of childhood innocence functions ideologically in ways that ultimately hurt kids: by commodifying youth and youth sexuality; by shifting the blame for social problems onto one of the least powerful segments of the population; by expanding youth consumerism; by accomplishing what Patricia Williams has called "innocence profiling"—that is, by affirming white privilege and power, assuming the culpability of non-white kids.

BACK TO BUSINESS: ERADICATING POLITICS

Alongside these films on fascism, other films use childhood innocence to intimate the impossibility of politics. The film *Election*, for example, shows childhood innocence endangered by the corruption of the electoral process. Unlike films such as *Cecil B. Demented*, *Election* suggests that political participation resides solely in electoral participation, whereas, in many other recent films (e.g., *Bulworth; Primary Colors; Oh, Brother Where Art Thou*), electoral participation appears as a bad joke, an illusion, dysfunctional, an opening for deceit and criminality, and an erasure of the potential for substantive social change. The corporate media's incrimination of politics aligns private life with a benevolent and saccharine depiction of power devoid of political controls.

As *Life Is Beautiful* begins, Benigni and his friend are going to the town of Arezzo to try their luck. Benigni dreams of opening up a bookstore, and it is this endeavor that the state bureaucracy blocks. When Benigni marries and has a child, he acquires the proper permits, along with a house with ample, hard-wood furnishings and beautiful clothes for his wife. With marriage, then, comes freedom from the state, but freedom defined as business and the objects of class prestige. The sentimental family is tied to a critique of business regulation. Thus moralized, freedom of commerce is framed as family safety and the protection of family privacy. As in advertising, the hard and difficult cruelty of unfettered competition appears kind, made appealing and seductive as the soft and loving touch of the mother.

One of the main faults of the Fascist state in *Life Is Beautiful* consists in this imposition of regulations and licensing requirements which curtail entrepreneurial initiatives, making it harder to do business. The family in the film represents freedom and, particularly, freedom from state controls and interventions, in other words, the freedom of a liberalized economy without protections, regulations or redistributions, the freedom to practice business. Benigni's absolute anti-federalist moralism erroneously portrays market freedom, rather than state protection, as the freedom of expression leading to increasing forms of democratization and the eventual dissolving of racism. As Jameson writes in his critique of the anti-federalist bent in the cultures of globalization, "The market in the sense of exchange and commerce thus functions . . . as what also escapes the unenlightened domination of the state itself. . . ."[29] After all, when Guido wins his wife from the fascist bureaucrat through winning a fair competition, he at the same time acquires the permits for his private business from the same bureaucrat. The business, however, does not do well. It is restricted from fair competition because someone has painted the words "Jewish Business" on the outside, making them have to cut prices below a profit level. Aligned with the state, the racist slur performs the same function as the fascist bureaucracy and its licensing permits by inhibiting what is supposed to be the fairness of the market.

TRIUMPH OF THE WILL

In *Life Is Beautiful*, the humor is driven predominantly by the cleverness of the protagonist. Guido's cleverness is deeply tied to his indomitable will—a will that he explicitly derives from the philosophy of Schopenhauer and which helps him, in the first half of the film, to win the attentions of his future wife and, in the second half of the film, to shield his son from Nazi persecution. The way will works, Guido's friend tells him, is through thinking, and this particular type of thinking transforms the material world into the idea that the imagination has conceived of it so that the world itself becomes a projection of the mind. It is not simply Guido's cleverness that enables him to seduce and win his future wife, but rather this cleverness in addition to his unmitigated persistence and perseverance in wooing her, risking his own safety and disregarding public mores. Again, in the second half of the film, Guido's cleverness is bound to his unrelenting will in his trickery and gaming for the survival of his family. This triumph of the will that Guido displays often takes the form of magic and even divine intervention, as when he makes the key to Dora's heart fall from a window by having Dora ask for it from the Virgin Mary, or when he makes Dora herself fall into his arms from out of the sky. In fact, the film culminates in one of Guido's miracles that the game sets up—that is, the miraculous arrival of the rescuing tank materializing in the concentration camp.

Much of the humor in *Life Is Beautiful* is constructed through the conflict between Guido's will and the stupidity of political life. For example, Guido impersonates the inspector from Rome in order to surprise Dora, who is one of the teachers at the school. The inspector's job is to talk to the children about the superiority of their race. Guido is unprepared, but at the behest of the haughty principal, he jumps up on the table to everyone's surprise, and starts driveling on about the superiority of his ear, fondling the bell-shaped cartilage at the end, and getting the children to follow suit. Next, he starts to undress. After the cut, he is in his underwear, dancing around on the table tops and pointing to his belly button, praising it as the belly button of the superior race. At this point, the real inspector from Rome steps in, and Guido grabs his clothes and flees out the window, yelling a promise to Dora that he will see her next time in Venice (and, of course, this is what happens).

Guido's will marks him as a radically free individual, free of the public mores and public institutions that he flouts, free even of material restraints. Guido can simply will change, prosperity, happiness, and abundance as his mind transcends the limitations of the material and political world, even outsmarting public officials and magically making eggs appear for his omelets and escapades. Yet individual liberty, as Zygmunt Bauman points out, *"can only be a product of collective work. . . . We move today though towards privatization of the means to assure . . . individual liberty."*[30] Indeed, Guido's acts of will conform to the cunning and deceit that Horkheimer and Adorno have identified as the nexus of the entrepreneur's *ratio,* the ability to use magic to produce a rational way of thinking. For Horkheimer and Adorno, fascism marks the culmination of rational thought, where rational thought, like the commodity, imitates and absorbs the transformative capabilities of "primitive," magical thought (accordingly, Guido's will would not oppose Fascism as much as reflect it under a different name: Fascism, too, magically transforms reality through the rules of scientific rationality and cunning).[31] Guido's acts of will even exceed the ultimate hindrance to transcendence: Guido's fantasy is realized after his death when, as Giosue acquires the prized tank, Guido's ever-generative mind magically realizes the outcome of the game as no longer a figment or a spell but a real object. Becoming real, the fantasy toy displaces what Giosue feared as the real: the Nazis and the concentration camp become the unreal, pieces of Giosue's long-gone paranoid fantasy rather than instruments of death. In order to assure his own freedom, Guido needs neither God, the attentions of the state, nor the aid of his fellow prisoners, but simply the realization of his own desire. Guido's indomitable will allows him to choose the outcomes of his actions while at the same time denying him the possibility of transforming his own life conditions by connecting his political will with the transformative desires of others.

The game is premised on the assumption that it is a choice and it can be ended at any time. If Giosue had gotten sick, the lie that Guido's choice and will transcended these social conditions would have been exposed because Guido's impotence in the face of these social conditions would have made apparent to the child his father's lack of choice and control. However, Guido's indomitable will transcends all social conditions; that is, his freedom of choice depends only on himself, despite his death. In effect, the supreme value of freedom of choice transcends even the grave. William E. Connolly has argued that the will, the very basis of Western civilization and philosophic thought, is currently in crisis, and so has become an overly emphatic, even paranoic source of cultural anxiety: with the popular understanding that, in the age of globalization and the rise of corporate power, the nation-state and public life do not provide the conditions in which citizens' wills are expressed, negotiated, voted on, and legally enacted, the individual will is more riotously accentuated in cultural forms, reaching even monstrous and mythic proportions. "According to the logic of democratic sovereignty," Connolly writes, "*I* am free when I can choose among several life options in a variety of domains; *we* are free when the state formally accountable to us through elections can act to protect both its standing in the world and the institutional conditions of nationhood. But the globalization of economic life deflates the experience of a sovereign, democratic state by imposing a variety of visible effects upon it that the state is compelled to adjust to. . . . The tendency to shift burdens to the most vulnerable constituencies is accentuated by the widespread tendency to blame the state for the limits it faces while celebrating the market as a potential site of freedom."[32] At present, the single biggest threat to basic freedoms and civil liberties stems from the over-extension of the corporate sector and its control over the state and civil society. With the ascension of the market, there has been a diminishing of participatory forums, a limiting of public debates on vital issues, and a large mainstream media initiative to make corporate control look natural and inevitable, beneficial to everybody, and objective, outside of politics. The will itself has been reduced to the exercise of consumer choice defended by the ever-diversifying "selection" that individuals can make between items on display in a constant parade of dazzling promotions.

In the face of the nation-state's retreat before transnational capital, the insecurity of the citizens' political will is redefined in myriad defenses of the individual's will constantly being thwarted. This was strangely showcased in the election battle of 2000 between Al Gore and George W. Bush. Electoral politics was presented in the news media as a threat to the stock market, a danger to the economy, and as one Chicago parent revealingly testified on CNN, political fighting threatened to keep her child from learning who the president was by Christmas. The point not to be missed in this statement is that politics, not the market, has been neatly framed as a forum for individual selfishness, greed, and a threat to childhood innocence: in this statement, childhood innocence indicates the magical perseverance of the people's will through the individual's transformative choice.

Like *Life Is Beautiful, American Beauty,* winner of the 2000 Academy Award for best picture, represented politics as absent and hence impossible or alternately present only as the worst form of politics, totalitarianism. A white middle class corporate man stands to be fired after years of loyal service to his company. In response to the insecurity of his work and the boredom of suburban life, he quits his job and reverts to the adolescent consumerist escapism of muscle cars, rock 'n' roll, marijuana, pumping iron, pursuing high school girls, and, oh yes, the *freedom* of working flipping burgers for minimum wage at a fast food joint. Collective action, worker solidarity, or political action as a response to the threatening labor conditions and repressive culture of the suburbs never appear as an option to the protagonist. Politics here is not only impossible as a choice to address the conditions of unfreedom, but when politics does appear it takes the form in which all choice is eradicated—fascism. What is so repulsive and desirable to Kevin Spacey's neo-Nazi neighbor in *American Beauty* is the possibility of choosing freely one's sexual practices as Kevin Spacey appears to. The skillful ideological work of *American Beauty* lies in its successful displacement of the conditions that limit individual choices onto the realm of individual, privatized concerns and extremist politics, whose major error is in denying innocence to children. Films such as *American Beauty* translate private anxieties about public issues into matters of private concern—most commonly concerns with individual and family security. As in *American Beauty,* and many shows on TV from the news to the true crime documentaries, the enemy is clearly shown to be your neighbor. And the remedy can only be less collective action rather than more. In this way, the representation of choice is a highly privatized affair, functioning pedagogically to frame not only the range of choices that individuals have but to define choice itself in individualized ways. What *American Beauty* shares with *Life Is Beautiful* is the refusal to admit that freedom comes from collective action, not from the will promised in the individualizing rationality of consumer desire.

MAKING RACISM INNOCENT

Guido's entertaining romance can and should, according to the logic of the movie, shield kids from knowing what is going on in Rome, what the Inspector was really going to talk about during his visit to the elementary school where Dora worked—racism, cruel authoritarianism, the Aryan dream, ideology, and power. This comedic critique of biological racism is also embroiled in a discussion of standards. The film uses the standard nineteenth century discourse on degeneracy, which the Nazis inherited, in order to show how very foolish the Nazis were in attributing intelligence as a racial trait. At the engagement dinner, the principal starts a conversation about third graders, and how preposterous it is that they cannot solve a problem of simple algebra. The problem given to them was about how much money the state would save if, instead of hospitalizing the mentally unfit and epileptic patients, it would, quite simply, eliminate them. Figures were provided about costs of care, and the other guests nodded that it was a question of simple algebra, while Dora shook her head in incredulity. The fact that German third-graders could solve such a problem while the Italians could not was given as proof that the Germans were, indeed, a superior race.

What is missing here is that the assumption that intelligence is linked to race is not only a ridiculous and laughable nineteenth-century doctrine, but has not stopped guiding policy. Teachers are being moved around, and schools are being closed up, in inner city and mainline Philadelphia for instance, because average test scores are deemed too low, while the effects of funding distributions on student performance is strategically all but disregarded. Standards are cited to justify unequal funding distributions. Educational agendas are being redesigned to motivate rising test scores instead of on the basis of what makes students better able to understand and live in the world, or what makes them able to have some control over their environments and livelihoods, or, still, what makes them able to identify and resist oppressions and work collaboratively to transform the conditions that give rise to their lived experiences. In *Life Is Beautiful*, the joke about standards displaces the reality that standards are, in fact, on the rise as a principal educational measure, not just in Nazi Germany, but also in the contemporary United States. It obscures the fact that racial inequalities and racism are still being justified through recourse to standards, and that this is neither a ridiculous historical aberration that our better moral senses tell us is obviously wrong, nor is it a joke. The standards fetish in educational reform policy that rages across the political spectrum eclipses more meaningful public discussion of whose standards and whose knowledge counts and why. As the standards movement shuts down such discussion it natural-

izes as most valuable the curriculum representative of groups with the
most power. Within the logic of the standards movement the political
agency of youth has no place because youth are to consume properly the
correct knowledge in the tradition of what Freire called banking education or what Donaldo Macedo has called "a pedagogy of stupidifica-
tion."[33] Thus, for example, youth struggles and organizing against racism
that are very seldom a part of standards movements appear as disruptive
rather than as vital democratic and defining pedagogical activities.

The focus on biological racism in the film obscures the way that racism
currently operates on a largely culturally based register by defining non-
whites as cultural pathologies. While Benigni's mockery of eugenics and
biologically based racism is well taken, particularly at a time of its resurgence with the publication of *The Bell Curve*, such a criticism shown to
contemporary liberal audiences, in fact, betrays a deeper analysis of the
way racism operates at present through cultural as well as biological figures of race.

The same is also true of another film released in the same year, *American
History X*. This film is about a neo-Nazi, Derek (Ed Norton), in Venice
Beach, Calif., who kills two black men for vandalizing his truck, and it is the
story of how Derek reforms in prison, leaves the movement, and tries to
save his younger brother Danny (Ed Furlong) from following in the same
path. This film takes a strong stand against neo-Nazis and their brand of
white supremacy by making it impossible to identify with Derek and his
neo-Nazi friends when they are performing acts of torture and evil. In the
scene where Derek murders the two black men as in another scene where
Derek rallies his followers to torture a black woman in a Korean super-
market, the camera's sympathy is with the victims, as the camera zooms in
to close-ups of emotion, panic, and pain. These practices of racism are so violent, extreme, and incomprehensible that they wipe out any possibility, on
the viewers' part, of considering complicity. The film clearly relies on visions of fear so that the viewer can rest easy knowing that his/her better
judgment and values are in opposition to the violence on the screen. *American History X*, however, does not put forth a political means of resisting,
overcoming, or changing white supremacy, but only of reacting to it affec-
tively. At the same time, the neo-Nazis in the film, including Derek himself, are able to articulate, very clearly and convincingly, the reasons for
joining white supremacist activities. Derek's father has died because, as a
firefighter, he was not protected and backed up, we are told, by the
most qualified job applicants, but rather by those chosen by affirmative action initiatives. This signifies, more broadly throughout the film, that
lower-middle-class white people are losing out economically and territori-
ally to blacks and immigrants like the Koreans (the film thus disregards that
the fire department is chiefly—over 90 percent in New York City—

composed of whites and, as even municipal governments are currently being forced to admit, this is due to continuing racism in hiring practices).

Derek therefore develops a carefully elaborated and thought-out political and social platform for hate for which the film never presents an opposing critical view but only an emotional one. The reasons for Derek's
decision to leave the movement were personal: the neo-Nazis he met in
prison were not committed enough, dealt drugs with Hispanic prisoners,
and in the end raped him. Then Derek meets and befriends a black prisoner who tells him a few jokes and protects him from potential assault by
the tough black gangs who intimidate prisoners across the color line.
There is no mention here of any political opposition that Derek could
form against neo-Nazism, but rather he changes his mind overnight because of the physical pain of the rape, a pain that makes him see that black
people (or at least one of them) can be nice too. In the end, after everybody is turned back onto the righteous path (Derek decides to help the
police to infiltrate the neo-Nazi movement), Danny gets shot and killed
by a black youth in school. The film is saying here either that the cycle of
violence will inescapably and inevitably continue or that the Nazi is redeemer (as in *Schindler's List*), hero, and victim rolled into one, and, ultimately, that blacks deserve the ill-treatment. Like *Life Is Beautiful*, *American History X* links politics to Fascism while reducing the idea of political
opposition to emotional and sentimental responses.

Most racist practices are not purely emotional or sensational bursts of
violence carried out by disturbed individuals or confused kids. Rather,
racist practices—evidenced in welfare cuts, challenges to affirmative action, unequal distributions of funds for schooling, racial profiling, the
continued impoverishment of inner cities, and the like—are integrally in-
sinuated within law, policy, and institutions. Culturally based racist discourses, in the form of the Moynihan Doctrine, and talk about the dysfunctional non-white family, justify attacks on social policies designed to
remedy racial inequalities. As Richard Lynn wrote in defense of Murray
and Herrnstein's *The Bell Curve: Intelligence and Class Structure in American
Life*, "There is one thing the underclass is good at, and that is producing
children. These children tend to inherit their parents' poor intelligence
and adopt their sociopathic lifestyle, reproducing the cycle of deprivation
from generation to generation."[34] Such attitudes are actually guiding public policy, as attacks on welfare, for instance, are justified in public rhetoric by calling the African American family a "tangle of pathology" as former New York Democratic senator Daniel Patrick Moynihan has been
claiming since 1965.[35] Affirmative Action and Aid to Families with Dependent Children have been subject to attack on the basis of the narrative
of the black welfare queen and the stereotype of the dysfunctional non-
white and single-parent family. As Lawrence Townsend, Riverside, N.Y.,

county welfare director, says, "Every time I see a bag lady on the street I wonder, 'Was that an AFDC mother who hit the menopause wall—who can no longer reproduce and get money to support herself?'"[36] These cruel comments define the black woman's body—against the "normal hard-working American family"—as in a parasitical relationship to the state. What becomes obvious in these cruel statements is the relationship between family discourse and economic interest. By linking the black mother to the state, such insidious representations make the state seem utterly deviant, out of place, overloaded, too needy, too demanding (particularly in its roles of economic redistribution and defender of social equalities). Within these representations, the state itself becomes a parasite, eating away at independence and freedom.

Contingently, as soon as it becomes evident that the family is in need of the state, the family assumes an abject status. It is thereby inferred that the public should not have any interest or responsibility within the privacy represented by the family unit. This abhorrent image of the state as the refuge of the single black mother or welfare queen defines, through opposition, the "healthy family" as a family that does not need the state. As well, the "healthy family" comes to replace the state's functions of support, education, and the performance of justice.

Life Is Beautiful's restoration of biological racism as the dominant mode of racism obscures the way that cultural racism allows white middle class viewers to believe that their opposition to the Klan and neo-Nazis is as far as their anti-racism needs to go. As well, conservative and liberal support for the dismantling of welfare, the weakening of affirmative action, the worsening of apartheid-style school and housing segregation testify to the ways in which anti-federalist projects are steeped in racist practices that need to be undone and challenged. In its liberal confidence and assumed innocence, *Life Is Beautiful* does not stop with displacing and silencing a critique on the ways contemporary institutional and culture-based racism fuels unjust educational funding. The sense that the public function is malignant continues inside of the film's conception of all public institutions. In the exchange at the engagement party about how the state should eliminate epileptics, as well as in the terror of the Nazi medical inspection, the film also stages an attack on state involvement in health care, where the state is seen to function as a killing machine targeting the marginal and the weak. One could almost argue here that it would be better, and safer for the patients, for state-supported mental health hospitals to close and turn the patients, out into the streets, as many politicians are currently arguing in the name of "fiscal responsibility."

Life Is Beautiful succeeds in making racism seem as just a stupid and false understanding of biology based on a discarded nineteenth century doctrine. Also, as it makes the audience laugh at the racism of others, it exculpates the audience from complicity in the racism that structures the everyday. Racism as archaic, elsewhere, and entertaining fosters the denial of contemporary racism as a social reality that needs to be changed through popular political force.

FUN AND GAMES FOR THE WHOLE FAMILY

In *Life Is Beautiful*, the game grants the possibility of hope in the face of extreme hardship, pitting the will to survive against the power of cruelty. Entertainment is the key to the child's survival, and thus preserves the innocence of everybody. However, games and entertainment are currently, in today's political climate, seen as a hazard. Movies like *The Matrix* (a convergence of film and videogame) are blamed for school shootings, while computer games like *Doom* are seen to create the kind of aggression in men that leads to war, murder, domestic abuse, and the stockpiling of weapons, or, as Justine Cassell and Henry Jenkins contend, "socializing boys into misogyny and excluding girls from all but the most objectified positions,"[37] promoting violence and exclusions by reinforcing destructive gender norming. An article in *Time* warns parents about the "Pandora's hard drive . . . the appalling filth, unspeakable hatred and frightening prescriptions for homicidal mayhem"[38] which are available on the Internet, where all knowledge is equally suspect, "ruled obscene or otherwise objectionable,"[39] from pornography to instructions on how to build bombs to correspondence from the Ku Klux Klan to gay and lesbian politics interchangeably. *Time* gives guidelines to parents on how to censor or monitor their kids—from buying software to checking recently visited Web sites to actually reading their kids' e-mail files (behind all this is an idea that kids' civil liberties are negligible). *Time* basically infers that kids are endangered by their exposure to the democratic public culture and free interactions that the Internet might offer them, and that it is up to parents to clamp down, discipline, and limit access to this knowledge. The responsibility for saving children from the violence and the sex of the Internet lies solely with the family, and particularly with their surveillance techniques: "But schools and libraries stake a claim on too little of the child's time, and inescapable First Amendment issues make it unlikely that any public agency will be or should be able to play an effective role in controlling Net access and content. That can happen only at home."[40] Knowledge is dangerous here because it is besmirched with public sensibilities and institutional protections. It is only by reconnecting with the privacy of the family that children will be saved.

How does *Life Is Beautiful*, then, manage to contend and avoid this logic, which says that entertainment and games are the corrupters of youth, offering kids a vile kind of escapism that fries their minds, makes them pathological, captures them in fantasy, destroys their ethical judgment, disorients their sense of reality, and propels them towards deviant behaviors? *Life Is Beautiful* adopts a mainstream ambivalence found in such discussions of games, where, as even Cassell and Jenkins point out, games are good to teach the values of competition and begin to assimilate kids into professional careers like engineering and computer science. The game in *Life Is Beautiful* works: Giosue hides from the Nazis because he thinks he is earning points, and laughs at the cruelty. He does not cry, call for his mother, or complain of hunger because these actions, as Guido had translated the rules of the "ones who yell," would make him lose points. In the end, the Americans come and, finding Giosue standing alone in the camp, invite him to ride in their tank. Giosue calls this his victory. "We won! We won!" he yells as the frame stills and the credits begin to roll. The game has completely erased the history of cruelty, and, unlike the kids who are losing their minds over *Doom*, Giosue's complete absorption in the game guarantees his and, by extension, all of our survival.

The U.S. Army has learned well Hollywood's skillful depoliticization[41] of war that turns war into a loving game. Ads for the Marines show a lone Marine going to war against a computer-generated dragon in a video game format.[42] Likewise, the TV show *Boot Camp* advertises the military as a game modeled on its competition, the TV show *Survivor*. As in *Survivor*, the competitors on *Boot Camp* must perform various feats efficiently or face punishment. The losing team has to vote out one of its members. The voting-out ritual is accompanied by a series of vignettes or confessions of how the players feel about their fellow team members, including about such irrelevant factors as their sexualities.[43] This serves to psychologize conflicts, showing them as part of random personality quirks and differences rather than about sociopolitical disagreements, ideological clashes, resource distributions, and tendencies towards territorial expansion and acquisition. In addition, the personal confessions make collective action and teamwork seem impossible, as close affiliation tends to turn people against each other. The difference between the two "Reality" programs, *Survivor* and *Boot Camp*, however, is that in *Boot Camp* the playing field is a facsimile of war, and the players must strategize about how to defeat an invisible enemy, or how to get by some obstacle in order to attain a military objective.[44] What is missing is a humanization of the enemy in terms of what the enemy represents and what makes the enemy into an enemy. Instead, war, like business, is conceived of as simply the development of competitive strategies for discipline and for winning, even for beating out friends and neighbors for the glory of it. Nonetheless, military activity as fun, games, and entertainment does more than obscure the purpose of the military as neither fun nor innocent and as hardly about uniting families, but rather exists to kill people efficiently.

The game in *Life Is Beautiful* poses a competition for points as the principle of salvation against a cruel and all-powerful state. In other words, the central metaphor of the game functions to place free and unfettered competition of individuals as the good fighting and winning against the evils of an insanely powerful federalism. Giosue is an example of a character whose true individualism saves him. When the Nazis come to take all the children to the showers, Giosue escapes, runs into the work camp to announce to his father, as he does an adorable childish dance and stamps his feet, that he does not want to take a shower. It is Giosue's childlike refusal—his "natural" effusion of independent thought and action—to give in to the conventions of adulthood that saves him, making his lack of knowledge seem all the more important and vital. Unlike the other children, Giosue has outsmarted the Nazis, and in this he seems to deserve his survival and the viewer's sympathy in ways that the other children do not.[45]

This fashioning of the individual within a competition for points and survival is distinctly opposed to the world of labor which the film depicts. Whereas the game is shown as fun and elevating (unlike in *The Matrix*, where it marks the end of the human as such and the coming of age of machines), labor is shown as sordid, dirty, and dehumanizing. Additionally, as playing the game is an act of resistance against state power, labor is a mechanism through which the state enacts its power, evincing the way the state claims the bodies of its citizens, marking them with numbers, coercing their compliance. As in the popular imaginary about Communist regimes, working for the state is shown to create utter conformity among people, a long line of automation where everybody is and does the same in a work world controlled from above (the likeness of this image to assembly-line production and Fordism—actually U.S. phenomena rather than Communist ones, arising out of industrial capitalism—is effaced in the very bleakness of the light here, the sense of desperation rather than fulfillment and glory). In a line of similarly grungy men wearing the same striped suits, Guido carries heavy anvils from one place to another where they will be built into Nazi military equipment. The work is hard and heavy; Guido and the other men finish the day exhausted, spent, and all but wasted.

In *Life Is Beautiful*, the crux and goal of the game is to get the family back together and reconstruct the fable. Dora does not really play a role during this second half except as the serene image of future hope, her eyes lifted and sometimes teary, her face somber and reflective of abundant devotion to the singular purpose of returning to the fold. The film shapes the State's attack on the private enterprise of individual subjects into a threat on the familial order when it is really the new age of global capital and markets themselves that are undermining familial relations,[46] substituting instead nostalgic, even fetishistic images of belonging and warmth. It is significant here that Miramax's chief Harvey Weinstein insisted on including the ending, where Giosue's grown-up voice-over thanks his father for this "gift." As in Disney's products (Disney owns Miramax), the real in *Life Is Beautiful* is reinstated as the innocence of children in the haven of the nuclear family. Most important, the G. I. Joe American hero rescues Giosue from the camp and restores him safely to his mother. The military and its technologies here promise the triumph of the United States and its families. *Life Is Beautiful* and films like it contribute to creating the new ethics of globalization as a glorious triumph of love, maligning the state instead of indicating its historical role of providing possibilities of social justice and democracy. As Horkheimer and Adorno say, "Donald Duck in the cartoons and the unfortunate in real life get their thrashing so that the audience can learn to take their own punishment."[47] Educators need to develop a counter-discourse, one that is able to show the fallacies of anti-federalism and shore up different types of histories and alternative visions for states of the future.

CONCLUSION—TRANSLATING THE PRIVATE TO THE PUBLIC

What might it mean for educators to develop a pedagogy that counters the privatizing tendencies of corporate cultural products and that translates private anxieties and insecurities into matters of public concern? We would like to take this issue up in relation to corporate curriculum by situating a film such as *Life Is Beautiful* within corporate cultural production more generally. As Henry Giroux argues, "corporate interests represent a new stage in an effort to abstract the notion of the public from the language of ethics, history, and democratic community."[48] What is needed is a concerted vitalization of the public sector through strengthening public sector institutions such as schools. This can be set in motion through developing and celebrating a discourse of the public to counteract the ideological projection of the corporate sector as the loving redeemer.

First, corporate curricula in the form of films, literature, and school materials need to be understood in relation to the broader corporatization of civil society and the broader privatization movement that is global and that threatens not only actually existing public institutions but the viability of the very notion of the public. Some of the necessary investigation into the ways corporate culture works must involve not only the study of the political economy of corporations but such study in relation to how corporations (1) frame issues and information in the corporate interest, (2) produce identifications with the corporate sector and with values and beliefs consistent with corporate control and against collective action and communitarian values, and (3) produce student identities.

Second, by understanding multiple forms of corporate cultural products such as film, TV, literature, museum exhibits, etc., as corporate curricula, cultural workers can focus on the cultural politics of these products relationally to see the ways broader public discourses about class, race, gender, sexuality, and nation are being produced and deployed pedagogically. Such a shift away from ascribed disciplinary boundaries encourages the emphasis on the political workings of these products.

Third, corporate curricula need to be combated both by attempting to replace them with public culture and by using corporate cultural products to teach those public values that corporate culture seeks to eradicate: collective action; communal work; critical citizenship; civic hope; political struggle; dissent; the radical indeterminacy of the future; the relationship between knowledge and power—that is, the political dimension of knowledge. Such combat against corporate culture needs to be understood as a part of a broader struggle to expand the public sector locally, nationally, and globally.

It is, of course, not enough simply to analyze representations and critique their ideological import and the institutions that they benefit. Indeed, the ideological power of such mass-mediated products is so strong that it cannot be simply dismantled with textual readings and counterdiscourse. Not only do the mechanisms for creating consent for neoliberal policies need to be revealed for what they are, not only do the cracks in its logic need to be exposed, not only does its control of information need to be unlocked and its performances of atrocities unveiled for public judgment, not only do alternatives need to be formulated, but also cultural workers need to start changing the material circumstances of neoliberal culture through direct interventions and public outcries. When corporations take over schools and curricula, they jeopardize the public and its institutions as a source of knowledge, as the present debate threatening the status of public school educational funding demonstrates.[49] What is at stake in the struggle over cultural curricula is participatory democracy itself and the possibility of the school as one public forum for democratic deliberation and one site for expanding the public sector.

NOTES

1. Zygmunt Bauman, *In Search of Politics* (Stanford, Calif.: Stanford University Press, 1999), 62.

2. Bauman, *In Search of Politics*, 5. "People feeling insecure, people wary of what the future might hold in store and fearing for their safety, are not truly free to take the risks which collective action demands. They lack the courage to dare

and the time to imagine alternative ways of living together; and they are too preoccupied with tasks they cannot share to think of, let alone to devote their energy to, such tasks as can be undertaken only in common."

3. Bauman, *In Search of Politics*, 195–96.

4. Bill Martin, *Politics in the Impasse: Explorations in Postsecular Social Theory* (Albany: State University of New York Press, 1996), 213.

5. For detailed coverage of the way information is framed and filtered by corporate media in ways that inhibit democratic participation and favor elites, see Robert McChesney, *Rich Media, Poor Democracy* (Urbana: University of Illinois Press, 1999); Don Hazen and Julie Winokur, eds., *We the Media: A Citizens' Guide to Fighting for Media Democracy* (New York: New Press, 1997); Edward S. Herman and Robert W. McChesney, *The Global Media: The New Missionaries of Corporate Capitalism* (London: Cassell, 1997).

6. Herman and McChesney, *The Global Media*, 35–36.

7. Herman and McChesney, *The Global Media*, 32.

8. Kenneth Turan, "The Improbable Success of '*Life Is Beautiful*,'" *Film Quarterly* 53, no. 1 (Fall 1999), 26–34.

9. Sharon Johnson, "'*Life Is Beautiful*'—Every Taste Satisfied with Italian Movie," *Harrisburg Patriot*, 17 February 1999, C5.

10. Richard Schickel, "Fascist Fable: A Farce Trivializes the Horror of the Holocaust," *Time*, 9 November 1998, 116.

11. Schickel, "Fascist Fable," 116.

12. Cited in Stuart Liebman, "If Only Life Were So Beautiful," *Cineaste*, 22 March 1999.

13. Cited in Maurizio Viano, "Life Is Beautiful: Reception, Allegory, and Holocaust Laughter," *Film Quarterly* 53, no. 1 (Fall 1999), 30.

14. Cited in Liebman, "If Only Life Were So Beautiful."

15. Henry Giroux, *Stealing Innocence: Youth, Corporate Power, and the Politics of Culture* (New York: St. Martin's Press, 2000), 2–6. Henry Giroux has talked much about the ambiguities in the myth of childhood innocence. He shows how at the same time as children are romantically idealized as the target of evil pornographers, teachers, and other neighborhood dangers, and depicted as completely without resources to deal with these threats, they are being blamed for a wide range of social problems from inner city violence to gang warfare, weapons and drug trafficking, and pregnancies, which drain the public coffers. Giroux writes, "Marked as innately pure and passive, children are ascribed the right of protection but are, at the same time, denied a sense of agency and autonomy. Unable to understand childhood as a historical, social, political construction enmeshed in relations of power, many adults shroud children in an aura of innocence and protectedness that erases any viable notion of adult responsibility even as it evokes it. In fact, the ascription of innocence largely permits adults to not assume responsibility for their role in setting children up for failure, for abandoning them to the dictates of marketplace mentalities that remove the supportive and nurturing networks that provide young people with adequate health care, food, housing, and educational opportunities. . . . Without understanding the experiences of actual children, contemporary society confronts the sometimes perilous, although hardly rampant, consequences of drug use and violent behavior by stiffening jail sen-

tences for teens, trying them as adults, and increasingly building new prisons to incarcerate them in record numbers."

16. Lauren Berlant, *The Queen of America Goes to Washington City: Essays on Sex and Citizenship* (Durham, N.C.: Duke University Press, 1997), 3. Lauren Berlant has attributed this popular cultural nostalgia for youth and intimacy to the growing politics of privatization and depoliticization emerging out of the Reagan years: She writes, "A conservative coalition formed whose aim was the privatization of U.S. citizenship. One part of its project involved rerouting the critical energies of the emerging political sphere into the sentimental spaces of an amorphous opinion culture, characterized by strong patriotic identification mixed with feelings of personal powerlessness." Precisely what *Life Is Beautiful* does is to suggest that politics is defined only through its sentimentalization in the family.

17. Henry Jenkins, "Introduction: Childhood Innocence and Other Modern Myths," in *The Children's Culture Reader,* edited by Henry Jenkins (New York: New York University Press, 1998), 2.

18. The discourse of childhood innocence is both historical and cultural. It becomes increasingly crucial in the debates over child labor, psychoanalysis, mandatory education, and children's consumer culture during the heyday of the Industrial Revolution in the late nineteenth century. See Henry Jenkins, ed., *The Children's Culture Reader* (New York: New York University Press, 1998). In particular, see Philippe Ariès's groundbreaking essay "From Immodesty to Innocence" as well as Stephen Kline's "The Making of Children's Culture" and Viviana Zelizer's "From Useful to Useless: Moral Conflict over Child Labor." Additionally, for a discussion of how the myth of childhood innocence was implemented to enforce colonial power, see Ann Laura Stoler's *Race and the Education of Desire: Foucault's History of Sexuality and the Colonial Order of Things* (Durham, N.C.: Duke University Press, 1995), which references Foucault's *History of Sexuality,* vol. 1, with its ideas about the discourse of the masturbating child and attempts to police it. Gail Bederman's *Manliness & Civilization: A Cultural History of Gender and Race in the United States, 1880–1917* (Chicago: Chicago University Press, 1995) also draws on Foucault to analyze how the innocence of white boys was seen to be threatened by the stresses of modernity. She discusses how Theodore Roosevelt and G. Stanley Hall, among others, suggested that the requisite toughness to carry on the white man's burden of advancing civilization could be acquired by white boys by accessing their "primitive" unconscious through activities such as were developed in the Boy Scouts and at the YMCA.

19. Ben Dworkin, "'*Life Is Beautiful*'—Cinematic Attempt to Tackle Shoa's Issues," *New Jersey Jewish News* LII, no. 44 (29 October 1998), 38. As one commentator remarks, "*Life Is Beautiful* is not a fairy tale, but more of a Chaplinesque fable— a unique and bittersweet story with a message about innocence, love, loss and hope that delicately balances both tears and smiles. All the while it manages to treat an emotional and difficult subject with respect."

20. Turan, "The Improbable Success of '*Life Is Beautiful.*'"

21. Henry A. Giroux, *The Mouse that Roared: Disney and the End of Innocence* (Lanham, Md.: Rowman & Littlefield, 1999), 20.

22. Viano, "Life Is Beautiful: Reception, Allegory, and Holocaust Laughter," 32–33.

23. Instead of a clean, hard look at the Holocaust as the culmination of capitalist progress and colonial ideologies that need still to be resisted, the movie says that only the sentimental love of family will get us through, using the family fable as a diversionary tactic to undo the possibilities of a political engagement or critique.

24. Bob Fenester, "Humor, Horror: A Part of *'Life'* Superb Italian Film Takes Radical View," *Arizona Republic*, 30 October 1998, D1.

25. One could argue that there is "bad knowledge" that harms youth. We contend, however, that knowledge is made meaningful by being contextualized. A democratic approach towards knowledge production involves the pedagogical task to help youth understand the power relations that inform the way representations and knowledge are made meaningful. This suggests that critical engagement with multiple forms of knowledge offers youth the possibility of political agency. The current media monopoly functions as de facto censorship preventing diverse viewpoints and ideological positions from being widely distributed. Rather than turning to censoring "dangerous knowledge," dismantling the corporate monopoly on knowledge production would promote the likelihood of vigorous public participation and debate vital to the possibility of a genuine democracy.

26. Liebman, "If Only Life Were So Beautiful."

27. See McChesney, *Rich Media, Poor Democracy.*

28. Daniel M. Kimmel, "'*Life Is Beautiful*' a Moving Film," *Telegram & Gazette* (Worcester, Mass.), 17 February 1999, C5.

29. Fredric Jameson, "Notes on Globalization as a Philosophical Issue," in *The Cultures of Globalization,* edited by Fredric Jameson and Masao Miyoshi (Durham, N.C.: Duke University Press, 1998), 72.

30. Bauman, *In Search of Politics,* 7.

31. Max Horkheimer and Theodor W. Adorno. *Dialectic of Enlightenment,* translated by John Cumming (New York: Continuum, 1991), 77–78.

32. William E. Connolly, "The Will, Capital Punishment, and Culture War," in *Cultural Studies & Political Theory,* edited by Jodi Dean (Ithaca, N.Y.: Cornell University Press, 2000), 35.

33. Paulo Freire, *Pedagogy of the Oppressed* (New York: Continuum, 1970, 1993); Donaldo Macedo and Lilia Bartolome, *Dancing with Bigotry* (New York: St. Martin's, 2000).

34. Richard Lynn, "Is Man Breeding Himself Back to the Age of the Apes?" in *The Bell Curve: History, Documents, Opinions,* edited by Russell Jacoby and Naomi Glauberman (New York: Times Books, 1995), 356.

35. Robin D. G. Kelley, *Yo' Mama's Disfunktional!: Fighting the Culture Wars in Urban America* (Boston: Beacon Press, 1997), 2.

36. Cited in Patricia Williams, *The Rooster's Egg: On the Persistence of Prejudice* (Cambridge, Mass.: Harvard University Press, 1995), 6.

37. Justine Cassell and Henry Jenkins, "Chess for Girls? Feminism and Computer Games," in *From Barbie to Mortal Kombat: Gender and Computer Games,* edited by Justine Cassell and Henry Jenkins (Cambridge, Mass.: The MIT Press, 1998), 3.

38. Daniel Okrent, "Raising Kids Online: What Can Parents Do?" *Time,* 10 May 1999, 38.

39. Okrent, "Raising Kids Online," 42.

40. Okrent, "Raising Kids Online," 42.

41. One way the Army's ideological production has depoliticized war is by re-tooling its slogan from a message of individual self-actualization, "Be All That You Can Be," to the more explicitly individualistic "Army of One." While the prior slo-gan was highly individualistic it still allowed the possibility of teamwork as the ads emphasized visually. The new Army slogan is accompanied by such scenes as a fully outfitted soldier double-timing it across a desert on his lonesome.

42. Like the convergence of video games and film showcased by such produc-tions as *The Matrix* and *Tomb Raider,* the Navy commercials advertised the film *Men of Honor* that in turn advertised the Navy on big and small screen and in the content of the film.

43. One woman, for example, tells that she wanted to be on *Boot Camp* because it was the only way she could do military training as an open lesbian. The pro-gram cuts to various team members talking about what they feel about her sexu-ality, mostly agreeing that her coming-out in front of the whole team was "unnec-essary." Nobody ever tells why it was so "necessary" for the whole team to be considered straight.

44. Lev Grossman, "In Brief," *Time.com,* www.time.com/time/magazine/arti-cle/0,9171,98961,00.html, 19 February 2001. The U.S. military created an Internet-based promotion that, like *Boot Camp,* follows the private lives of privates in the service by following their every action with spy cameras—a format that has been predominantly the domain of Internet pornography fetish sites ("Basic Training: The Making of an Army of One," www.goarmy.com/basic). Advertises Time Inc., "SURVIVOR III Apparently eager to cash in on two trends—reality TV and the Web—at once, the Army has launched a website called Basic Training that will fol-low the real-life, real-time adventures of six young recruits as they make their way through the trials and tribulations of the first nine weeks of Army life, from their first haircut to their last push-up. The recruits—four men and two women—will go through training at Fort Jackson in South Carolina. The show, which promises 'uncut, unfiltered glimpses of life in the Army,' premieres Feb. 16. Any moles will be summarily court-martialed."

45. This scene references another scene prior to Guido's imprisonment, when Dora was trying to get Giosue to take a shower, and Giosue impishly refused, hid-ing in a cupboard. The scene of Giosue's refusal to conform to the Nazi orders as the other children did links his extremely individualistic responses to the sweet re-membrances of family life and, through them, to a sweetly nostalgic idea of indi-vidual privacy as safe and free from state power.

46. Grace Chang, *Disposable Domestics: Immigrant Women Workers in the Global Economy* (Cambridge, Mass.: South End Press, 2000), 124. Writes Grace Chang, "When wages and food subsidies are cut [through global structural adjustment programs implemented by the World Bank and the IMF in the Third World], women as wives and mothers adjust household budgets often at the expense of their own and their children's nutrition. As public health care and education van-ish, women suffer from lack of prenatal care and become nurses to ill family mem-bers at home, while girls are the first to be kept from school to help at home or join the labor force. When export-oriented agriculture is encouraged, indeed coerced, peasant families are evicted from their lands to make room for corporate farms. Many women are forced to become seasonal workers in the fields or in processing

areas, or to find work in the service industry in manufacturing, or in home work producing garments for export. When women take on these extra burdens and are still unable to sustain their families, many have no other viable option but to leave their families and migrate in search of work."

47. Horkheimer and Adorno, *Dialectic of Enlightenment*, 138.

48. Henry A. Giroux, "Consuming Social Change: The United Colors of Benetton," in *Disturbing Pleasures: Learning Popular Culture* (New York: Routledge, 1994).

49. George W. Bush's proposal to give more funding to public schools to support standards testing does not, to us, mean that public schools are getting more educational funds. Standards testing does not fit our definition of education.

Conclusion

A s the preceding chapters illustrate, popular culture and new curricula are largely functioning pedagogically to create consent for neoliberal policies. Yet, as we have discussed and demonstrated, cultural workers including teachers can use cultural artifacts both to contest capitalism, white supremacy, and patriarchy, and to arrest current oppressions through participating in building a viable, democratic public. We turn now to the question of how current academic work, as one site of cultural production, expands or shuts down the possibilities for developing a critical democracy.

Much academic writing tends to evade the traumas of globalization or to undertheorize the relationship between cultural production and the increasing concentration of wealth in the hands of a few, the increasing disparity of rich and poor, and the increasing levels of poverty and insecurity on a global scale. This evasion on the level of theory is currently weakening the political potential of both higher and secondary education as sites of counterhegemonic knowledge production, refusing to address the economic situation that is harshly afflicting the possibility of free thought. Even as postmodernism celebrates cultural difference and marginal voices, it does not concern itself with privatization schemes including commercialization, vouchers, and for-profit charter schools, university downsizing, outsourcing, corporate infiltration through long-distance learning, the shrinking of full-time faculty and growth of contingent labor, the privatization of performance and curriculum assessment, standardization, the business of accreditation, and the reformulation of administration on the model of management systems and investment portfolios—all processes that will undermine if not totally negate access to education for the poor and minority students who supposedly compose these voices.

We have shown how this macro-restructuring of education in the age of globalization affects the content of what counts as knowledge. The new shape of education within a global economy envisions social values in corporate rather than democratic terms. This suggests the dire necessity to reclaim schools and mass media as places to foster community responses, democratic dialogues, common-cause alliances, and the revitalization of public and political action to face off against globalization, rather than as arms of the very power structure that is crushing them and thereby dimming imagination about a more just future. This reclamation must be done simultaneously at the level of unionization, protest, and revolt as well as in a vital rethinking of hegemony, theory, media, and culture—their roles, their ownership, their meanings, and their futures.

Since the publication of Lyotard's *The Postmodern Condition*, postmodern thought has been claiming that the current situation of culture is characterized by fragmentation, as the master narratives unifying human history—such as progress, subjectivity, and knowledge—have been dismantled. Cultural theorists have argued that the master narratives of history have been exclusionary, projecting a white male subjectivity as universal. This work has been useful and necessary, as it has inspired the production of diverse histories, a serious consideration of cultures explicitly not based in whiteness and/or Westernness, and a contingent exploration of the ways cultural canons have produced exclusions that have, in turn, fed unfair practices of justice and economic distributions. However, problematically, the question remains as to whether these new philosophies offer any basis for empathetically engaging the suffering of the other when one of the primary master narratives which these theories have disallowed is the narrative of human emancipation.

For example, Deleuze is a postmodern theorist who writes about fragmentation and multiplicity as a form of liberation. Deleuze follows a Nietzschean logic of affirmation where things are pushed to the point where they transform, deterritorialize, or become-other. Deleuze rejects political strategies of contestation in favor of affirming what appears as an oppressive force so that it becomes something else, allowing transformation. In the case of capitalism, for Deleuze and Guatarri the radical political move is to push capitalism forward to the point that it mutates. This renders a politics based in contestation inoperative. "It is wrongly said," state Deleuze and Guatarri in *A Thousand Plateaus*, for example, "[in Marxism in particular] that society is defined by its contradictions. That is true only on the larger scale of things. From the viewpoint of micropolitics, a society is defined by lines of flight. . . . There is always something that flows or flees."[1] The current, almost obsessive turn towards Deleuze in continental philosophy and literary studies witnesses an abstraction of contemporary problems of human suffering by avoiding consideration of who and what is producing enclaves of misery and ignorance, or how and in whose interests does racism, sexism, classism, homophobia, and economic inequality more generally get formed and supported by power.

Deleuze and Guatarri's refusal to theorize beyond desire and the socius yields an inability to theorize political agency, the subject, or to distinguish private from public as this distinction plays out in actual institutions. As well, the diminishing of oppositional political power that Deleuze's vision presages symptomizes a serious movement towards the complete abolition of public institutions for learning. Such institutions are gradually being broken down and transformed as public funds are transferred to private initiatives, and labor in general becomes more fluid, newly configured as temporary, partial, and multiply situated. Affirming flexibility serves here to affirm flexible labor.

Deleuzian ideas of change and flexibility feed a corporate logic of endless capital flow and commodity transfers. "Today we can depict," Deleuze and Guatarri write in *A Thousand Plateaus*, "an enormous, so-called stateless, monetary mass that circulates through foreign exchange and across borders, eluding control by the States, forming a multinational ecumenical organization, constituting a de facto supranational power untouched by governmental decisions."[2] The idea that things, people, concepts, and forces are constantly and inherently in flux conforms to the unchecked world of the commodity, as even Deleuze and Guattari recognize: "[Capitalism's] power of deterritorialization consists in taking as its object, not the earth, but 'materialized labor,' the commodity."[3] Impossible to differentiate and equally affirmed, labor and capital are simply coextensive, deterritorialized flows of desire.[4] Like capital, labor is constantly moving, decoding and recoding the forces of production. The shortcomings of the logic of affirmation become readily apparent in immediate political questions such as labor strikes or affirmative action, questions that cannot fit into a Deleuzian vision because of their oppositional quality or because they demand an ethical judgment evaluating types, forms, rules, and methods of capital flow. Struggles for wages, benefits, contracts, fair labor practices, and security all appear as "molar" or territorialized, arresting flows and transformation, while Deleuzian logic embraces change and flexibility. Redistributive politics, too, inhibits the flow of money by imposing the despotism of state taxation,[5] just as justice and politics obstruct the mobility of objects that the purely economic guarantees: "When the flows reach this capitalist threshold of decoding and deterritorialization (naked labor, independent capital), it seems that there is no longer a need for a State, for distinct juridical and political domination, in order to ensure appropriation, which has become directly economic."[6] Would education, then, have to be privatized as teachers and schools are moved around according to the intensities and new geographies of capital? Would capital regulate itself?

Additionally, as various feminists have noted, Deleuze's thought has posed problems for action as it denies the identities by which coalitions are formed as well as the subjectivities which might allow a common cause, a common goal, and a common language in which to analyze and undo oppressions. Jerry Aline Flieger, for example, writes, "[Deleuze] seems to be resolutely opposed to any form of what we have come to call identity politics, presumably since this politics necessitates 'territorializing'—staking out one's turf in the social hierarchy. In fact 'identity' itself is a notion that Deleuze wants to undercut or complicate, as do other poststructuralists."[7] And Alice Jardine states, "There is no room for new becomings of women's bodies and their other desires in these creatively limited, monosexual, brotherly machines."[8] In fact, Deleuze and Guatarri directly doubt the effectiveness of feminist politics because the positing of an identity of women would arrest the flows of desire and transformation: "It is, of course, indispensable," they argue, "for women to conduct a molar politics, with a view to winning back their own organism, their own history, their own subjectivity: "we as women . . ."" makes its appearance as a subject of enunciation. But it is dangerous to confine oneself to such a subject, which does not function without drying up a spring or stopping a flow."[9] The impossibility of identity and subjectivity within Deleuze's world also has implications for resistances based on race, class, sexuality, nationhood, or other types of group alliances and anti-discrimination movements.

Instead of being governed through a centralized consciousness which can make principled judgments, the social field in Deleuze's is constituted in abstract, de-gendered assemblages and machines of desire which, as Paul Patton indicates, are not "internal to the subject" or tending towards "the formation of a fixed or centred subjectivity"[10] but rather exist and operate separately from human agency, control, or intentions in the "entire surroundings that it traverses, the vibrations and flows of every sort to which it is joined".[11] Deleuzian logic incapacitates a center or standpoint from which to make decisions about fairness, and places in its stead a never-ending transformation, always moving, motivated by desire and abstract machines which exist devoid of subject or consciousness. "There are no revolutionary or reactionary loves," they contend, for example, "which is to say that loves are not defined by their objects, any more than by the sources and aims of the desires and the drives."[12] Indeed, Deleuzian desire is another strange love. Deleuze and Guatarri's "critical freedom," Paul Patton has noted, "is indifferent to the desires, preferences and goals of the subject in the sense that it may threaten as much as advance any of these. As a result, whereas the normative status and the value of liberal freedom is straightforwardly positive, critical freedom is a much more ambivalent and risky affair: more ambivalent since it involves leaving behind existing grounds of value, with the result that it is not always clear whether it is a good, or indeed by what standards it could be evaluated as good or bad; risky because there is no telling in advance where such processes of mutation and change might lead, whether at the level of individual or collective assemblages."[13] While, as Elizabeth Grosz observes, Deleuzian thought does open the possibility of change by foregrounding "the question of futurity" and committing "to the task of thinking the new,"[14] this is certainly not Deleuze's nor postmodernism's innovation. André Bréton, Ezra Pound, and other artistic theorists of the time put "the new" at the center of the modernist project of counterbourgeois collective human freedom, rather than in an obscure promise of partial and temporary displacements. As well, Deleuzian thought completely leaves out the possibility of judging what kind of change guides towards social justice and what kind of change, on the contrary, guarantees the expansion of capitalist oppressions.

Deleuze's anti-identity, anti-subjectivity philosophy might seem to offer escape or reprieve from the so-called prisonhouse of language, or tools with which to think anew the isolation of various identity-based actions. However, it does not account for by whom and on what basis transformation and mobility are currently motivated, not even when it comes to how "lines of flight" are resituating institutions of knowledge production. As flexible labor is filling university staff positions with undercompensated and undercommitted teachers, schools themselves are following the lead of corporations in outsourcing the labor of learning to poorer nations where teachers work for even less and discipline is tighter. An article in *Time* magazine celebrates a program that sends troubled inner city youth from Baltimore to Kenya where their behavioral disruptions and truancy are brought under control by stricter rules and surveillance:

> [Robert Ebry, head of the Abell Foundation, which invests $5 million a year in education in Baltimore] chose a spot beneath the foothills of Mount Kenya, where land is cheap and his teachers, half of whom are Kenyan, are willing to work for salaries as low as $5,000 a year. . . . Baraka [the school in Kenya] tries to save the boys with strong discipline. . . . "It was hell," says Brandon of his first year at Baraka. He kept talking back to his teachers, again and again, and landed in the "boma," a crude, isolated group of tents surrounded by thornbushes that Baraka used for punishment.[15]

Time lauds the program not only because it cures the kids from resisting an education that has become meaningless to them, but also because it shows an instance where labor laws and unionization do not interfere in cutting the public costs of teaching. The kids return to Baltimore, now obedient and dressed in suits as they blend into a service-oriented work-force, despising their old neighborhoods which are now more run-down than ever:

> Passing near Harlem Park, his old middle school, he seems embarrassed by the boarded-up row houses, the trash-strewn streets, the bars on the windows. Like a nervous out-of-towner, Brandon begs a visitor to speed up the car. "I never go outside," he says. "I ain't associatin' with them hoodlums."[16]

Not even opening the option of improving the Baltimore system, *Time* does not mention the connections between the city's decrepitude and the decaying of public supports like schools, even as it offers such deep praise to the private business that has deemed public schools unworthy beyond repair by sending kids abroad. "The pattern for a lot of our kids is so devastating. They don't just need smaller classes and better schools. They need to get *out*," as Baltimore middle-school teacher Kristi Ward confesses to *Time*.[17]

Such efforts demonstrate how the very structure of schooling, consciousness, and knowledge itself adheres to the movements of capital. *Time* exposes and affirms how schools are caught within a repetition of colonial logic as they exploit cheap, unprotected, and (at least in terms of *Time*'s photographic exhibit) female labor in Third World contexts. Deleuzian reason does not fundamentally offer a way of critique, nor a normative call to justice, by which to combat this remodeling of school as offshore production, nor does it theorize the possibility of creating social movements to stop and resist the mobility of public institutions like schools along the lines of capital flight and colonial flow. In her essay "*Goodbye America* (The Bridge Is Walking . . .)," Camilla Benolirao Griggers makes an attempt to apply Deleuzian analysis to denounce U.S. military presence in the Philippines, the subsequent transformation of women's work with the growth of the entertainment and sex industries, the severe economic crisis warranted in the U.S. withdrawal as Philippine macro-economic policy was forced into an IMF straightjacket, and the resulting crisis leading up to the Asian devaluation. However, Deleuzian concepts do not seem to provide any oppositional narrative but rather to affirm through description capitalism's predictable, preordained, and inevitable journey through atrocities. "It would be a mistake," Griggers argues, "to confuse machinic effects for individual agencies, both on the side of the Filipinas who are victimised and on the side of Americans who perpetrate. . . . The concept of machinic assemblage in this regard suggests Deleuze and Guattari's negation of bourgeois individualism."[18] The lack of subjectivity in the Deleuzian tableau means that the critic's job is only to observe and describe the stronghold of capital, applying concepts whose movement into the different scenes of capitalist abuses ensures an opening towards some unspecifiable sort of change. Such analysis stifles, for instance, thinking of how the IMF could make different decisions and force different types of change that would not cramp government's interventions in support of its citizens. It says no one is to blame for gutting inner city programs so that schools need to be shipped abroad to become affordable and effective. Rather, capitalism itself appears the only force of change. This implies that these colonial practices simply reflect a transformation towards new meanings induced by capitalism's constant and automatic appropriation of new sites and methods of exploitation.

It is not enough to celebrate diversity, fragmentation, and mobility if such terms are reduced to a purely abstract and linguistic basis. Will the rhizome, with its multiple roots and plethora of unintended destinations, help the immigrant fleeing economic oppression to avoid deportation? Is the body without organs, with its myriad movements and deracinations, beneficial for a *maquiladora* laborer who can be easily deracinated from her job because she works without a contract or the right to organize, or useful for considering the politics of AIDS and contesting the corporate control of pharmaceutical distribution? The academic interest in diversity and fragmentation tends to obscure the economic basis of oppression, rendering it purely a new type of aesthetics and representation rather than a question of the way institutions function to produce differences and silences which augment some people's power over others'. As Peter McLaren points out, "Ironically, postmodernism has become the new doxology of the Left only to impede our ability to understand the current historical juncture as inscribed in the uneven and unequal development of the capitalist world system."[19] In other words, in the wake of the postmodern and with the rise of neoliberalism, cultural studies needs to take seriously the ways it can challenge the material basis of inequality and implement a more just and democratic distribution of power, knowledge, and the means to acquire them.

The rise of globalization studies in academia marks a hopeful shift away from some of the more depoliticizing aspects of postmodern theory. As well, the turn to globalization in cultural theory has the potential to expand the project led by Noam Chomsky and Robert McChesney that engages the political economy of neoliberalism, communications, and corporatism. As important as this work is, it has yet to link political economy and policy formation to cultural, representational, and discourse politics. Unfortunately, rather than make this needed link, much recent work in cultural theories of globalization has done little more than merely overlay the conceptual categories and metaphors of postmodernism (fragmentation, fluidity, multiplicity, hybridity, etc.) onto a discussion of global economy and culture, limiting economic effects to purely cultural phenomena, aesthetic images, methods of reading, or movements in theory. "So polysemous was globalization," begin, for example, contributors Toby Miller, Geoffrey Lawrence, Jim McKay, and David Rowe in *Social Text's* issue on globalization, "that it included sameness, difference, unity, and disunity—in short, globalization, like postmodernity before it, had come to stand for nothing less than *life itself*."[20]

In another appropriation of postmodern terminology, globalization has meant a celebration of fragmentation and diversity where the geopolitical context influencing what gets recognized in and what gets excluded from these new canons seems less relevant than the accumulation and interaction of expressions from an endless array of cultures. Even when, for example, a keynote writer in the *PMLA* has noted that globalization has meant that "the gap between rich and poor in the world is still being widened by forces of economic and cultural globalization, and these forces, largely reflecting the dominance of the United States, need to be thoroughly reorganized if this gap is not to become catastrophic,"[21] there is very little sense of how a "new sensitivity to the interconnections among discursive fields and expressive practices, in and across cultures and in and across periods"[22] could either exacerbate that gap or be part of how it gets reorganized because it connects integrally to such production of poverty.

The Deleuzian term *deterritorialization* has been specifically appealing to critics formulating descriptive terms for new global movements, but such terminology often serves to blunt theories of access and political agency. "The world we live in now seems rhizomic," suggests, for example, Arjun Appadurai, "even schizophrenic, calling for theories of rootlessness, alienation, and psychological distance between individuals and groups on the one hand, and fantasies (or nightmares) of electronic propinquity on the other."[23] True enough, but Appadurai goes on to profess that the contemporary large-scale migrations of people and electronic networks at ever increasing rates across regions and national borders calls for a reconceptualization of the public sphere through the new possibilities offered in new media. These new media have granted expanded imaginary landscapes (labeled ethnoscapes, mediascapes, technoscapes, financescapes, and ideoscapes), each interacting and constituted through the shifting locations of friends, relatives, exiles, tourists, and immigrants. These landscapes, augmented by images of the world brought back through newspapers, cinema, and the like, give people, according to Appadurai, an increased sense of possibility.

Appadurai's theory does provide a way out of the despairing stringency of the iron cage idea of culture imagined by the Frankfurt School and its followers, where agency is denied as the culture industry becomes purely authoritative and determining of consciousness. However, it performs the opposite mistake of positing the individual as radically free, and therefore inferring that the individual has purely free choice among the imaginary landscapes displayed for its delight. This means that freedom is viewed as an act of consumption. "There is growing evidence," Appadurai continues,

> that the consumption of the mass media throughout the world often provokes resistance, irony, selectivity, and, in general, *agency*. Terrorists modeling themselves on Rambo-like figures (who have themselves generated a host of non-Western counterparts), housewives reading romances and soap operas as part of their efforts to construct their own lives. . . . : these are all examples of the active way in which media are appropriated by people throughout the world. T-shirts, billboards, and graffiti as well as rap music, street dancing, and slum housing all show that the images of the media are quickly moved into local repertoires of irony, anger, humor, and resistance. . . . Where there is consumption there is pleasure, and where there is pleasure there is agency.[24]

Certainly, housewives, for example, have been reading romances since the eighteenth century, and it has not helped to end the growing world poverty of women and children, and hanging Bruce Springsteen posters on the cardboard walls of temporary dwellings has not stymied the growth of shanty-towns outside of large urban centers developing globally. Appadurai's theory does not account for how the mass media are working to narrow the possibilities of the imagination *and* movement. As the large corporations controlling the media have consolidated, ideas, themes, debates, narratives, values, and, yes, possibilities have been ever more restricted. Appadurai's theory needs to consider how these migrations are not really induced by the free choice of individuals to select the grounds of their imaginary travels, but rather set in place by powerful institutions designed to defend property, to provide labor, to create surplus, and to extend territories of profit. It is not enough simply to claim that the imagination, "in its collective forms, . . . creates ideas of neighborhood and nationhood, or moral economies and unjust rule, of higher wages and foreign labor prospects . . . [and] is today a staging ground for action, and not only for escape,"[25] in other words, simply to imagine away the immense power interests who are dazzling the public with distractions and selling the tragedies of capitalism as sweet, as though individuals can simply select another channel. One needs rather to talk about how individuals can negotiate meanings which counter corporatism from within a world governed by a strengthening corporate power. The iron cage of the corporate media is, as yet, not absolute or determining of consciousness, but still exhibiting gaps in logic from which to theorize (not assume) freedom and transformation.

Postmodernism has definitely granted valuable insights in such areas as representation, identity, culture, history, nation, language, difference, and power, insights that have completely changed the way human relationships, politics, and progress can be thought. However, transposing postmodern theory onto a description of globalization means also transferring the problematic absences and conditions of postmodern theory into the thinking through of economic processes. The most important of these concerns the position of agency and the contingent necessity, abolished in most postmodern thought, of theorizing or assigning blame for economic inequalities and social injustices. If, as perhaps the legacy of Foucault warrants, power can be located in the multiple social interactions between subjects, then the grand mechanisms and institutions of power under world capitalism become equal to the power an individual wields. This means that capitalism cannot be centralized as a world force all but determining the direction of history, or that there can be no transcendent ethical subject and so moral judgment is reduced to a limited, local, regulatory, and/or relative field. Or if, as Baudrillardian philosophies of simulation would profess, reality has disappeared in the face of the production of images, then reality itself cannot be subject to change. Or if, as Derridian logic assumes, the world is a text and society simply the relationships between floating signifiers, then the difficulty for the postmodern theorizer is how to find a stable point beyond language from which to launch critique.

There seems to be a current tendency within academic treatments to construct descriptions of globalization from the residues of postmodern theory. This often means that theoretical descriptions of globalization inherit from postmodernism the difficulties of thinking political agency. In the book *Empire*, for example, Michael Hardt and Antonio Negri adopt Deleuzian thought in order to talk about a resistance to the powers of global capital. Instead of a critical or negative power from below, they propose to conceive of revolution as a positive power, a just force which transcends both capital and the rational subject in an intensity of productive life. This power of the multitude is not outside of the power of global capital, which they call Empire, but rather is within the system and ferments in the implosion of a capitalism pushed to the extreme, "a constituent counterpower that emerges from within Empire,"[26] "an absolutely positive force that pushes the dominating power toward an abstract and empty unification, to which it appears as the distinct alternative."[27]

This perspective on globalization starts effectively in offering the idea of theorizing a universal justice, "the validity of right situated above the nation-state," a "global constitutionalism," a "global civil society," and a "new transnational democracy."[28] Yet, the authors disappointingly do not give a sense of how the intensity of productive life will come about, or of how justice will operate once the very idea of the subject has been dissolved and negativity as the source of critique, opposition, and historical change has been denied. Additionally, because there are no limits to Empire, imagining an outside to Empire—utopian or not—is rejected as impossible: "The transcendental fiction of politics can no longer stand up and has no argumentative utility because we all exist entirely within the realm of the social and political."[29] In *Empire*, a power without name composes "social life in its entirety" as a "regime with no temporal boundaries . . . dedicated to . . . perpetual and universal peace outside of history."[30] Agency, like subjectivity, is reduced to a metaphysical and arbitrary flow of forces, an effect of a creative energy which is produced by capital but for which no particular capitalist configuration or institution can be held responsible. Denying the possibility of politics, *Empire* cannot tell where there are real agents really profiting from capital movements, or where there is real suffering, and that capitalist power can and must be named, exposed, and actively contradicted by real agents of opposition.

There have, in fact, been efforts to fight back at the realigning of knowledge production along lines of capital flight. At New York University, the graduate students unionized and their union was approved by the National Labor Relations Board, and then they forced the administration to recognize their union as a negotiating body. At the City University of New York, the faculty took over the union, demanding faculty governance, tuition reduction, and wage parity for part-time staff, among over 170 other acts in the name of ensuring universal access to education for all New Yorkers and the fostering of democracy. Through protesting and picketing, students at Adelphi University in Long Island managed to halt the transformation of their university administration into a shelter for heavy investors, gift takers, financial squanderers, and budget-cruncher. Students at Syracuse joined physical plant, food service, and library workers to denounce subcontracting and outsourcing of university employees against an administration claiming that "modern institutions need flexibility . . . to do the things they didn't want to do because they might want to do them at some point."[31] It is clear from such initiatives that knowledge workers are insisting on returning subjectivity and thus ethics to politics and posing normative principles with which to evaluate and contest lines of change. The corporation's work, as Fanon says of colonialism, "is to make even dreams of liberty impossible."[32] Organizing for change and linking knowledge production with broader social movements will open up the very content of knowledge to imagining alternatives.

Political action requires the exertion of force. While most of this book has focused on the possibilities for cultural struggle, we realize that some historical moments demand more potent forces than those rallied through discursive and hegemonic initiatives. We recognize the materiality of discursive engagement. Yet, we also discern that there are moments when language fails to produce conditions of freedom. Now at the dawn of the new millennium, such conditions require international organizing and regulatory mechanisms (in conjunction with the cultural struggle this book has advocated) to address injustices and inequalities and to face off against corporate power in an age of globalization. In other words, international bodies of governance must be formed both at the grassroots level and at the level of institutional justice and law, bodies with the power, initiative, and backing to negotiate and enforce ethical principles. The multinationalization of capital must be countered by multinational checks-and-balances as well as multinational resistance. Furthermore, discursive struggle is most likely not an adequate force to reverse the violence of corporate globalization and the symbolic violence of neoliberal ideology. The impending impossibility of thinking in terms of the public threatens to render discursive struggle an insufficient force to reverse the violence of corporate globalization and the symbolic violence of neoliberal ideology.

If the eradication of the public tends towards the hateful inevitability of violence, then, strangely, the politics of expanding the public may be the most potent form of love.

NOTES

1. Gilles Deleuze and Félix Guatarri, *A Thousand Plateaus: Capitalism and Schizophrenia,* translated by Brian Massumi (Minneapolis: University of Minnesota Press, 1987), 216.

2. Deleuze and Guatarri, *Thousand Plateaus,* 453.

3. Deleuze and Guatarri, *Thousand Plateaus,* 454.

4. Deleuze and Guatarri, *Thousand Plateaus,* 453.

5. Gilles Deleuze and Félix Guatarri, *Anti-Oedipus: Capitalism and Schizophrenia,* translated by Robert Hurley, Mark Seem, and Helen R. Lane (Minneapolis: University of Minnesota Press, 1983), 197.

6. Deleuze and Guatarri, *Thousand Plateaus,* 453.

7. Jerry Aline Flieger, "Becoming-Woman: Deleuze, Schreber and Molecular Identification," in *Deleuze and Feminist Theory,* edited by Ian Buchanan and Claire Colebrook (Edinburgh, Scotland: Edinburgh University Press, 2000), 40.

8. Alice Jardine, *Gynesis: Configurations of Woman and Modernity* (Ithaca, N.Y.: Cornell University Press, 1985), 223.

9. Deleuze and Guatarri, *Thousand Plateaus,* 276.

10. Paul Patton, *Deleuze and the Political* (London: Routledge, 2000), 71.

11. Deleuze and Guatarri, *Anti-Oedipus*, 292.

12. Deleuze and Guatarri, *Anti-Oedipus*, 365.

13. Patton, *Deleuze and the Political*, 87.

14. Elizabeth Grosz, "Deleuze's Bergson: Duration, the Virtual and a Politics of the Future," in *Deleuze and Feminist Theory*, edited by Ian Buchanan and Claire Colebrook (Edinburgh, Scotland: Edinburgh University Press, 2000), 216.

15. Andrew Goldstein, "The Africa Experiment," *Time*, 9 Oct. 2000, 75.

16. Goldstein, "The Africa Experiment," 76.

17. Goldstein, "The Africa Experiment," 76.

18. Camilla Benolirao Griggers, "*Goodbye America* (The Bridge Is Walking . . .)," in *Deleuze and Feminist Theory*, edited by Ian Buchanan and Claire Colebrook (Edinburgh, Scotland: Edinburgh University Press, 2000), 200–01.

19. Peter McLaren, *Che Guevara, Paulo Freire, and the Pedagogy of Revolution* (Lanham, Md.: Rowman & Littlefield, 2000), 107.

20. Toby Miller et al. "Modifying the Sign: Sport and Globalization," *Social Text* 60, 17, no. 3 (Fall 1999): 15. Emphasis in original.

21. Giles Gunn, "Introduction: Globalizing Literary Studies," *PMLA* 116, no. 1 (January 2001), 19.

22. Gunn, "Introduction: Globalizing Literary Studies," 19.

23. Arjun Appadurai, *Modernity at Large: Cultural Dimensions of Globalization* (Minneapolis: University of Minnesota Press, 1996), 29.

24. Appadurai, *Modernity at Large*, 7.

25. Appadurai, *Modernity at Large*, 7.

26. Michael Hardt and Antonio Negri, *Empire* (Cambridge, Mass: Harvard University Press, 2000), 59.

27. Michael Hardt and Antonio Negri, *Empire*, 62.

28 . Michael Hardt and Antonio Negri, *Empire*, 6–7.

29. Michael Hardt and Antonio Negri, *Empire*, 353.

30. Michael Hardt and Antonio Negri, *Empire*, xv.

31. Frantz Fanon, *The Wretched of the Earth: The Handbook for the Black Revolution that Is Changing the Shape of the World*. Translated by Constance Farrington (New York: Grove Press, 1968), 93.

Coda

On Sept 11, 2001, as this book was being sent to press, a tragic event occurred which changed the political landscape.

We do not want to minimize the pain and suffering that people experienced in the wake of the attack. Nor do we want to dismiss the very real terror that many feel in its aftermath. Nor do we want to cancel out the shock and anger resulting from witnessing such massive destruction to two inspirational cities. Nor do we want to promote a "just cause" knee-jerk reaction with the many clichés that have historically been useless to garner political opposition, clichés like "the chickens come home to roost" or "you reap what you sow." Nobody deserves this sorrow.

However, "national community" is currently being evoked in order to win the support of the public for war (full scale conventional war or smoldering guerrilla war) that will unleash the barbarism that, according to its designers, it is supposed to be combating to uphold a civilization defined as the right to a violent supremacy. Some of the central themes of this book—the legitimation of violence through sentimental stories, the justification of global aggression for corporate expansion, the mobilization of compassionate narratives to arouse citizens towards public distrust, killing, and outrage—suddenly jump forward on the national and international stage. Issues of national security eclipse questions of civil liberties, education, and social security, and the public interest is almost universally equated with military power. It is good to teach children, said one news report, that it is OK to feel anger. A little boy confesses to the microphone, "I just want to kill 'em." As *Strange Love* argues, the stage has been set for decades to galvanize the population for a war that will not benefit the people in whose interest it is being advocated.

Time will tell if the United States will continue its murderous interventionist policies that, many say, brought about this event. Meanwhile, U.S. leaders continue to deny the social and political context and the consequences. The media cries that this event represents a loss of innocence, and that the terrorists destroyed two of the most potent symbols of U.S. life. While exhorting the public to return to normal, newscasters do not relegate a good deal of broadcasting time to explaining the murderous implications of "business as usual," for example, how the marginalization of the public from politics allows the defense sector and the state to be the world's leading weapons seller, arming poor nations to the teeth thereby creating regional arms races, wars, and impoverishment. Citizens are told that patriotism is getting back to normal when normal means 5.4 million U.S. families are classified as having "worst case housing needs," which "means they pay more than half of their income to live in substandard housing."[1] Normal means citizens allowing the government to spend "hundreds of millions of dollars to eradicate coca production in Colombia (including parts of the Amazon) through the aerial spraying of crops with chemicals that are believed to cause human health and environmental damage."[2] Normal also meant the destruction to security, freedom, and lifestyle that happened when businesses in the Trade Towers hired non-unionized labor (now left with little access to the huge sums of aid pouring in or to job placement services) when the airlines contracted out airport securities to cheap, pay-by-the-hour cops or when the city could only afford to pay starting fire fighters $30,000. Was this the type of "U.S. way of life" to which the Trade Towers served as monument? New York City's mayor Rudolph Giuliani has rallied in support of New York and New Yorkers—evincing, in the eyes of many of even his staunchest former critics, both eloquence and leadership. Is it so easy to forget that Giuliani ruined housing prospects for many in New York City long before the attacks, or that he supported the police as it terrorized African American communities?

President George W. Bush told the nation that the imminent war was a war of fear against freedom. What he did not mention, however, was not a major consideration in the U.S. support of oppressive regimes in Saudi Arabia, for example, or even, formerly, in Afghanistan, but rather, the United States has historically been on the side of curtailing the freedoms of peoples around the world in the name of fear. Nor has the U.S. leadership sincerely explained to the U.S. public the repercussions of an all-out military response, where not only is it likely that militant fundamentalist regimes will gain even more support from the desperate, not only will the world' most impoverished people find themselves targeted by its strongest military power, but also it is possible that the war will escalate towards intensified retaliations, biological or chemical strikes, and nuclear devastation.

If the Trade Towers and the Pentagon represent the most potent symbols of American life then American life is high finance, the lifestyles of the rich and famous, and the militarism to back U.S. economic and political power. The destruction of these buildings has led to the intensification of practices which have been questioned ethically for their contradictions to democratic governing—practices like phone tapping, racial profiling, and censorship. In the aftermath of the attacks a central question has been how to balance civil liberties with national security while preserving the "American way of life."We are suggesting that this tragedy opens the possibility for posing a series of far deeper questions about how to rethink and transform this way of life. What of democracy? What of equality? What of government by the people? If the Trade Towers and the Pentagon represent anything, they represent the possibility to reconsider where we are and how far we have gotten from the core ideals of the nation, not to mention how far we must go in striving to realize these ideals.

October 1, 2001

Robin Truth Goodman
Kenneth J. Saltman

NOTES

1. Congresswoman Jan Schakowsky's Report to Illinois' 9th District September 2001, Volume 3.
2. Ibid.

Index

About the Authors

Robin Truth Goodman is assistant professor of English at Florida State University. She is the author of *Infertilities: Exploring Fictions of Barren Bodies* (2001).

Kenneth J. Saltman is assistant professor in the Social and Cultural Studies in Education program at DePaul University. He is the author of *Collateral Damage: Corporatizing Public Schools—A Threat to Democracy* (2000).